1992

THE COLLECTOR'S
TWENTIETH-CENTURY MUSIC
IN THE WESTERN HEMISPHERE

Keystone Books in Music

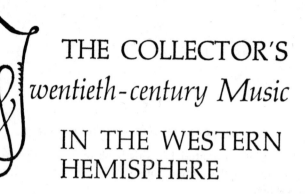

THE COLLECTOR'S
Twentieth-century Music
IN THE WESTERN HEMISPHERE

by Arthur Cohn

J.B. Lippincott Company

Philadelphia and New York

To my wife
Lois

Contents

Foreword

THIS BOOK DISCUSSES THE RECORDED MUSIC OF TWENTY-SEVEN CON-temporary composers of the Western Hemisphere—twenty-three Americans, one Argentinian, one Brazilian, and two Mexicans.

Selection, in such a book, is a dangerous diversion. There is no problem in the choice of such men as Aaron Copland or Heitor Villa-Lobos. It is the young composer and the well-ensconced older colleague who pave the hell of a critic's good intentions. The recording companies have anticipated and in some instances solved the problem by giving no attention to certain composers. Further, it is obvious that a single recording of a composer's work would not warrant his inclusion. Beyond this, there is the simple fact of lack of space; and the argumentative one—the subjective view of any critic. It is an author's privilege to cast his vote as he pleases. The important thing is to cast it with conviction, plus the hope that readers will derive value from the commentary offered, and then, after reading—listen! Further, one man's choice does not gainsay the creative abilities of composers such as Berger, Harrison, Moore, Persichetti, Porter, Stevens, and others not included.

A second volume along similar lines is projected, covering the important twentieth-century composers of Western Europe, and a third will deal with Soviet composers and the music of Stravinsky. Such a scheme gives no place to the music of Morton Gould, Ferde Grofé, Kurt Weill, George Gershwin, Richard Rodgers, and others. Their works for the most part represent a fusion of popular style with serious forms, or are music designed primarily for the Broadway stage. A separate study would be required to cover their output adequately.

The objective in the present book has been to treat each composer and his music in relation to the recordings, rather than the reverse. Very little biographical data has been given; such information is plentifully available elsewhere. A general discussion on each composer is followed by a capsule survey of his recorded music, covering all releases issued up to May, 1960.

Each composer's works are discussed in the following order: *orchestral* (full, chamber, string, brass or band, percussion); *solo instrument with orchestra* (concertos, other works); *works for solo instrument* (with or without accompaniment); *chamber music; vocal and choral compositions; sacred;* and finally *complete ballets, operas, and other dramatic works.* Each of these categories is arranged alphabetically, save for chamber music, where the order is according to the number of instruments involved.

Some surprise may greet the inclusion of short pieces. These minute works, or excerpts, are usually completely ignored, unmentioned in discographies and other surveys. Most of them are hidden away on recordings with extremely odd catch-all titles. To ferret out such works is a task for which most listeners have little time or inclination; even if willing, they usually lack the necessary catalogue information. But interest in a composer often extends to his complete recorded output—minor compositions as well as major ones. A small deed is just as noble as a large one. These smaller works are covered here as thoroughly as possible, though some omissions were unavoidable through inability to hear the recordings.

Some of the compositions discussed are available only on recordings containing more than two works, issued under an inclusive title. In such cases the record title is given, preceded by the word "in," without indicating the other contents of the collective release. Where only one other work is involved, or where there is no overall title, the accompanying compositions are naturally noted, but without indicating the conductor, organization, etc., if different from those in the performance under discussion, the effort being to focus only upon the music of the composer in question.

The emphasis throughout is on the aesthetic pattern and logic of the music, rather than on recorded sound. It can be taken for granted that most recordings are acceptable, give or take a decibel or two. When a disk is less than should be expected, the scalpel has been wielded. In cases where there is more than one recording of a work (the most exciting development in contemporary music is this slowly building duplication, no longer limited to the "favorite fifty" pieces), comparisons are drawn, and the recordings are listed as far as possible in the order of preference.

A word about stereo. The quality of a performance is not improved by stereophonic recording; neither is poor sound quality disguised by the multitrack technique. A good reading will be enhanced on stereo, if the composition is for more than the average chamber-music total; it will not be minimized if it is played on a monaural machine. By all means go stereo, but don't think the miracle of electronics will make up for an inept or only average performance. Since most contemporary music is not available stereophonically the entire matter is academic anyway. As proof of this, the very latest release described in this book, issued by RCA Victor in May, 1960, includes two works by Paul Creston; it is only available monaurally.

Since this survey is devoted principally to the men and the music, little is made of the difference between stereo and monaural releases. All stereo catalogue numbers follow the monaural numbers, and are enclosed in parentheses. If, as is sometimes the case, only a stereo version is available, the single number is given in parentheses.

No codes, and only a few very obvious abbreviations, have been used in this book. The necessity for turning pages to decipher cryptic listings is as wearying to this author as to the reader.

Practically all of the recordings listed are available in most record stores. While some are no longer listed in the important Schwann catalogue, a number of stores still carry stock; if not, such recordings may often be obtained from one of the out-of-print specialty shops (the "we supply your wants" type). Moreover, one does not have to own a record to hear it at a friend's or on the radio, or obtain it from a record club or a library. When a record no longer in the catalogue is discussed the purpose is to emphasize its importance; however, this book does not attempt to cover every record that has been deleted. It is a survey of current recorded contemporary music with a glance at the past.

Acknowledgments

No critic can possibly own every record discussed in a large discography. The scope of this book was made possible only through the cooperation of a number of people in the recording industry, whose names are given below. To them, I express my thanks, and regrets for the trouble involved. If some have been overlooked, I hope they will freely accept my apology as they so freely offered their assistance.

The luxury of helping also signifies tolerance. When recordings are compared conscientiously, critical judgments follow. My appreciation for understanding this fact is warmly given to: Richard C. Burns (Overtone), Emory Cook (Cook), Walter Diehl (Vox), Ben Deutschman (Everest), Sidney Finkelstein (Vanguard), Peter Fritsch (Lyrichord), Roger Goeb (Composers Recordings), Louise Goodman (Boston), Horace Grenell (Westminster), Sol Handwerger (MGM) and his most cooperative aide Shelley Wapner, Herb Helman (RCA Victor and Camden), John Hurd (London and Richmond), Debbie Ishlon (Columbia and Epic), Erna Lynn Katz (Decca), Irving Kratka (Classic), John C. Long (University of Oklahoma), E. D. Nunn (Audiophile), Marion B. Phillipps (Acta Corporation), Jack Romann (Angel and Capitol), Clair Van Ausdale (Mercury), Earl Walker (Music Library), Richard H. Wangerin (Louisville Orchestra), Sol Weinstein (Trans Disc Corporation), Ernest Walker (United Artists).

Anonymous personnel of the following firms were also generous in tending my wants: Dot, Folkways, Unicorn, Urania, and Washington. (Since discredits cannot be mingled with credits, I abstain from listing companies who turned down my pleas for loan material. Their records were considered without prejudice.)

I am especially in debt to my friend, the brilliant publisher-editor of *The American Record Guide*, James Lyons. His suggestions of recorded source material solved many a problem, and his willingness to permit me the use of recordings from his magnificent collection illustrates his unselfish spirit. I also wish to thank him for permission to use material which originally appeared in his publication. (Printed acknowledgment of his understanding of my failure to deliver reviews on time while this book was in progress clears my uneasy conscience.)

There must be noted some further expressions of gratitude: to my publishers, who have given me a free hand in the writing of this book, and more time than they normally would permit a procrastinating author; and to my wife, with whom I discussed many points of this work. The latter's understanding patience is a talent not many women possess. Her willingness to labor over a typewriter is no less a rarity.

ARTHUR COHN

New York City, 9 May 1960

Music in the Americas

MUSICAL COMPOSITION IN AMERICA FOLLOWED A SORT OF DOG-chasing-its-tail pattern. It began with European influence. To that continent went many young American composers in search of musical know-how. Their studies in Germany and France were reflected in the work they produced. The trend toward emancipation took hold finally, reaching its peak in the 1920's, when a purer type of music appeared, much of it displaying genuine American "rugged individualism." With the advent of Nazism, there came an influx of important European composers into the United States. In their wake followed pedagogical influence. One noted the appearance of Hindemithian and Bartókian techniques, in addition to Schoenbergian tendencies. But the individual artist makes his way, regardless. There are a large number of American composers who cannot be called imitators (then again, many imitators do write quite decent music). No matter how much individuality is manifested, one can always trace the heritage and background.

The music of the Americas displays more different idioms and techniques than that of any other one country. American composers, as well as Mexican, Brazilian, and the large number from other countries of North, Central, and South America, have absorbed all the international musical techniques, and at the same time have made use of indigenous materials from their own lands. Nationalism in music is a matter of intention, a devotion to characteristic creative devices, and the American school of composers has followed this pattern. Much of their music has, however, become known and recognized outside its national boundaries. By becoming a part of the international scene, it loses its complete insularity and takes its place among the many musical dialects. Nationalism is not a primary requirement for any country in achieving its creative goals. The art, craft, and intelligence shown by composers, painters, and writers is all important. But if a specifically national orientation develops, as it has in American music, it does not stem the creative current, but rather enlarges it in a way not possible with other musical modes. American music is by and large of the first rank; that it is nationally relevant is only part of the reason

13

for its acceptance. The Western Hemisphere has kept pace artistically with the world, producing its European equivalents and its own pure products. It is represented in world music by compositions utilizing every idiomatic possibility.

Whether from all of this musical activity there will emerge a *great* composer is impossible to estimate, nor, actually, does it matter. A country as wealthy in creative individuals as the United States will, considering the number of worthy works that already exist, be bound to produce lasting art. Villa-Lobos has led the way in Brazil, Chávez in Mexico, and there are outstanding artists in the other countries, plus an amazing number of young talents.

Musical composition in the Western Hemisphere is in a flourishing condition, aided by a growing public which no longer mistrusts its homemade product. Much American music is now a standard part of the contemporary musical repertoire. More of it will enter that category, one can be certain. At the moment, music being composed on the American continent is the equal (qualitatively speaking) of that produced by any other countries. If, in the United States, this is a coming of age, all the better, although such a phrase, if correct in the 1920's, is inapplicable to the mature creations of the present day.

The recorded-music picture is just as healthy. More and more American works are being placed on disks. While no contemporary Colombian or Nicaraguan musician (to cite but two nationalities) has been accorded this type of prominence, there is growing representation of the countries that lie south of the United States. The amount of music that has not reached the desks of the artists-and-repertoire men is startling. Nevertheless, the hundreds of works now available to the listener comprise a wealth that was unimaginable in the past. The mechanical age which brought the radio and the sound film into existence has harmed the performers of music, but it has rewarded today's composers quite handsomely. These rewards are due to a disk that revolves electrically at thirty-three and one-third revolutions per minute. Despite the reactionaries and the limited viewpoint of the commercial interests, the fields of music have never been so green. The recorded music of the twenty-seven composers covered in the pages that follow is a part of this exciting chronicle.

1. Samuel Barber
(1910—   )

BROADLY SPEAKING, THERE ARE TWO TYPES OF COMPOSERS: THOSE who work on the definite principles brought to fruition by the previous generation (as Strauss's music is based on Wagner's, early Stravinsky modeled on Rimsky-Korsakov); and those—a minority —who cast off, almost ruthlessly, the fetters of the past and strike out for richer newness (though, contrary to what the graybeards say, there is always some connection with the past).

Barber clings to his classical and romantic forebears. He is an American composer who has assimilated the creative habits of the past, and is content. And this conventional demeanor makes him a composer without distinguishing characteristics. This is not so much a criticism as it is an artistic judgment on the term "American music." In its sound a great part of American music is as much French, Russian, Swiss, or Scandinavian as it is American. Yet it has as much claim to the label "American" as do works based on Negro or Indian themes, jazz speech, or sounds descriptive of Times Square on parade. Regardless of the difference between those who utilize folklore and those whose aesthetics preclude the use of indigenous materials—regardless of the creative philosophy —because of its birth and growth in a country of conglomerate cultures, American music is simply music written by Americans.

Lyricism is the dominant feature of Barber's output. He knows how to spin a real melody—among contemporary composers this is no small achievement. His strongest link with the past is in his formal practice: the classical concept of the sonata remains the point of emphasis, even when Barber reshapes it to suit the work at hand. There is more freedom in his harmonic language, yet it retains a basic romantic accent, even when some salty polytonal words are utilized. Barber is never academic; he is merely concerned with earlier times, though he is of the twentieth century.

Barber's major works are fairly well represented in the record catalogues, with too much attention being given, however, to the "Adagio" for string orchestra. This is a haunting little piece, but is, nonetheless, of minor importance. We should have fresh recordings of the violin and cello concertos and their chamber relative, the "Capricorn Concerto." Anyone who can locate a Concert Hall (E-8) copy of the violin concerto will be struck both by the beauty of the work and by its solo realization by Louis Kaufman. The old London LPS-332 spread the cello concerto over two sides of a ten-inch disk, but even with the bother of the break this record is worthy, in view of Zara Nelsova's magnificence as a cellist. And Concert Hall again (this firm is no longer active, so one must search for its releases), via its A-4, will satisfy on the "Capricorn," until Mercury's plan to record this is carried out. No weapon slays the composer as neatly, deftly, and completely as the withdrawal of his work from the record catalogue. In this respect Barber has suffered less than many, yet he too is being deprived.

ORCHESTRAL

Essay for Orchestra, No. 1, Op. 12

The only slightly off-the-beaten-track feature of this work is the use of a literary title to describe a musical design, and an exceedingly "slight" one at that; the theme and elaboration of the prose form are paralleled by the unfolding of a somber subject, with some development, plus a short recapitulation to prove the point. Barber's second "Essay" is a better work but until it is recorded one will have to be satisfied with the initial effort. The collector has two choices: an all-Barber record, or one which gives equal billing to Morton Gould. Hanson does both offerings exceptionally well.

——Eastman-Rochester Symphony Orchestra, Howard Hanson, cond. Mercury 50148 (with Adagio; Overture to *The School for Scandal*; Symphony No. 1).

——Eastman-Rochester Symphony Orchestra, Howard Hanson, cond. Mercury 50075 (with Adagio; Overture to *The School for Scandal*; and Gould: Latin-American Symphonette).

Intermezzo from Act IV of "Vanessa"

Comparison with the complete opera recording under Mitropoulos (*see below, under* Opera) shows quite vivid differences. Kostelanetz spreads the music, intensifies it by his choice of tempo, whereas Mitropoulos takes it much faster and is apparently concerned with the support it gives to the opera as a whole. If Mitropoulos played the Intermezzo by itself one wonders whether he would not have a different conception, for the mood set by Kostelanetz allows the music to sing much more effectively.

——New York Philharmonic, André Kostelanetz, cond. COLUMBIA ML-5347 (MS-6040) (with Copland: A Lincoln Portrait, and Schuman: New England Triptych).

MEDEA (BALLET SUITE), OP. 23

This score of archaic and modern contrasts is Barber at his most violent, and though the composer-led orchestra could have proposed more shadings the music comes through in a satisfactory manner. Barber's usual romantic harmony has a polytonal tang in this opus.

——New Symphony Orchestra, Samuel Barber, cond. LONDON LL-1328 (with Symphony No. 2).

MEDEA (MEDEA'S MEDITATION AND DANCE OF VENGEANCE)

The portion of the suite that Munch plays is fast becoming a modern perennial. Its performance is worthy of the Bostonians' reputation, but having the complete score makes the London release above preferable.

——Boston Symphony Orchestra, Charles Munch, cond. RCA VICTOR LM-2197 (with Prokofiev: Piano Concerto No. 2).

OVERTURE TO "THE SCHOOL FOR SCANDAL," OP. 5

Do not be misled by the early opus designation. Although this was Barber's graduation piece at the Curtis Institute in Philadelphia, it is far from pedantic. No attempt is made to delineate any of the characters or scenes in Sheridan's play; rather, the overture depicts the general light mood of the work. No one who has heard the elegant and sensitive second theme can forget it. Hanson's orchestra gives a clearly enunciated performance. The sound is excellent also. As with the "Essay" (*see above*) the choice is only between companion pieces and not performances.

——Eastman-Rochester Symphony Orchestra, Howard Hanson, cond. MERCURY 50148 (with Adagio; Essay No. 1; Symphony No. 1).

——Eastman-Rochester Symphony Orchestra, Howard Hanson,

cond. MERCURY 50075 (with Adagio; Essay No. 1; and Gould: Latin-American Symphonette).

SOUVENIRS (BALLET SUITE), OP. 28

These are rather plain, almost dry considerations of dance forms ranging from a waltz through a galop. Barber is altogether too well-tailored in this work. Kurtz's performance can't do much for the music, since its wit seems labored. The companion piece is the opposite.

——Philharmonia Orchestra, Efrem Kurtz, cond. CAPITOL G-7146 (with Shostakovich: Age of Gold).

SYMPHONY NO. 1 (IN ONE MOVEMENT), OP. 9

Barber's initial symphony was written in 1936. It had the distinction of being the first work by an American composer to be performed at the Salzburg Festival, in 1937. Though it combines classical ideology with a romantic enlargement of harmony, it also has some latter-day touches—the orchestration contains Sibelian colors and the lusty drive of many a passage is kin to the music of Shostakovich.

The usual four movements are rolled into one in this work, but are sufficiently demarcated to be identified—thus making a synthesis of classical patterns. But this formula is not new. Hanson performs the symphony with care for each of the separate divisions as well as for their integration. As is often the case, there is a choice in accompanying works—either by Barber or by the conductor.

——Eastman-Rochester Symphony Orchestra, Howard Hanson, cond. MERCURY 50148 (with Adagio; Essay No. 1; Overture to *The School for Scandal*).

——Eastman-Rochester Symphony Orchestra, Howard Hanson, cond. MERCURY 50087 (with Hanson: Symphony No. 5; The Cherubic Hymn).

SYMPHONY NO. 2, OP. 19

This work was composed in 1944, during Barber's Army service. It was commissioned by the Army Air Force, but has no extra-musical (programmatic) connotations. There is, however, a tragic air about the symphony that shows Barber was not aloof from the emotions of wartime. Ostinato patterns serve both for rhythmic drive and for purposes of expression; the composer's usual warm lyricism is darker, more impetuous. Set forms contain the symphony, yet some unorthodox handling of the designs makes the work much more direct and personal than Barber's other compositions. The lines sing but have sting, and forceful harmony heightens the drama. Although the performance is acceptable the sound is not as spacious as one might desire. A newer recording of this symphony would be welcome.

——New Symphony Orchestra, Samuel Barber, cond. London LL-1328 (with Medea).

String Orchestra

ADAGIO FOR STRINGS, OP. 11

This is Barber's "Prelude in C-sharp Minor," and doubtless it has caused him as much chagrin (why do composers decry the success of a work of small proportions?). But the fact is that the "Adagio's" multitudinous performances and recordings—currently the most numerous of any of Barber's works—have banished from consideration its original place as the slow movement of the String Quartet, Op. 11 (recorded by Stradivari—*see below under* Chamber Music). The "Adagio" is string music that is liturgical in sound, with chordal placements enriching the ever-repeated monorhythmic theme.

The choice of recording must also (especially in the case of a short piece) be based on the other works on the record, and in this case pairing has not become stereotyped—as it has, for instance, on records where Bartók is always found shaking hands with Kodály. The buyer is offered combinations as disparate as Barber plus Tchaikovsky or Barber plus Honegger's numbered locomotive. As to performance, first place may go either to Ormandy or Hanson. The latter is more precise; the former has better players; both display an emotional affinity with the work. On the Ormandy disk all the music is in the string-orchestra medium; on the Hanson, the Mercury 50148 version, the offerings are closely related (all Barber music). The schmaltziest effort is by Stokowski and the driest comes from Golschmann, but the differentiations are minute and not worth arguing. Munch and Slatkin offer thorough readings,

while Page's is somewhat disappointing—he doesn't mind the score.
——in "The Strings of the Philadelphia Orchestra," Philadelphia Orchestra, Eugene Ormandy, cond. COLUMBIA ML-5187.
——Eastman-Rochester Symphony Orchestra, Howard Hanson, cond. MERCURY 50148 (with Essay No. 1; Overture to *The School for Scandal*; Symphony No. 1).
——Eastman-Rochester Symphony Orchestra, Howard Hanson, cond. MERCURY 50075 (with Essay No. 1; Overture to *The School for Scandal*; and Gould: Latin-American Symphonette).
——Boston Symphony Orchestra, Charles Munch, cond. RCA VICTOR LM-2105 (with Elgar: Introduction and Allegro, and Tchaikovsky: Serenade).
——in "Strings by Starlight," Hollywood Bowl Symphony Orchestra, Felix Slatkin, cond. CAPITOL P-8444 (SP-8444).
——in "The Orchestra," Leopold Stokowski, cond. CAPITOL SAL-8385 (SSAL-8385).
——in "Modern Orchestral Textures," New Orchestral Society of Boston, Willis Page, cond. COOK 10683 (RONDO 502).
——in "Contemporary American Music," Concert Arts Orchestra, Vladimir Golschmann, cond. CAPITOL P-8245.

Band

COMMANDO MARCH
Composed during Barber's term of service in the Army during World War II. A band march written by a leading contemporary composer is an extraordinary incident in any case, but unless one has the particular talents of a Sousa the incident is a waste of musical powder and shot. "*Gebrauchsmusik*" is not for this composer.
——in "American Concert Band Masterpieces," Eastman Symphonic Wind Ensemble, Frederick Fennell, cond. MERCURY 50079.

CHAMBER MUSIC

SONATA FOR CELLO AND PIANO, OP. 6
An important point of this sonata's design is the telescoping of the slow and scherzo movements into one. The two outer move-

ments are in set forms; the first is in sonata arrangement, with lines that sing in a traditional manner, and neat romantic harmony; the last consists of a series of connected variations on a theme, though not so titled. But this movement's construction is exceedingly tight-knit. Its sections unfold with no recapitulated material. This type of romantically constructed music suits Piatigorsky. Ricci does just as well, but Stradivari's sound cannot compare with Victor's.

——Gregor Piatigorsky, cello; Ralph Berkowitz, piano. RCA VICTOR LM-2013 (with Hindemith: Sonata).

——George Ricci, cello; Leopold Mittman, piano. STRADIVARI 602 (with String Quartet, and Wolf: Italian Serenade).

STRING QUARTET, OP. 11

Styled with excellence of design and a neutral regard for specific complexities of technique, Barber's quartet exemplifies his fine training and conservative outlook. The Stradivari group is well schooled and performs with proper style. Sonics are not too luscious, however. Thus, dating unfairly penalizes this type of recording, because so many buyers are concerned with acute sound fidelity and don't consider the music behind (or ahead of!) the engineering. The famed "Adagio" is heard here in its pristine, four-stringed state.

——Stradivari Records String Quartet. STRADIVARI 602 (with Sonata for Cello and Piano, and Wolf: Italian Serenade).

SUMMER MUSIC FOR WOODWIND QUINTET, OP. 31

The term "new music," once considered a signal for the critic's cannon and musketry to open fire, needs redefining. Many new works are dated at birth; few are dateless.

Barber's music shows craftsmanship, but it is less than acutely creative. His latest compositions are angled toward acceptance, rather than letting acceptance come from the music itself. The coterie of the eclectic is a substratum of composers, though good ones at that. Barber illustrates such eclecticism in this opus, written in 1956. In a review that appeared in September of that year I prophesied dozens of performances for it. I damn myself, willingly, by asserting that the symphonies of Joachim Raff also obtained (once upon a time) a wide hearing. Better to be played now than never is an argument I cannot discount, however.

If diplomatically written music is your taste, then this quasi-impressionistic, one-movement quintet will certainly please you. Acquiring it will serve, in any event, to let you hear at the same time a work of glistening liquidity, its sonorities a constant joy of fresh discovery (Etler's Quintet for Winds), as well as Dahl's composition. The last is chamber music without emotional heat, put together by the hand of a master. This type of music has sensual appeal too.

——New York Woodwind Quintet. CONCERT-DISC (CS-216) (with Dahl: Allegro and Arioso, and Etler: Quintet for Winds).

VOCAL

HERMIT SONGS, OP. 29

A set of ten songs set to texts by anonymous Irish monks and scholars living between the years 700 and 1300. Barber's ability to set words to music was proven in his early opus, "Dover Beach." These songs are sung exquisitely; the words (earthy, in many instances) are not very clear.

——Leontyne Price, soprano; Samuel Barber, piano. COLUMBIA ML-4988 (with Haieff: String Quartet No. 1).

CHORAL

THREE REINCARNATIONS, OP. 16

Somewhat bland mixed-voice settings of poems by James Stephens. The Hufstadter group projects this neo-Renaissance contrapuntalism with taste, but the occasion does not make for celebrations. The record includes gorgeous examples of Lassus, Palestrina, and the like, but its over-all title oddly refers only to the harpsichord portion. Queer cataloguing indeed!

——in "The Forgotten Pedal Harpsichord," The Hufstadter Singers, Robert Hufstadter, cond. COOK 11312.

OPERA

VANESSA

A company with the resources of RCA Victor would be loath to pass up the opportunity of a possible recording gold mine, represented by a four-act opera composed by America's very successful Samuel Barber, with a libretto by the just as successful, immeasurably more widely recognized Gian-Carlo Menotti, first performed in January, 1958, by the venerable Metropolitan Opera, awarded the Pulitzer Prize in the same year, and chosen for presentation in the staid Mozart-laden atmosphere of Salzburg. Victor tended its potential lode by using the same Metropolitan cast, orchestra, and conductor as that which gave the première. The vocal artists (especially Elias and Gedda) are excellent, and Barber's scheme makes vocalists (and many a listener) happy, for he adheres to set operatic standards: arias, duets, etc., with a culminating quintet which turns out to be the best chunk of the entire five sides.

The performance is stunningly controlled and unstinting preparation (the rehearsals and performances at the Met played a great part) shows from start to finish. Why so many of the words don't register is a vocal curse that haunts us everywhere, be it *Traviata* or *Vanessa*. But musically and dramatically *Vanessa* is somewhat of a grand operatic potpourri, with its material fused into a general style that is not recognizable as anything but patly eclectic. This makes for undiluted frustration on the part of anyone who seeks the impact of a *Wozzeck*, or even of a *La Bohème*. And it must mean further frustration for those American composers who have operas unperformed, unexamined, unrealized, untouched by human hands.

Victor's set has class and is packaged to fit. Why the sixth side was filled with oddments is perplexing. If one goes with Barber five-sixths of the way, why not entirely?
——Metropolitan Opera Orchestra and Chorus; Eleanor Steber, soprano; Rosalind Elias, mezzo-soprano; Regina Resnik, mezzo-soprano; Nicolai Gedda, tenor; Giorgio Tozzi, bass; George Cehanovsky, baritone; Robert Nagy, tenor; Dimitri Mitropoulos, cond. RCA Victor LM-6138 (LSC-6138) (with excerpts from Donizetti: *Lucia di Lammermoor* [Act 2], and Mascagni: *Cavalleria Rusticana* [Duet]).

Vanessa (abridged)
A shorter version of Barber's opera is also available.
——(Same as above). RCA Victor LM-6062 (LSC-6062).

2. Ernest Bloch
(1880—1959)

AMONG THE WORKS OF IMPORTANT CONTEMPORARY COMPOSERS, those of Ernest Bloch are among the most personal. Without adapting his music to any of the established modes such as linear counterpoint, twelve-tone technique, neoclassicism, or chordal continuums of any particular sort, he produced a number of masterworks. Two of these are already termed classics in their particular mediums. The Viola Suite and "Schelomo," for cello and orchestra, are considered to be two of the greatest and most individual works conceived for their respective instruments.

Bloch, a Swiss Jew who resided in the United States after his thirty-sixth year, early in his career expressed the desire to render the Jewish soul in his music; not to imitate chants and the like, but to give voice to the racial consciousness that flowed through him. He succeeded so admirably in this that the Jewish coloration is evident in most of his works, even though they have many other attributes. Nor have critics apparently ever forgotten his statement, for he has become to them a "Jewish" composer regardless of the fact that only *some* of his works were written with this intention in mind. However, the eloquence of Hebraic speech is heard in all of his music.

Yet, if Bloch's music is fundamentally Hebraic, it is also Oriental, and Swiss as well. The last strain is least significant in his multilingual music; yet it appears in the impressionistic accent, and at the same time the classic solidity, to be heard, to a degree, in every one of his works. His is a rare individuality, not affiliated with any particular school; the wonders of Bach and Beethoven are his Book of Psalms, sung in his own fashion.

During his last years Bloch undertook a remarkable series of works for unaccompanied violin and cello (one for solo viola remained unfinished). Realizing that the composer was very ill and could not live long, his publisher attempted to have some of these works recorded in Bloch's lifetime, but failed. Since important art often remains unrecognized until attention is given it posthumously, we may hope to see these fine works appear soon. The deletion of important recordings of contemporary music has been harmful to Bloch, as to others. The quartets (which London had issued in one package) have been discontinued and not a single one of these wonderful works has been issued since; also the pleasures of such important pieces as the "Suite Symphonique" and the "Three Jewish Poems" have never been ours to enjoy on records. And where is the opera *Macbeth*? The fate of this man's stunning individuality reminds one of the Biblical phrase: "They have ears, but they hear not."

ORCHESTRAL

ISRAEL SYMPHONY

One half of this work is symphonic, the other includes voices used with almost symphonic effect. Describing the Jewish people's most sacred day, Yom Kippur, and its antithesis, the feast of Succoth, Bloch displays a multiple personality: he prays and declaims; he is tender and barbaric; and he is rhapsodic. But above all he is preaching the faith.

This extremely moving work is given a well-directed performance, with carefully regulated sound that balances the large forces of orchestra and five solo voices. It represents Bloch's single work in the symphonic category available on records as of this date.
——Vienna State Opera Orchestra; Friedl Helsing, soprano; Helga Augsten, soprano; Elfriede Hofstaetter, alto; Lore Doerpinghaus, alto; Leo Heppe, bass; Franz Litschauer, cond. VANGUARD VRS-423.

Chamber Orchestra

FOUR EPISODES FOR PIANO, WINDS AND STRINGS

Bloch was a Jewish cosmopolitan who refused to travel along a single track. The greatness of his work lies in the fact that he never abandoned his own distinctive personality; the style of his music never disintegrated into snippets of various styles. The Chinese vignettes, the picture of ostinated obsession, and the other two episodes in this suite all have the tincture of Bloch himself. Though a lively performance, the fusion one expects is not always present and the sound is rather dead. Neither major-league Bloch nor a major-league recording.

——Knickerbocker Chamber Players, Izler Solomon, cond. MGM
E-3245 (with Berger: Serenade Concertante; Britten: Sinfonietta;
and Pinkham: Concertant for Violin, Harpsichord and Strings).

String Orchestra

CONCERTO GROSSO FOR STRING ORCHESTRA AND PIANO OBBLIGATO

Bloch's initial composition in concerto grosso style is a valuable
commercial property. When the original publisher discontinued his
business all the orchestral works were returned to their composers,
with one exception—Bloch's, which was sold to another firm. And
publishers do not buy twenty-two-minute string orchestra works
unless there's money in those strings!

This music is a magnificent treatment in the classic style, displaying a fervent voice through the sophisticated musical sounds
of this century. Bloch writes with a fresh viewpoint though his
four-movement work is rooted in designs of an earlier time. Mass
chordal writing marks the opening; the "Dirge" is searching, beautiful music. This entire second section is one difficult to forget.
Swiss recollections are basic to the third movement, and the concerto is completed by an exciting fugue, employing all the manifold techniques of the form.

Despite Hanson's performance, a recent release, the most fully
developed rendition remains the much older recording made by
Kubelik. Mercury goes all the way and honors it by giving the
purchaser a choice of companion pieces. In the fourth recording,
under Steinberg's baton, Bloch's music is played too formally.

——Chicago Symphony Orchestra; George Schick, piano; Rafael
Kubelik, cond. MERCURY 50001 (with Bartók: Music for Strings,
Percussion and Celeste).

——Chicago Symphony Orchestra; George Schick, piano; Rafael
Kubelik, cond. MERCURY 50027 (with Hindemith: Symphonic
Metamorphosis on Themes of Carl Maria von Weber).

——Eastman-Rochester Symphony, Howard Hanson, cond. MER-
CURY 50223 (SR-90223) (with Concerto Grosso No. 2).

——Pittsburgh Symphony Orchestra, Harry Franklin, piano; William Steinberg, cond. CAPITOL P-8212 (with Schuman: Symphony
for Strings).

CONCERTO GROSSO NO. 2 FOR STRING QUARTET AND STRING ORCHESTRA

Bloch's expertness in writing for string instruments is nowhere better evidenced than in this contemporary interweaving fashioned on classic models. The gentle climaxes are not the Bloch of the Jewish inspiration but there are Hebraic qualities within the work. The technique is resourceful; intellectualism does not rule merely because of the formal objective. This is one of the best recordings Solomon turned out during the halcyon days when MGM was sympathetic to matters contemporary. The Hanson recording has beautiful sound; it lacks urgency—the climate of performance is too temperate.

——MGM String Orchestra; Guilet String Quartet; Izler Solomon, cond. MGM E-3422 (with Antheil: Serenade for Strings, and Richter: Lament for String Orchestra).

——Eastman-Rochester Symphony, Howard Hanson, cond. MERCURY 50223 (SR-90223) (with: Concerto Grosso No. 1).

SOLO INSTRUMENT WITH ORCHESTRA

SCHELOMO—HEBRAIC RHAPSODY FOR CELLO AND ORCHESTRA

With the deletion from the catalogue of Bloch's Violin Concerto, this remains the only solo-with-orchestra work obtainable. (The "Voice in the Wilderness" [*see below*] is not a pure solo vehicle, though it is placed in this section for convenience.) Happily, the recording companies have cooperated with the cellists they have under contract and numerous versions are therefore available. We would be grateful for fewer with more disks of hitherto unrecorded Bloch.

"*Schelomo*" was composed in 1916, at the request of the cellist Alexander Barjansky. It is probably Bloch's most important and communicative work and doubtless his lasting testament. The heart and sincerity of the man were never so potently expressed. The music of this rhapsodic proclamation-declamation has the full cry, the self-revelatory insistence, and the sumptuousness of the Jewish race within it. Few Jews fail to be filled with emotion on hearing this work of secular-sacred incandescence; few non-Jews do not react similarly.

Any recording of the work must be measured against the blazing performance recorded by Feuermann and the Stokowski-led Philadelphia Orchestra, in the old wide-groove days. Victor transferred this first to a ten-inch LP, then onto one side of a twelve-inch Camden record, but it is no longer on the counters.

The choice among currently available performances must go either to Rose, who plays with dignity, sensitiveness, gorgeous tone, and careful phrasing, or to Piatigorsky, but the drenched thrills come from the younger man. The Bostonians are held too much in check by Munch and the microphoning has overemphasized the percussion in places where it should be a subtle shading and not a glaring highlight. Piatigorsky plays with superb skill, but while recognizing his status as musical elder statesman, one prefers the exultancy of younger blood. Neikrug does not portray a Solomon of passion, but a character who speaks in rubato; the performance is a small splash of cool water in place of a warm bath with scent. Stokowski's handling of the orchestra in this recording leaves the wonders of the score undiscovered—difficult to understand since he all but owns the work.

The remaining four are simply not in the race. Nelsova is uneven, too bravura, with insufficient melismatic projection. Navarra seems removed from the score's ecstatic proclamations; Janigro is not keyed to the style, while De Machula overplays, overweeps, overstates his role and edits as he draws his bow. Each version has a different companion work, which may influence one's choice, but *the "Schelomo"* reading credits belong to Leonard Rose, Dimitri Mitropoulos, and the New York Philharmonic.

——Philharmonic Symphony Orchestra of New York; Leonard Rose, cello; Dimitri Mitropoulos, cond. Columbia ML-4425 (with Saint-Saëns: Concerto No. 1 in A Minor).

——Boston Symphony Orchestra; Gregor Piatigorsky, cello; Charles Munch, cond. RCA Victor LM-2109 (with Walton: Concerto for Cello and Orchestra).

——Symphony of the Air; George Neikrug, cello; Leopold Stokowski, cond. United Artists UAL-7005 (8005) (with Ben-Haim: From Israel).

——London Philharmonic Orchestra; Zara Nelsova, cello; Ernest Ansermet, cond. London LL-1232 (with Voice in the Wilderness).

——London Symphony Orchestra; André Navarra, cello; Richard Austin, cond. Capitol P-18012 (with Tchaikovsky: Variations on a Rococo Theme).

——Philharmonic Symphony Orchestra of London; Antonio Janigro, cello; Artur Rodzinski, cond. Westminster XWN-18007 (with Bruch: Canzone; Kol Nidre).

——Hague Philharmonic Orchestra; Tibor De Machula, cello; Willem Van Otterloo, cond. Epic LC-3072 (with Lalo: Concerto in D Minor for Cello and Orchestra).

Voice in the Wilderness—Symphonic Poem
with Cello Obbligato

In a sense, a sequel to "*Schelomo*," but far more introverted in spirit, with visionary meditations in place of glowing splendors. Bloch's rhapsodic shapes are placed properly in perspective in the single recording listed. Cellists seem to shy away from this work, for they must accept the secondary role of an instrumental commentator.

——London Philharmonic Orchestra; Zara Nelsova, cello; Ernest Ansermet, cond. London LL-1232 (with Schelomo).

INSTRUMENTAL

Cello

Prayer from "Jewish Life"

One of a group of three pieces Bloch wrote in 1924. (The others are titled "Supplication" and "Jewish Song.") Since the style is precisely the same as the work for violin and piano bearing the subtitle "Three Pictures of Chassidic Life," this set could be termed Bloch's "*Baal Shem*" for cello.

The encore collection in which the "Prayer" is contained is much better than is usually the case. Other contemporary composers represented are Ravel, Falla, and Nin. Janigro and Bagnoli team well together. The engineering is a credit to Westminster; the instruments are perfectly balanced and the resonance quotient is excellent.

——in "Cello Encores," Antonio Janigro, cello; Eugenio Bagnoli, piano. Westminster XWN-18004.

Piano

ENFANTINES

Though children's pieces, Bloch's set of ten sketches is not limited to any age. The *"Enfantines"* were originally written as exercises for Bloch's two daughters but, as with the music for children produced by such important composers as Bartók, Prokofiev, Shostakovich, Stravinsky, Toch, and others, the suite has a rich musical quality for listeners as well as meeting the needs of students. Pressler performs poetically; Ajemian is direct and plays the dynamic spades as they turn up, as spades. Obviously, the choice of recording will be governed by the desire either for a cross-section of first-rate contemporaries or for music exclusively by Bloch.

——in "Piano Music for Children," Menahem Pressler. MGM E-3010.

——in "Piano Music by Ernest Bloch," Maro Ajemian. MGM E-3445.

FIVE SKETCHES IN SEPIA

Bloch was attracted to the piano only mildly; his important music lies in other media. This set of pieces (a cyclic suite, since the final movement quotes material from the previous portions) tends toward impressionism. Ajemian plays with certainty and sensitive use of the pedal; vagueness and inanition defeat the other listing.

——in "Piano Music of Ernest Bloch," Maro Ajemian. MGM E-3445.

——LeRoy Miller. MUSIC LIBRARY RECORDINGS MLR-7015 (with Poems of the Sea; Sonata).

POEMS OF THE SEA

The genesis of this work is descriptive material: "Waves," a "Chanty," and "At Sea." The rich sonorities of the pieces are styled cogently by Ajemian. Miller plays just acceptably.

——in "Piano Music of Ernest Bloch," Maro Ajemian. MGM E-3445.

——LeRoy Miller. MUSIC LIBRARY RECORDINGS MLR-7015 (with Five Sketches in Sepia; Sonata).

SONATA FOR PIANO

Bloch in a stormy mood, despite a more relaxed central ("Pastorale") section. The music is conceived on an orchestral scale and demands much from the performer. He must clarify the various masses of sound, which quite often are heard contrapuntally. However, Bloch's plan of composition makes everything as clear as a gigantic Gothic structure.

Cumming, himself a composer, has given the work a clean performance, and done so without fuss. Nádas has the requisite technique, but not much affinity for Bloch. The sonata requires a virtuoso—a red-blooded, born-to-the-keyboard performer. A number of such artists appear in our concert halls and make recordings. Why is this work unheeded by them?

——Richard Cumming. MUSIC LIBRARY RECORDINGS MLR-7015 (with Five Sketches in Sepia; Poems of the Sea).

——István Nádas. PERIOD 736 (with Bartók: Sonata; Prokofiev: Sonata No. 7; and Stravinsky: Sonata).

Viola

MEDITATION

Composers' short pieces sometimes tend to be set in a different, somewhat lighter frame, but this is not true of Bloch. This short mood piece is as Blochian as are his large works. The plan of presenting four of the composer's works for viola and piano on one record presents a unique opportunity for comparison.

——William Primrose, viola; David Stimer, piano. CAPITOL P-8355 (with Processional; Suite Hébraïque; Suite for Viola).

PROCESSIONAL

A somewhat impressionistic piece. However, Bloch's impressionism is more earthbound than Debussy's. The Jewish characteristic is not paramount, neither is it absent. Beautifully performed.

——William Primrose, viola; David Stimer, piano. CAPITOL P-8355 (with Meditation; Suite Hébraïque; Suite for Viola).

SUITE HÉBRAÏQUE

This suite was composed in 1951; it is therefore Bloch's second suite for viola and piano. However, unlike his initial work in the form, the stringed instrument is here in the spotlight; the piano is principally a background voice. For that reason it is discussed as instrumental music, rather than chamber music.

In this "Hebraic" suite Bloch's Jewish musical thoughts are mingled with medieval modes and contemporary mannerisms. None of the latter are utilized haphazardly; in every case they are expressive.

Primrose's recording is a "first." No better performer could be named. His interpretation of the three movements, "Rhapsodie," "Processional" (not to be confused with the separate piece bearing the same title), and "Affirmation," demonstrates the highest type of stringed-instrument art.

——William Primrose, viola; David Stimer, piano. CAPITOL P-8355 (with Meditation; Processional; Suite for Viola).

Violin

BAAL SHEM—THREE PICTURES OF CHASSIDIC LIFE

Shofar-like calls and intervallic spans taken from the Hebrew ritual abound in this suite. But, despite the Jewish melos, the augmented (crying) intervals, the heavy melancholy and despair which seep through the music's tissues, the sounds this Blochian Jewish credo makes have much in common with music of the other Semitic races. Bloch's music is, however, the first and most important example of modern secular Hebraic music. But this is not to limit its significance. "*Baal Shem*" is a nationalistic work, but its Hebraic dialect is only one aspect of the international music speech it employs.

Eudice Shapiro's is the only complete recording. Her playing is rare in the violin world, for technical power is subordinated to the musical objective. The kaleidoscopic colors and free rhapsodizing of the Bloch suite are beautifully framed in her performance. And if one wishes a "*Nigun*" superior to any of those listed below, this recording is "*prima la musica.*"

——in "Modern Masterpieces for the Violin," Eudice Shapiro, violin; Ralph Berkowitz, piano. VANGUARD VRS-1023.

NIGUN FROM "BAAL SHEM"

The "Improvisation" (*Nigun*) from the "*Baal Shem*" triptych is quite often played separately. Its recitative-cantillative quality originated in the synagogues of Bloch's forefathers. One would expect a Russian-Jewish violinist to display expertise in such a piece and Elman's fervor is magnificently in keeping. Kogan has more repose and a beautiful tone, hard to better, while Milstein combines fastidiousness and rhythmic excitement with regal tonal splendor. Since Bloch had written in the cantillated retards, and other gradations of tempi, Bezrodny's amplifications overdemonstrate the sacred passion of the piece almost to the point of sensuousness. Too much of a muchness in his case.

——Mischa Elman, violin; Joseph Seiger, piano. LONDON LL-1467 (with Achron: Hebrew Melody; Josten: Sonatina; and Korngold: Suite from *Much Ado about Nothing*).

——in "Encores by Kogan," Leonid Kogan, violin; Andrei Mitnik, piano. RCA VICTOR LM-2250.

——Nathan Milstein, violin; Carlo Bussotti, piano. CAPITOL P-8259 (with Brahms: Allegro in C Minor; Paganini-Milstein: Paganiniana; Pergolesi: Sonata No. 12; Schumann: Intermezzo; and Suk: Burleska).

——in "Bezrodny Plays Gershwin," Igor Bezrodny, violin; Abram Makarov, piano. MONITOR MC-2028.

CHAMBER MUSIC

SUITE FOR VIOLA AND PIANO

This work's winning of a $1000 award in the Berkshire Chamber Music Festival Competition of 1919 did more to bring Bloch's music to the attention of the world than any of his other compositions. Though in Bloch's second version of the suite the piano is replaced by a large orchestra, the original chamber-music setting is not to be considered supplanted. The amplified form, however, is in the frustrating category of "unrecorded" literature.

Without musical scene-painting or programmaticism of any kind, this suite is a composite of Oriental sounds, suggesting Java, India, and China. That a Swiss Jew could produce such music is not odd at all, however, since Hebraic expression is cognate with Eastern music.

The Oriental musical language will be recognized in the augmented intervals that characterize many of the melodic lines. The introductory slow section of the initial movement is a foil for the primitive dance of the Allegro portion. The second part of the suite is a biting, caustically accented scherzo. The preoccupation with bare intervals results in tightly bound sonorities, especially in these fast-tempoed sections.

All composers have their harmonic and formal mannerisms. Bloch's slow movements are always nocturnal, the melodies emerging from embedded chordal arpeggios, and ostinated rhythms, over which the song runs its course. To emphasize the melancholy mood of the Lento (third) movement, Bloch mutes the solo string voice; he follows his habit of recalling themes of previous divisions in the finale.

According to Joan Chissell, a British authority, the titles of the movements were to be (1) "In the Jungle," (2) "Grotesques," (3) "Nocturne," and (4) "Land of the Sun." That Bloch in the end eliminated these titles means that the listener should not consider them. On the other hand, they are central to the composer's line of musical reasoning, and if one must have the aid of picturization of one sort or another, then these headings are certainly not incorrect, unofficial though they may be.

Primrose is truly magnificent in his conception of the work. His playing has meaning, it has dramatic sweep, and he defines the assorted colors of the viola with minute sensitivity. Stimer's musicianship cannot be questioned, but his dynamic contrasts are rather weak. The Classic release gets more than a passing grade, yet is not fully satisfactory. Gromko does not have enough bite in the ironic scherzo. His somewhat narrow tone does not do full justice to the virility of Bloch's work.

——William Primrose, viola; David Stimer, piano. CAPITOL P-8355 (with Meditation; Processional; Suite Hébraïque).

——William Gromko, viola; Harriet Wingreen, piano. CLASSIC EDITIONS CE-1038 (with Vaughan Williams: Suite for Viola and Piano).

SONATA NO. 1 FOR VIOLIN AND PIANO

The keynote of this work is its emotional barbarism, evident immediately in the opening fortissimo declaration. The same elemental savagery is called on in the final (third) movement. There is a prophetic bitterness that bespeaks the Biblical robes worn by this composer. There are moments when the violin and piano function like tribal instruments, giving evidence of Bloch's racial characteristics, which include that of dogged perseverance. If Druian and Simms seem to be striving for more than they are capable of, they are simply playing Bloch's music as it was written. Theirs is an engaging recording, fully displaying the architectural clarity of the sonata and with hearty, correct sound. A better version is hard to imagine.

——Rafael Druian, violin; John Simms, piano. MERCURY 50095 (with Sonata No. 2 ["Poème Mystique"]).

SONATA No. 2 ("POÈME MYSTIQUE") FOR VIOLIN AND PIANO

The relationship between the first and second violin and piano sonatas is similar to that between the pair of works for cello and orchestra, "*Schelomo*" and "*Voice in the Wilderness*." In both instances the later work is cooler and more serene than the earlier one. The second sonata also differs formally from the first, its material being designed in one extended movement.

It is to Druian's credit that he styles his performance with sharpness, bringing out as many of the details as does Heifetz. The latter's tone is rounder but not much more so than his younger colleague. As for the pianists, Simms is a much better musician than Smith in terms of his understanding of Bloch's aims.

——Rafael Druian, violin; John Simms, piano. MERCURY 50095 (with Sonata No. 1).

——Jascha Heifetz, violin; Brooks Smith, piano. RCA VICTOR LM-2089 (with Grieg: Sonata No. 2 in G, Op. 13).

STRING QUARTET No. 1, IN B MINOR

Bloch has said that his quartet was composed to express his outlook on life (*Weltanschauung*) at the age of thirty-six; that no work of his "can be compared to it in this respect." There are semiprogrammatic infiltrations in the four movements, conceived in classical form, plus a summarization of thematic reflections that ties the work's final movement in with the previous sections. But beyond this, the work is bound up with Bloch's racial consciousness: the intoning of the Hebrew cantor, laments derived from the liturgies of Bloch's ancestors, echoes of the *chazzanim* with their fervid chants of prayer, the *Chassidim* with their wailing and riotous dances, are heard throughout this quartet. Bloch's opus, a remarkable work in chamber literature, is intensely rooted in the Hebraic tradition. Yet, as with all nationalistic music that spills over its boundaries and becomes international, so the vocabulary of this quartet is universal, understandable to all.

Which means that a quartet team such as the Grillers plays the piece with authority, despite some convolutionary rubati that are not among the minutely detailed directions given by Bloch on his score. The same practice of adding rhapsodic items to a work conceived with controlled fantasy is heard in the Roths' performance, but much more so. The Roths' unison playing is not all it should be. Now, microtonal differences are important, since they not only can play havoc with the diatonic system, but because they are particularly noticeable in the purity of the string-quartet medium. In the performances under review the intonation is tampered with by the Roth group and tempered by the Griller foursome. Both disks have good sound, but the miking of the Roth performance gives one the added distraction of fingering and bowing noises. (To secure the Griller record one must purchase the entire set of three records, and even these are not readily available. In view of Bloch's reputation it seems proper to raise the question of re-releasing the London set in individual records.)

——Griller String Quartet. LONDON LLA-23 (with Quartets Nos. 2, 3, and 4).

——Roth String Quartet. MERCURY 50110.

STRING QUARTET NO. 2

At this advanced date, musical forms have been more or less freed of strict interpretation. A quartet composition rarely duplicates a scheme used by Mozart, Brahms, or Franck. However, structural balance must be preserved, and even in a rhapsodic design there must be a unifying basis. The plan of an art work can be complex. The fact that such complexity can be analyzed does not make the work inferior to a composition employing simple musical speech which reaches heavenly heights.

Bloch's plan for his second quartet consists of two main themes, the first of these subsidiary to the second; the themes are related in various ways, the first beginning and ending the work, and the second developed constantly so that the four movements are tied together as one, regardless of change of mood, pace, and style. The overall design is like a gigantic held-in-check variation, not developed sectionally but on a large mural basis. The form has that intellectual honesty without which a work cannot survive, or, for that matter, be considered worthy in any respect. Its combination of emotion and creativity distinguishes this work among the quartet literature.

Given such a formal design, a performer must be creatively responsive, must understand the equating of emotion and intellect. The recording by the Musical Arts Quartet rates the highest recommendation, save that the copy I have shows a peculiar decline in sonic strength for the last inch or so on both sides of the record. The buyer is warned to check this point lest this defect be present in all the pressings. London's recording is good but far less impressive. The Grillers play meticulously but without sufficient discernment, in this instance.

——Musical Arts Quartet. Vanguard VRS-437.

——Griller String Quartet. London LLA-23 (with Quartets Nos. 1, 3, and 4).

String Quartet No. 3

Bloch's third string quartet was completed in 1952. In it a change of philosophy is evident. There are no Hebraic-Talmudic accents, traces of which were evident in the second quartet, written seven years previously. This quartet is much more reserved; declamation has given place to continual, expressive string conversation. The Grillers' reading is impressive.

——Griller String Quartet. London LLA-23 (with Quartets Nos. 1, 2, and 4).

String Quartet No. 4

Instrumental coordination and timbre balance are accompanied by a distinctive performance of this last of Bloch's quartets to be placed on records. (For a time it was thought that Bloch had produced only four quartets; after his death it was found that he had written a fifth.) Bloch's development as a composer of quartets is marked by ever-increasing use of polyphony in place of direct thematic statement; cyclic form is also important. The Grillers are somewhat sharper in their playing here than in the other three quartets with which this one is packaged.

——Griller String Quartet. LONDON LLA-23 (with Quartets Nos. 1, 2, and 3).

QUINTET FOR PIANO AND STRINGS

This lean yet rugged work is considered one of Bloch's best. It also is one in which the Hebraic influences are rather negligible. Instead, Afro-Indian elements are much in evidence. Eastern exoticism always held a fascination for this composer; it was only in his very last compositions that he eliminated both Judaic and non-Western musical speech.

In many of Bloch's works, there is an unstated, shadowed type of programmaticism (similar to that hinted at by Beethoven, especially in some of his late-period compositions). This programmatic element is suggested in the quintet by the use of quarter-tones, the semi-outlined *Dies Irae* theme, the succession of moods ranging from the barbaric to the most serene. These, together with Bloch's manifold colors, place this work midway between absolute and programmatic music. The latter quality depends on the auditor; no explanation being made by the composer, the performers must convey the story by the use of the stringed instruments' microtones (well-registered on the record), by varying specific string qualities, striking with the wooden part of the bow, using mutes, chained trills, and playing on the fingerboard. All these, and many more, are anatomical marks on the organic body of the work. They cannot be considered merely as technical effects. The single recorded performance of the quintet does not fulfill these requirements. The Waldens with Mrs. Roy Harris play with a too-relaxed quality, the frictions are glossed over, the grain of the music does not show. There is too much polish. In some music, roughage is essential. Some intonation mishaps and shaky balances indicate hasty editing.

——Johana Harris, piano; Walden String Quartet. MGM E-3239.

SACRED MUSIC

SACRED SERVICE (AVODATH HAKODESH)

Music in the ancient synagogue consisted of abundant traditional melodies and cantillations handed down almost by rote. The organized synagogue musical service is a fairly recent development. In the first quarter of the present century improvisation gave way to formally composed works for the Hebrew liturgy. Before this, works with religious content had been composed by men such as Sulzer and Nowakowsky, but these composers are important only to Hebrew liturgical musical history, not to the world at large. Because of its more modern outlook, the Reform movement within the Jewish community encouraged the composition of original synagogue music. Achron, Diamond, Foss, Freed, Jacobi, Saminsky, Weiner, and others also composed such works, but those by Ernest Bloch and Darius Milhaud are considered to be the most important (Milhaud's remains unrecorded).

Bloch's work is unique in that it discards the set orientation of Eastern decorative ("old style") music in favor of a more neutral method. It is Hebraic at its roots, but completely universal in its appeal. It is music that combines the dignity and quietude necessary for worship with the drama and power that aid in its projection from the concert platform. Spiritually, it is Bloch's counterpart to Bach's great B Minor Mass.

The London performance is magnificent and the principal solo parts, sung by the bass-baritone, Marko Rothmuller, have a stirring vividness and keen personality. It is interesting to note that Rothmuller is the author of a definitive survey, *The Music of the Jews— An Historical Appreciation*, which was published in 1954.

——London Philharmonic Orchestra; London Philharmonic Choir; Marko Rothmuller, bass-baritone; Dorothy Bond, soprano; Doris Cowan, contralto; Ernest Bloch, cond. LONDON 5006.

3. Elliott Carter
(1908—   )

ELLIOTT CARTER IS ONE OF THE MOST LEARNED OF AMERICAN composers. Most of his music tends to be philosophic, its emotion almost repressed in favor of the purest logical handling of the material and the shaping of the architectural proportions. But his musical credo is not to be intellectually pigeon-holed. Carter's music is philosophic in the sense that it avoids parochialism. He knows that creative growth requires constant renewal. His profound music constantly brings new problems to light, relates them to previously solved ones and sends out new refractions.

A listener to Carter's music will find emotion within it—dynamic not synthetic. But there is no compulsion on his part to serve the public in its predilection for singable melodies. Totally absorbed in the creative process, he has the virtue of refusing to be anything but a serious composer. If the listener will devote himself to Carter's purposes, the music will bring its own particular satisfactions.

Only five works (two for orchestra and three chamber-music pieces) constitute the recorded-music catalogue of this composer, but each holds an important place in his total output. Furthermore, each of these compositions is of a different construction, formally and in terms of instrumentation.

ORCHESTRAL

THE MINOTAUR—SUITE FROM THE BALLET

The post-Stravinskian sounds which convey this story based on a Greek legend have an intensity derived from complex sonoric tenets. The tonal territory is wide, the music fluid without over-astringent dissonance. This is due to the chromatic range of the harmonies, but let it not be thought that this music is (to use the loosest term in music) "atonal." Carter makes the key pole vibrate but it is not loosened by the chromaticism. Thus, this is music related to the past, yet new. In terms of orchestration the suite is multi-hued. It is expertly performed and clearly recorded save for an occasional "boom" that is certainly not in the score. The companion piece is a kind of encyclopedic synthesis of Balinese musical art in Western translation.

——Eastman-Rochester Symphony Orchestra, Howard Hanson, cond. MERCURY 50103 (with McPhee: Tabuh-Tabuhan, Toccata for Orchestra).

VARIATIONS FOR ORCHESTRA

Of primary importance here is the fact that none of the simple catch-alls of variation design are present. Nor does the work fit into any type of routine technical elaboration. The formal balances are achieved by a strong sense of stylistic unity and organic growth whereby one statement leads to another, which in turn produces other, related propositions: i.e., the variations come from within and from without and are combined as well as compounded in multitudinous ways. Despite the constant mutations (an aggressive fluidity), the color and rhythmic juggling give the music its principal strength, its coherence.

The Louisville Orchestra does itself proud with this work. Not a top-drawer outfit by any means, the group conquers the complex problems of Carter's score in a most astounding performance. The sound equations are acute. This record holds interest from every angle of consideration: Carter writes with freshness of constructive expansion and the Louisville Orchestra illustrates this beautifully.

——Louisville Orchestra, Robert Whitney, cond. LOUISVILLE COMMISSIONING SERIES LOU-58-3 (with Helm: Second Piano Concerto).

CHAMBER MUSIC

EIGHT ETUDES AND A FANTASY FOR WOODWIND QUARTET

By concentration on a single line, an etude formulates its own coherence. The great majority of etudes are products of technical apprenticeship; only the brilliant masters of musical composition have been able to combine craftsmanship with creative meaning in this form. The contemporary composer has not been much inclined to enter this field of endeavor; in chamber music the possibilities have hardly been touched. Carter's "Fantasy" is a contrapuntal summation of the previously stated eight-chapter text, and here too the etude style prevails. Heard separately, one might define this ninth movement as a *quodlibet*; heard as a postscript, it gives the work a valid conclusion. The performance is superb and a credit to the unselfish CRI firm.

——Members of the New York Woodwind Quintet. COMPOSERS RECORDINGS CRI-118 (with Porter: String Quartet No. 8).

STRING QUARTET

Approximately three-quarters of an hour in length, this quartet marks one of the high points in American chamber music; artistically, historically, and—most significant—technically. The innovation here is permutative rhythm, designed to function with thematic content as a second dimension of continuity, parallel to the basic matters of melody, harmony, counterpoint, form, and color. This rhythmic empathy which is developed alongside all the other elements (as well as complementing them) gives rise to a tremendous sense of freedom, almost of exploratory improvisation. Carter's quartet is not, as some critics have incorrectly stated, a twelve-tone work—it is as far from Schoenbergian doctrines as it is from Stravinsky. The music is a synthesis of the classical symmetries of control and balance, paradoxically obtained by asymmetrical means.

Carter's quartet is of excruciating difficulty for the performers. The Waldens do a herculean job and prove their transcendent abilities to cope with the score. Carter's music demands and takes much from the listener. This quartet is a new musical phenomenon and it must be judged according to a new scale of values. Heard sufficiently often, these will be recognized.

——Walden Quartet of the University of Illinois. COLUMBIA ML-5104.

WOODWIND QUINTET

Form, with this composer, is best described by the German *fortspinnung*—"spinning forth." This process of creating continuity by dynamic attention to growth within a single, compact unit rather than symmetrical disposition is uncompromising. But it is not the mark of an unyielding composer. Rather, Carter is constructively outspoken, refusing to work according to precepts that can be catalogued under precise, formal headings. His work is perhaps quite intellectual, but it is also quite an art experience—

and includes, in this piece, the kind of pert humor only woodwinds can convey.

The disk has excellent sound plus balance and the performance displays a first-class ensemble who know their way around a recording studio.

——in "An American Woodwind Symposium," New Art Wind Quintet. CLASSIC EDITIONS CE-2003.

4. Carlos Chávez
(1899—   )

CARLOS CHÁVEZ IS NOT ONLY MEXICO'S FOREMOST MUSICIAN, BUT A master in the international musical field. He is a distinguished composer, conductor, and educator; and above all, a warm, intelligent, and forcefully honest human being. Chávez became one of the most important of all musical pioneers through his industrious efforts to make Mexico a great musical country, with the artistic profits to be shared by all the people of the land.

Without any creative cerebration and without deliberately using arid and stark tonal combinations merely for the sake of being known as a contemporary voice, Chávez has composed "abstract" works which are as basically Mexican as his nationalistically-titled productions, the only difference being that they are less sensuous (if any of Chávez's music can be described as sensuous).

With more and more of this composer's compositions being published, his recording total may be increased. As of now, the pickings are very lean, save for the unique status of the "Toccata" for percussion instruments. This has already been recorded by Boston, Capitol, MGM (available in two different albums), Urania (twice), and the University of Illinois. (The latter's small but selective CRS series is worthy of consideration by anyone interested in contemporary art. Unfortunately, these recordings have not been publicized and are therefore little known.) Truly the number of "Toccata" recordings is a remarkable acknowledgment of an equally remarkable composer.

ORCHESTRAL

OBERTURA REPUBLICANA
Rampant nationalism in plain, unadorned (un-Chávezian) musical diction. A real band-in-the-park march, plus a waltz, and a song are combined in forthright pops-program manner. Not the most exciting fare, but an interesting example of light Mexican music.

——in "Music of Mexico," Symphony Orchestra of Mexico, Carlos Chávez, cond. DECCA DL-9527.

44

SINFONIA DE ANTIGONA (SYMPHONY No. 1)

Contemporary archaic solidity and austerity characterize this eleven-minute, one-movement symphony. In 1932 Chávez composed music for a Jean Cocteau production of Sophocles' *Antigone*. It was from this score that he drew (in 1933) the material for the symphony. There is no programmatic basis; the symphony expresses a harsh, almost bitter pessimism. It has acidity and acridity; it has a power that is eloquent. The prickling iciness of this work is an important contribution to the music of the century.

Chávez has explained that ancient Greek music was his source —"the themes all are modal, and the harmony is in fourths and fifths, thirds having been avoided because the Greek musical system treated them as dissonant." This restricted plan has sufficient sting in its harmony. It is orchestrated with equal power, the orchestra being very large, including bass flute, heckelphone, and two harps.

Himself a first-rate conductor, Chávez's performance with the Stadium group (alias New York Philharmonic) is superb. Everest's sound is brilliant and rich.

——Stadium Symphony Orchestra of New York, Carlos Chávez, cond. EVEREST LPBR-6029 (SDBR-3029) (with Sinfonia India; Sinfonia Romantica).

SINFONIA INDIA (SYMPHONY No. 2)

Like the composer's "*Antigona*" this is a single-movement symphony. It has design, it has formal balance; neither is dependent on textbook formulas. Chávez resists being diverted from his goal by marking of time, by patch-work. There is a complete lack of fussy figuration, ornaments, or padding in this music. In Chávez's Mexican style native art is conveyed through the use of indigenous materials, blended spiritually (not literally) with the composer's aesthetic. The "*Sinfonia India*" has flaming color that can only be described as Igor Stravinsky in the land of Mexico, but this is not to question Chávez's originality in any way. The proof lies in the performances: since its première in 1936 the "*Sinfonia India*" has been performed on a worldwide basis. It remains Carlos Chávez's most brilliant, most individual composition.

Both recordings are under the direction of the composer. The first is *the* recording. It has magnificent sound and virtuoso performance. The Decca release has dated sonics, though the sharpness of the scoring comes through presentably.

——Stadium Symphony Orchestra of New York, Carlos Chávez, cond. EVEREST LPBR-6029 (SDBR-3029) (with Sinfonia de Antigona; Sinfonia Romantica).

——in "Music of Mexico," Symphony Orchestra of Mexico, Carlos Chávez, cond. DECCA DL-9527.

SINFONIA ROMANTICA (SYMPHONY No. 4)

Chávez employs his usual methods in this work, the result of a Louisville Orchestra Commission. The material is given a sonorous setting that is as strong and personal as that expressed in the orchestral colors of the first two symphonies. Chávez's rhythmic slant actually slants; no pedestrianism in this orbit. The melodic lines are somewhat short, save in the aria-like middle movement; they have an urban drive with a suburban spaciousness. Throughout a compactness of thought marks the inventiveness that this composer's music always displays.

A single slip in the recording caught the ear of this reviewer—all else is top-flight. The engineering skill in producing the disk deserves its own laurel wreath.

——Stadium Symphony Orchestra of New York, Carlos Chávez, cond. EVEREST LPBR-6029 (SDBR-3029) (with Sinfonia de Antigona; Sinfonia India).

String Orchestra

SINFONIA No. 5

A work of color and rhythm with a lean sonority of taut percussiveness. Chávez's extremely inventive mind is illustrated here. The nondescriptive title signifies his brand of neoclassicism. Top-rank performers are required since the instrumental demands are of virtuoso order—not, however, for purposes of display. Chávez's instrumentational directions are always aimed at the musical purpose and nothing else.

The MGM release is unfortunately not first-rate. The mishaps in the playing have been permitted to stand as they fall out of intonational focus and the clarity is far from what the score indicates. Since this is an important Chávez work and as important an addition to the string-orchestra catalogue, it is a shame the performance was not scrubbed clean. Should one wish to own a recording for the sake of the composition, not the performance, choose E-3423, since the Ben-Haim is performed much better (it's much simpler) than the Toccata, even though the Israeli's work cannot be rated in a class with Chávez.

——MGM String Orchestra, Izler Solomon, cond. MGM E-3423 (with Ben-Haim: Concerto for Strings).

——MGM String Orchestra, Izler Solomon, cond. MGM E-3548 (with Toccata for Percussion).

Percussion

TOCCATA

If the percussion family were once merely metrical servants they are now mature musical beings. A strong group they are, ranging from the extreme soprano gamut to the lowest contrabass register. Their individuality is born of contrariety, being made of skin, wood, metal, glass, and other substances both rough and smooth, and the various instruments—drum, cymbal, bell and others—being pitched actually or simulatively by size.

Percussion music as a medium of artistic expression can no longer be thought of as *avant-garde* nonsense. The healthy condition of its literature, the several ensembles devoted to presenting this type of work make further preaching unnecessary. We now possess compositions in the medium that are outstanding. Two of these have become "classics"—Varèse's "Ionisation" and Chávez's three-movement "Toccata." (Additional proof: the published material for the Mexican's composition is well into its second edition!)

In the "Toccata" a membranous group is used exclusively in the opening movement; the dynamic power is tremendous, and ostinati drawn from Mexican Indian rhythmic patterns prevail. Bell and metal instruments hold the stage in the middle part; the music is quasi-threnodic and beautifully mysterious. Instrumental mixtures are the elements for the exciting fugal finale. Chávez is extremely resourceful in this work and has set a mark that it is difficult to imagine being excelled. This magnificent work belongs in every representative library of recorded music.

A buyer's decision should be governed not only by the quality of the "Toccata" performance, but by what is paired with it on each record. In this respect the all-percussion records, Urania's UX-134 and that on the CRS label, are tops. Although Boston's is a close second, it has a great deal of empty record space and is therefore no bargain. MGM has a discriminating combination of related works, though not totally percussion-concerned. It also offers the "Toccata" on a disk with another Chávez composition (but the string work is not done well). The Capitol release must be given careful thought since it also has Milhaud's seldom-heard concerto, while Urania's 7144 is least interesting since it throws Respighi and Granados into the same container and they just don't mix with Chávez.

The best performances are by the two ensembles conducted by Paul Price (who is the artistic father of the current interest in percussion teaching and performance) and by the Boston group. Urania's depth of sound, its acutely balanced resonance and the proportioned presence of each instrument results in an example not only of fine percussion reproduction but of recording art *in toto*. These factors, together with brilliance of execution, weigh so heavily that all the other recordings are completely overshadowed. Solomon is sympathetic but the sound is on the dull side. Slatkin has a certain sensitivity, minus pungent excitation. Urania's Gotham Players offer only an average performance.

——in "Percussion!," Manhattan Percussion Ensemble, Paul Price, cond. URANIA UX-134 (USD-1034).

——University of Illinois Percussion Ensemble, Paul Price, cond. UNIVERSITY OF ILLINOIS CUSTOM RECORDING SERIES CRS-3 (with Colgrass: Three Brothers; Harrison: Canticle No. 3; McKenzie: Introduction and Allegro; and Varèse: Ionisation).

——Boston Percussion Group. BOSTON RECORDS B-207 (with Farberman: Evolution).

——in "Spanish and Latin-American Music for Unusual Instrumental Combinations," MGM Percussion Ensemble, Izler Solomon, cond. MGM E-3155.

——MGM Percussion Ensemble, Izler Solomon, cond. MGM E-3548 (with Sinfonia No. 5).

——in "Percussion!," Concert Arts Percussionists, Felix Slatkin, cond. CAPITOL P-8299.

——Gotham Percussion Players, Milton Forstat, cond. URANIA URLP-7144 (with Granados: Two Spanish Dances, and Respighi: Brazilian Impressions).

CHAMBER MUSIC

SONATINA FOR VIOLIN AND PIANO

The Ajemians play with convincing style in this example of Chávez's non-lush style. The music is compact and sparsely woven, not heavily laced with harmonic bands. "Flinty" and "steely" are the words that best describe the stern profile of the piece. The violin's sound is expertly mastered, catching all the detonative effects and primitive sonorities.

——Anahid Ajemian, violin; Maro Ajemian, piano. MGM E-3180 (with Revueltas: Three Pieces, and Surinach: Doppio Concertino).

CHORAL WITH ORCHESTRA

CORRIDO DE "EL SOL"

The style is simple, and frames the prose clearly. It could well be mistaken for many another composer's romantic-nationalistic music. Not a revealing or deeply penetrating score, but engaging. The orchestra is somewhat subdued but the chorus registers well.

——in "Music of Mexico," Symphony Orchestra of Mexico; Coro del Conservatorio; Carlos Chávez, cond. DECCA DL-9527.

5. Aaron Copland
(1900—   )

COPLAND IS AN EXAMPLE OF A COMPOSER WHOSE WORK FALLS INTO three successive categories—imitative at the start, striving for individuality in the later years, and finally, reaching maturity.

His early works contained jazz distillations, followed by the abstract shaping of musical materials in a somewhat austere manner (for example, the steely-strong Piano Variations). The latter phase of this first period produced an independent music, not immediately comprehended, but time has shown these works to be enduring and among some of Copland's finest. Copland's second major stage was that of creative-wise, music-fed Americanism. Folk music's essences were integrated, hymnody was dipped into and reshaped. "Rodeo," "Billy the Kid," and similar compositions were produced. A transitional period was ushered in with the Third Symphony, wherein one perceives the end of one style and the beginning of another. The newest manner became evident in 1950, when Copland wrote his Quartet for Piano and Strings. This displays a judicious combination of melodic (somewhat chromatic) elements, harmonic resources of more abstract type, together with the use of a partial serial technique.

It is noteworthy that regardless of the changes in his style, at no time has there been a vestige of insecurity in Copland's work. His output, whether utilitarian or directed at the most serious goals, has always been distinctive, artistically conceived, and always bearing his own mark on its surface. This truly creative sincerity rewards the listener by giving him a music of direct expression, by a composer whose work is personal and minus the present-day striving for sensationalism.

These conclusions were evident quite some time ago. Copland is without doubt one of the world's most important living composers and in American music he strides as a giant. It goes without saying that his place is assured even if his musical fertility were to become watered down, or his invention cease. He has brought his country's music to a higher level than it had hitherto reached.

Every composer hopes that he may be recognized—not only through performance, but by his music's actual sound. This Copland has achieved, though it is rare for a contemporary. One can recognize his music as easily as one can identify the musical profile of Bach or Tchaikovsky.

A large catalogue of recorded Copland is available so that one can do more than merely sample his work. Deletion has made its sinister inroads: neither the early piano concerto nor the "Old American Songs" are obtainable from ordinary sources; but there is no doubt that the few major works still absent from the lists will soon make their appearance. In general, the important works are represented, and these in performances by major artists. Copland is not only valuable as an artist; he represents a money-maker for the musical entrepreneurs. Lately, also, he has been very much in demand as a conductor. There is little doubt that his value as a box-office attraction will act as a spur to the recording companies.

ORCHESTRAL

Appalachian Spring—Ballet Suite

If any one work exemplifies Copland, typifies the man's facts and fancies; if one wishes to know *what* is Copland's music, his general creative method, "Appalachian Spring" will supply the answers. It is music that vibrates from beginning to end with Coplandesque spirit. The musical prose of the composer is exhibited, as well as his rhythms, the nostalgic open-air quality of his retrospections and their homespun tenderness. "Appalachian Spring" is American to the core. Copland's music flows like a "Moldau," its tunes breathe the simplicity and spirit of folklore, absorbed to such an extent that it has become the composer's own.

Composed in 1944 as a ballet for Martha Graham, this work was originally for a baker's dozen instruments. In its transformation into concert music, via orchestral amplification, it has gained much, yet the tissue-like transparency of the original has been preserved. It stands as Copland's number one work.

The entire dance score has been recorded once and is the top choice (*see under* Ballet). From this Copland extracted a suite

of eight connected sections, which is the version heard with very
rare exceptions. Of the listings below Susskind's rendition and
Everest's sound are super in quality; the old Victor record has magnificent playing, but dry sonics; the Mitchell release has good
sound, but emphasizes instrumentational dressing over musical
content, and has some odd balances. The European recording
groups display an ability to read notes, but do not perform with
liquidity or proper style, and some of the playing is downright horrible. Copland requires a hybrid performance blending tension with
repose. He also needs (as does any composer) a conductor who
can read a score and understand it. Neither Rother's nor Litschauer's readings is acceptable. Of the two the Viennese are a shade
better than the Berliners, but don't bother with either.

——London Symphony Orchestra, Walter Susskind, cond. EVER-
EST LPBR-6002 (SDBR-3002) (with Gould: Spirituals).

——National Symphony Orchestra, Howard Mitchell, cond.
WESTMINSTER XWN-18284 (with Billy the Kid; El Salón México;
Fanfare for the Common Man).

——Boston Symphony Orchestra, Serge Koussevitzky, cond. RCA
VICTOR LCT-1134 (with El Salón México).

——Vienna State Opera Orchestra, Franz Litschauer, cond. VAN-
GUARD VRS-439 (with El Salón México).

——Symphony Orchestra of Radio Berlin, Arthur Rother, cond.
URANIA URLP-7092 (with Piston: The Incredible Flutist).

BILLY THE KID—BALLET SUITE

True Copland flavor and American savor. The connecting link
here is native speech rendered in Copland's own type of slang. One
is reminded of the relationship between New Orleans barrelhouse
and Kenton's "progressive" style; pure folk data is as apposite to
what emerges from Copland's artistic strainer. Aside from its indigenous subject, and a scenario made for rootin', tootin', and
shootin', the musical veracity and the verve of "Billy" make it a
unique contribution to musical Americana.

The recordings are as varied as Copland's picturesque ideas. Bernstein is "with it," save that the surface of the disk is not clean, due
to its transfer from a 78 r.p.m. version. Gould has understanding, as
do Mitchell and Levine. However, the first and last have had experience of a kind not shared by the Washington conductor; the

score's illustrative quality is keenly outlined by the former director of the Ballet Theatre's orchestra, and expertly indicated because of the diversified background (including the composition of several "hit" ballets) of the talented Mr. Gould. Both of them have also included the full suite, which Mitchell has not. Copland's own direction of his work is well-done, but the climate is too temperate for his orchestral cast of characters; the sound, however, is marvelous. The best playing comes (why not?) from the Philadelphians, but Westernese is lacking. On the other hand, Abravanel has quality but not the smooth expertise required from his players. Forget the Allegro version if you find it. It is pitifully dull and the tempos are run off in slow motion.

——RCA Victor Symphony Orchestra, Leonard Bernstein, cond. CAMDEN CAL-439 (with Gershwin: An American in Paris).

——Morton Gould and His Orchestra, Morton Gould, cond. RCA VICTOR LM-2195 (LSC-2195) (with Billy the Kid—Waltz; Rodeo).

——Ballet Theatre Orchestra, Joseph Levine, cond. CAPITOL P-8238 (with Schuman: Undertow).

——Philadelphia Orchestra, Eugene Ormandy, cond. COLUMBIA ML-5157 (with Appalachian Spring).

——National Symphony Orchestra, Howard Mitchell, cond. WESTMINSTER XWN-18284 (with Appalachian Spring; El Salón México; Fanfare for the Common Man).

——London Symphony Orchestra, Aaron Copland, cond. EVEREST LPBR-6015 (SDBR-3015) (with Statements for Orchestra).

——Utah Symphony, Maurice Abravenel, cond. WESTMINSTER XWN-18840 (with El Salón México; Rodeo). WESTMINSTER WST-14058 (stereo release with Billy the Kid—Waltz; Rodeo).

——Allegro Concert Orchestra, Alfred Van Weth, cond. ALLEGRO 1688 (with Rodeo).

BILLY THE KID—WALTZ

An extract from the complete ballet, not generally contained in the suite. It may be heard separately only on the Gould and Abravenel records, both of them also containing the usual ballet suite of six sections. (Levine does include the waltz within his version of the suite on Capitol—*see above.*) Note that Gould's performance of the waltz is available on both monaural and stereo,

Abravenel's only on stereo ("*El Salón México*" is substituted in
the monaural release).

——Morton Gould and His Orchestra, Morton Gould, cond. RCA
Victor LM-2195 (LSC-2195) (with Billy the Kid—Ballet Suite;
Rodeo).

——Utah Symphony, Maurice Abravenel, cond. Westminster
WST-14058 (with Billy the Kid—Ballet Suite; Rodeo).

Children's Suite from "The Red Pony"

The music from the film (not as successful as his other motion-
picture scores) is in summer-afternoon Copland style; the sonorities
captivate, but are restrained. Nevertheless, such musical economy
does not mean simple black-and-white playing, with loud or soft
dynamic planes and naught else. Scherman's performance does not
probe. Copland's music needs tenderness and strength with discreet
handling of the varying weights (disposed by the composer either
dynamically or texturally). These are absent from the one recording that has been made.

——Little Orchestra Society, Thomas Scherman, cond. Decca
DL-9616 (with Thomson: Acadian Songs and Dances).

Dance Symphony

Early Copland—its actual birth took place between 1922 and
1925, when the ballet "Grogh" was composed. This dance composition remains in manuscript, but Copland extracted his "Dance
Symphony," as well as a "*Cortège Macabre*" from it (the latter has
not been published). Detaching the symphony was a matter of ex-
pediency. The RCA Victor firm in 1929 offered $25,000 (no typo-
graphical error, if you please!) for a new symphonic work. Copland decided to enter the competition but the work he had planned
was not finished. He therefore extracted three dances from the
"Grogh" score, titled them collectively "Dance Symphony," and
made them his entry. The judges found their task somewhat difficult and split the prize money five ways. Copland's success was
emphasized by the company he was in: the co-winners were Ernest
Bloch, Louis Gruenberg, and Robert Russell Bennett, Bennett
receiving $10,000 since he had submitted two works.

The "Dance Symphony" is un-Coplandesque in its mixture of
French impressionism (Debussy) and the Stravinsky of the ballets.

Not until the final section does the composer's individuality break through; it does so there by way of jazz infiltrations, heard in the nervous, asymmetric rhythms. However, though the music does not display what has come to be recognized as Copland's personality, it is not a student opus.

The recording issued in 1960 shows that justice is done slowly in the field of mechanized music. The terms of the 1929 Victor contest included the recording of the prize-winning work. None of the five pieces ever received this promised reward. It has taken more than a quarter of a century for the initial recording of any of these outstanding compositions to be made, and then in—of all places—Japan! The record is a credit to the orchestra and its conductor, but only partially to the engineers; the heavy and loud passages are not at true pitch.

——Japan Philharmonic Symphony, Akeo Watanabe, cond. COMPOSERS RECORDINGS CRI-129 (with Stevens: Symphony No. 1).

DANZÓN CUBANO

Originally for two pianos; this work represents Copland the transcriber (not too often his practice) and Copland the temporary creative expatriate. It has no hyperbole and requires a neat tightness of statement—not heard in Dorati's performance.

——Minneapolis Symphony Orchestra, Antal Dorati, cond. MERCURY 50172 (SR-90172) (with El Salón México; Rodeo).

FANTACIA MEXICANA (*version by Johnny Green*)

A shameful idea, a seepy condensed soap-opera version of some portions from "*El Salón México*," adorned with a quasi-obbligato piano part. Too late for apologies.

(The MGM people recently began a series of re-releases of standard repertoire items and compilations such as that listed below under a subsidiary label, Lion, at much lower cost. Since the sound is just the same it follows that the choice would be Lion; the more expensive MGM disk is listed only for completeness.)

——in "Pop Concert Favorites, Volume 1," MGM Orchestra; Leonid Hambro, piano; Macklin Marrow, cond. LION CL-40007.

——in "Pop Concert Favorites, Volume 1," MGM Orchestra; Leonid Hambro, piano; Macklin Marrow, cond. MGM E-3136.

MUSIC FOR MOVIES

All of Copland's motion-picture music retains his personal flavor and creative quintessence, even though there is a sparseness of texture. The reasons for his success as a movie composer are here illustrated. The once-functional music is haunting and cannot easily be differentiated from his concert-hall compositions; indeed quite an achievement. All of the settings—sections from one documentary and two commercial film scores (including music from the famed score for *Of Mice and Men*)—are real jewels.

A larger string section would have removed the peculiar salon orchestra sound that prevails. The recording that gives a threefold view of Copland's music for screen, radio, and simulated stage is a clever and fascinating packaging idea.

——MGM Chamber Orchestra, Arthur Winograd, cond. MGM E-3367 (with Music for Radio; Music for the Theatre).

——MGM Chamber Orchestra, Arthur Winograd, cond. MGM E-3334 (with Weill: Music for the Stage).

MUSIC FOR RADIO ("SAGA OF THE PRAIRIES")

"Music for Radio" is a unified composition. (The subtitle, supplied by the winner of a contest held for that purpose, was originally "A Saga of the Prairie"; it has been slightly altered since.) Without depending on folklore for its content, the music's spaciousness is in the American (quotation marks should surround this adjective) style of the composer.

Winograd does a good job, permits the special quality of the music, its spacious and lean scoring, to remain untouched by any overloading. The recording has good musical sound; it is not super-hi-fi, but it frames the music acceptably.

——MGM Symphony Orchestra, Arthur Winograd, cond. MGM E-3367 (with Music for Movies; Music for the Theatre).

MUSIC FOR THE THEATRE

Read: "for the imaginary theatre," since no actual dramatic occasion is involved, but simply a view of jazz onstage. Imitations are always second best—this is not one. The opus shows Copland working from the source and amalgamating the soundmarks of the racy '20's into his music. It is his analogy to the period, written with no cold, academic attitude. The syncopations and other rhythmic flashes make an exhilarating essay including delineations of "burley-cue" and the night-club *viveur* (though the titles are very staid—"Prologue," "Dance," "Interlude," "Burlesque," and "Epilogue").

Those who recall the pre-LP days will remember Howard Hanson's excellent recording. Solomon's issue is even better. Of the pair of MGM choices the three-in-one disk is more interesting because it has composer continuity rather than contrast.

——MGM Chamber Orchestra, Izler Solomon, cond. MGM E-3367 (with Music for Movies; Music for Radio).

——MGM Chamber Orchestra, Izler Solomon, cond. MGM E-3095 (with Weill: Suite from *The Three-Penny Opera*).

ORCHESTRAL VARIATIONS

A transcription of the 1930 Piano Variations (*see under:* Instrumental), made 27 years after the fact. While a certain uncompromising hardness of piano texture is lost by the non-percussiveness of woodwind and string instruments, the orchestral version is convincing, and served to fulfill a Louisville commission. Copland's scoring has massivity, tensility, and strength. An assertive work and played in striking fashion.

——Louisville Orchestra, Robert Whitney, cond. LOUISVILLE COMMISSIONING SERIES LOU-59-1 (with Letelier: "Aculeo," Suite for Orchestra).

RODEO—SUITE FROM THE BALLET

Of all Copland's ballets "Rodeo" has the most inventive orchestration. The play of textures by the thickening and thinning of chordal combinations, together with the dovetailing and juggling of accents on the thematic lines is acutely perceptive. In this way Copland dressed his rowdy music for Agnes de Mille's lightly humorous ballet. The usual orchestra suite consists of four movements, called "Four Dance Episodes," but there are shorter extracts (*see below*).

Levine's performance takes top place. While Dorati's experience as a ballet conductor is exemplified in his reading, with every note and nuance measured exactly, a conductor's approach cannot be the same for concert purposes as it would be for stage performance.

The boldness and striking quality of this work demands that a
conductor unbend. Dorati does not. Abravenel does much better
and so does Gould, but Dorati has been given more entrancing
sound. The Allegro version is played fairly well, but it has under-
nourished sonics.

——Ballet Theatre Orchestra, Joseph Levine, cond. CAPITOL P-
8196 (with Bernstein: Fancy Free).

——Utah Symphony, Maurice Abravenel, cond. WESTMINSTER
XWN-18840 (with Billy the Kid; El Salón México). WESTMIN-
STER WST-14085 (stereo release with Billy the Kid—Ballet Suite;
Billy the Kid—Waltz).

——Morton Gould and His Orchestra, Morton Gould, cond. RCA
VICTOR LM-2195 (LSC-2195) (with Billy the Kid—Ballet Suite;
Billy the Kid—Waltz).

——Minneapolis Symphony Orchestra, Antal Dorati, cond. MER-
CURY 50172 (SR-90172) (with Danzón Cubano; El Salón México).

——Allegro Concert Orchestra, Alfred Van Weth, cond. ALLEGRO
1688 (with Billy the Kid).

RODEO—THREE EPISODES

A new conductor in the record lists and he performs these Copland extracts (the "Corral Nocturne" is the section eliminated
from the full suite) with young-blooded sympathy. The release also
contains a rarely heard Bernstein overture and splendid performances of items by Gould and Piston. Epic turns out beautiful
sound.

——in "Pop Concert U.S.A.," Cleveland Pops Orchestra, Louis
Lane, cond. EPIC LC-3539 (BC-1013).

RODEO—WALTZ AND SATURDAY NIGHT HOEDOWN

Top-flight, especially because of the colorful second piece of the
pair. The Waltz is rather stodgy. If a listener is satisfied with only
part of the "Rodeo" suite, Lane's larger quota plus the choice of
other music makes his release (*see above*) more enticing. The inevitable "Sabre Dance," and some "Three-Cornered Hat" are in
Fiedler's album and there are plenty of examples of these around.

——in "Slaughter on Tenth Avenue and Other Ballet Selections,"
Boston Pops Orchestra, Arthur Fiedler, cond. RCA VICTOR LM-
1726.

EL SALÓN MÉXICO

A colorful essay in Latinate-Coplandesque virtuosity which has always tempted the conductors (and their E-flat clarinet players). The music is a "pops" positive, but is not merely fanciful, displaying the composer's ability to synthesize any ingredient that he desires to utilize. Though not "American" and not one of his most impressive works, Copland's transmutation of Mexican colloquialisms is comparable to the foreign musical temper beautifully illustrated in the Frenchman Chabrier's well-known *"España."*

Rather than being a mere functionary with a baton, Bernstein functions almost as a proxy creator. In music as graphic as this such individuality is permissible. Fiedler's ideas are straightforward, but the playing has real zest; ditto Mitchell and Abravenel. Of these three the Bostonians have the Latin passion closer to their heart. Koussevitzky's record contains fantastic playing, but only average sound. Closest to Bernstein is the Dorati entry. Splendidly done, the acute measurement of Copland's inventive sound combinations is matched by Mercury's engineers; the squealy clarinet and the percussion are reproduced stunningly. A fat minus sign goes to Litschauer: the pedestrianism and the poorly recorded percussion deprives the music of scope and presence.

——Columbia Symphony Orchestra, Leonard Bernstein, cond. COLUMBIA CL-920 (with Bernstein: Fancy Free, and Milhaud: La Création du Monde).

——Minneapolis Symphony Orchestra, Antal Dorati, cond. MERCURY 50172 (SR-90172) (with Danzón Cubano; Rodeo).

——Boston Pops Orchestra, Arthur Fiedler, cond. RCA VICTOR LM-1928 (with Grofé: Grand Canyon Suite).

——in "The Tone Poem," Boston Pops Orchestra, Arthur Fiedler, cond. RCA VICTOR LM-6129.

——National Symphony Orchestra, Howard Mitchell, cond. WESTMINSTER XWN-18284 (with Appalachian Spring; Billy the Kid; Fanfare for the Common Man).

——Utah Symphony, Maurice Abravenel, cond. WESTMINSTER XWN-18840 (with Billy the Kid; Rodeo). WESTMINSTER WST-14063 (stereo release with Gershwin: Orchestra Suite from *Porgy and Bess*).

——Boston Symphony Orchestra, Serge Koussevitzky, cond. RCA VICTOR LCT-1134 (with Appalachian Spring).
——Vienna State Opera Orchestra, Franz Litschauer, cond. VANGUARD VRS-439 (with Appalachian Spring).

STATEMENTS FOR ORCHESTRA

Excellently wrought music is not always recognized. Too often the listener's ear is only open to murmuring sounds which follow the old rather than command the new. A composer's viewpoint is of no value if it be narrow and scanty, limited to recapitulation in place of exposition.

Copland's six-movement "Statements" has real adventure. But it has not met many adventurous conductors and almost repeats the "stay away from the score" history of his "Short Symphony" (*see p. 68, under* Chamber Music). It was commissioned by the now defunct League of Composers for performance by the Minneapolis Symphony, then directed by Ormandy. In 1936 he gave the première of one-third of the work. Six years later the entire piece was heard for the first time under Mitropoulos' baton with the New York Philharmonie. Since then it has rarely been programmed. This, its first recording, is long overdue.

This is truly an abstract work, despite the titles ("Militant," "Cryptic," "Dogmatic," "Subjective," "Jingo," and "Prophetic") given by Copland ". . . as an aid to the public in understanding what the composer had in mind." All the musical elements, from pitch level to dynamic intensity, are as poised as the many steel cables that separately and together hold a suspension bridge in place. It is a music of impressions, without the exterior effects and influences this word usually connotes. The descriptions are *general*, the arena and décor against which the music performs. And only in the "Jingo" (the fifth statement) is there a hint of the folksong period that was soon to follow in Copland's work. There, with an amusing scherzo briskness, "The Sidewalks of New York," a ditty in three-four time, is put into duple meter as a mischievous bit of counterplay.

Copland the conductor is not in the same league with Copland the composer, but he does well with his music, does not outsmart himself; the composer keeps the conductor in line. Though the companion composition is available in better performances by other conductors, Everest's record is highly recommended because of the unique "Statements."

——London Symphony Orchestra, Aaron Copland, cond. Everest LPBR-6015 (SDBR-3015) (with Billy the Kid).

Symphony No. 3

There are constant cries that the extension of musical language requires newer means, not newer uses of old means. This dignified, lofty work of Copland's is a telling piece of evidence for the latter position. The former position is valid also, but in fact there is room for both. The Third Symphony is Copland's major production in the area of absolute music, displays his desire to be other than a folk-symphonic statistician. It has staying power, it reveals a composer who has the knowledge (and courage, in these days when abnormality is a creative virtue) to write in a classical-romantic manner though still with quiet virtuosity. This music is tightly bound, though it has length; it is not shallow, is without the usual glittering sheen which rubs off easily. In a word, this *is* a symphony. It is Copland's example of expansively wrought music, written without stage directions or a motion-picture scenario to constrain him. (The beginning of the finale of the symphony is based on a fanfare which exists as a short, separate piece—*see under:* Brass Instruments.)

It is useless to compare the two recordings. Despite the composer-conductor surety, Everest's release is not the final word on the symphony, nor can any one version be that for a work of comparable breadth and importance. Dorati has a thrilling way with this work and yet where Copland moves he applies the brakes and vice versa. The disparity indicates that no important symphony has its single interpretational answer.

——London Symphony Orchestra, Aaron Copland, cond. Everest LPBR-6018 (SDBR-3018).

——Minneapolis Symphony Orchestra, Antal Dorati, cond. Mercury 50018.

String Orchestra

Two Pieces for String Orchestra

One of the results of the *volte-face* that took place after the compositional thicknesses of the late romantic period and the evocative leanness of impressionism was a refurbishment of musical materials in the direction of simplicity and nonscholastic classicism. In the '20's this produced music sharply engrossed with contemporary manners, morals and postwar freedom. Copland was conscious of these elements and jazz was one of the ways of affirming a new structural force. In 1923 he composed a string quartet piece, "Rondino," which he augmented for string orchestra and combined with a work written in 1925—"Lento Molto." Both of these have the rhythmic precipitancy which defines jazz. The first of these short pieces is an excellent example of sparseness, the effect is of a concert blues. The "Rondino" has jazz implications joined to a slightly nervous quality. Efficient and efficacious performance by Solomon.

——in "Contemporary American Music for String Orchestra," MGM String Orchestra, Izler Solomon, cond. MGM E-3117.

Brass Instruments

Fanfare for the Common Man

Eugene Goossens, then the conductor of the Cincinnati Symphony Orchestra, during World War II commissioned a number of American composers to write fanfares to begin his concerts. Copland's contribution (written in the fall of 1942) was one of the most successful and he thought sufficiently well of the piece to incorporate it in his Third Symphony. (The fanfare serves as the basis for the introduction to the finale of the symphony.)

——National Symphony Orchestra, Howard Mitchell, cond. Westminster XWN-18284 (with Appalachian Spring; Billy the Kid; El Salón México).

SOLO INSTRUMENT WITH ORCHESTRA

Concertos

Concerto for Clarinet and String Orchestra
(with Harp and Piano)

There may be those who disagree, but the concept of this work strikes me as second-rate Copland. It is almost a forced derivation from his own materials: the lyrical and the jazz, plus the south-of-the-border. The form of the work is interesting, however, consisting of slow and fast movements, joined by a cadenza for the solo instrument.

The performance does nothing to enhance the concerto. Copland is now a fairly experienced conductor, but at the time he recorded this work (in 1951) he was new at the baton game. This may well be the reason for a pale performance. Goodman doesn't seem at home with this music (or with Mozart either, despite all the past publicity).

——Columbia String Orchestra; Benny Goodman, clarinet; Aaron Copland, cond. COLUMBIA ML-4421 (with Quartet for Piano and Strings).

Narrator with Orchestra

A LINCOLN PORTRAIT

Though music can express the general aspects of specified emotions, it is, without an accompanying program that sets associations into mental motion, an abstract art. When joined with an expression of ideas and, as in this case, a great man's ideas (culled from his speeches and letters), then music becomes a representational but no less pure art. Copland's score is not a literal exposition of Lincoln's pronouncements, but an extraordinarily skilled way of applying and combining free-sounding music with specific prose meanings. It is as moving and significant as the words Lincoln wrote. For such an occasion no better narrator could be found than Sandburg. His declamation is beautiful, breath-catching. A genuine experience.

——New York Philharmonic; Carl Sandburg, narrator; Andre Kostelanetz, cond. COLUMBIA ML-5347 (MS-6040) (with Barber: Intermezzo from Act IV of *Vanessa*, and Schuman: New England Triptych).

Solo Wind and Brass with Orchestra

QUIET CITY

This searching, nostalgic, almost threnodic music, originally served as a piece of incidental music for Irwin Shaw's play of the same name. The play passed into oblivion after a pair of performances, but Copland's sensitive score has proven its lasting qualities. It receives a peak performance under Hanson and his solo players, Sidney Mear and Richard Swingley. The Capitol recording is quite prosaic (though not the trumpet!) by comparison. Hanson's collection of wind solo works is very interesting—the only one of its type on the market.

——in "American Music for Solo Winds and String Orchestra," Eastman-Rochester Symphony Orchestra; Sidney Mear, trumpet; Richard Swingley, English horn; Howard Hanson, cond. MERCURY 50076.

——in "Contemporary American Music," Concert Arts Orchestra; Harry Goltz, trumpet; Albert Goltzer, English horn; Vladimir Golschmann, cond. CAPITOL P-8245.

INSTRUMENTAL

Organ

EPISODE

Copland's only solo organ piece and neither important nor effective. The medium escapes him (as it does so many other composers). Ellsasser makes the music clear, but overdramatic by overcharging his dynamics, though his registration is firm and controlled. Miss Mason gives as much attention to clarity as does the liner copy on her recording, which gives notes on all the works save Copland's. Since the content of the "Episode" is mainly polyharmonic, this lack of refined performance defeats the music.

——in "Organ Music by Modern Composers—Volume 1," Richard Ellsasser. MGM E-3064.

——in "The King of Instruments—Volume VII," Marilyn Mason. WASHINGTON WAS-7.

Piano

FOUR PIANO BLUES

Dot Records and Leo Smit have come up with a scintillating idea in presenting music by serious composers which has been touched by (or bathed in) the waters of jazz. Smit's playing is unaffected, expert and not exaggerated; the recording is of sonic authority. Copland's pieces were written over a 22-year span: the first was composed in 1947; the second dates from 1934; the latest of the group is the third, written in 1948; and the earliest is the fourth, composed in 1926. They include the constructive earmarks of jazz—piquant, determined rhythm, the gliding melody, the half-step glance, the staccato determination, and the "blued" note that "sends" the triad this-way-and-that. Music with open-hearted kick. Heartily recommended.

——in "The Masters Write Jazz," Leo Smit. DOT RECORDS DLP-3111.

PASSACAGLIA

Not counting discarded juvenilia, this composition, written in 1922, is Copland's fifth recognized opus. An eight-measure subject is the basis for eight variations, each considered clearly and differently in terms of texture. However, the Passacaglia shows some stylistic errata, and none of the composer's credentials. Copland's curiosity makes him wander afield and there is an aesthetic unrest, illustrated by a mélange of romantic and latter-day sounds.

——Webster Aitken. WALDEN 101 (with Piano Variations; Sonata for Piano).

PIANO VARIATIONS

A view of Copland in a very austere and uncompromising attitude, the composition being the epitome of concentration and logic. Each sound is part of the argument—there are no ornamental fillers. Though not making use of serial technique, dealing with twelve tones, there is a resemblance to the Schoenbergian system, with a single unit of four sounds giving all the substance for the work's dyestuff. Copland recently orchestrated this work (*see under*: Orchestral). Aitken's logic is just as effective as Copland's. Walden produces rich sound and is to be congratulated for knowing how to record a piano, especially in a work as texturally sparse as this one.

——Webster Aitken. WALDEN 101 (with Passacaglia; Sonata for Piano).

SONATA FOR PIANO

Compared to the sternness of the Piano Variations, this is warm, rich-hued music, with a nice assortment of rhythmic spicing in the jazzy middle movement. There are a good number of contemporary piano sonatas and a fair total have been recorded, but few have touched the high point Copland's achieves. The sonata shows Copland the sophisticated folklorist being assimilated by Copland the composer of profound absolute music.

Sensitive playing on the part of Aitken, plus some editing that was unnecessary. Three viewpoints on a single disk of Copland as a writer of piano music—certainly a worthwhile release, plus the Walden brand of excellently recorded sound.

——Webster Aitken. WALDEN 101 (with Passacaglia; Piano Variations).

SUNDAY AFTERNOON MUSIC

Written in 1935 for inclusion in a collection of children's piano pieces by American composers, yet Copland to the core and utterly charming.

——in "Piano Music for Children by Modern American Composers," Marga Richter. MGM E-3147.

THE YOUNG PIONEERS

Another in the same series for which "Sunday Afternoon Music" was composed. Short and relatively simple, yet retaining the Copland touch. The "Pioneers" in the title refers to present-day music students, willing to play contemporary music.

——in "Piano Music for Children by Modern American Composers," Marga Richter. MGM E-3147.

Violin

HOE-DOWN FROM "RODEO"

The soloist's arrangement and a very vivid one. Transcriptions are rarely propitious, but what is better than a fiddle for swinging a square-dance tune? A quality performance, not readily available since Concert Hall was sold and its regular distribution ceased. But look and perhaps you'll find—worth it.

——in "International-Americana: A Program of Favorites for the Violin," Louis Kaufman, violin; Annette Kaufman, piano. CONCERT HALL SOCIETY CHC-58.

UKELELE SERENADE

Semi-sophisticated jazz (Copland at the age of twenty-six); the second of a pair of pieces written in Paris between January and

April of 1926. A Negro blues song is connoted by slides and slithering quarter-tones. Kaufman and wife do the piece to a turn.
——in "International-Americana: A Program of Favorites for the Violin," Louis Kaufman, violin; Annette Kaufman, piano. Concert Hall Society CHC-58.

CHAMBER MUSIC

Sonata for Violin and Piano

This sonata expresses a fairly close contact with the classical school in respect to the harmonic language. The classical composers having based their music on the triad, Copland continues this line. Thus it is a classical work, but not neoclassic, for Copland's forms are not as close to the former era as are the extensions he proposes of their harmonic resources. Triads are his prime harmonic conversation, but with the newer diatonic freedom. The result is dissonant but not bitonal. Bitonality is the expression of two opposed keys; Copland's combination is merely triadic ambivalence.

Despite a habit of using harmonic (denatured) sounds and thereby creasing a line by deflecting its proper dynamic course, Fuchs and his partner define the first movement with artistry. The second movement is performed properly as music of cool refinement contrasted with that of greater warmth. Both performers play the final movement with concentration of musical purpose and altogether deliver a performance that should make the composer happy. It should bring the same result to the listener.
——Joseph Fuchs, violin; Leo Smit, piano. Decca DL-8503 (with Stravinsky: Duo Concertant).

Vitebsk—Study on a Jewish Theme; Trio for Piano, Violin and Cello

Despite the fact that a creative artist will always, in some manner, show his heritage, Copland has never deliberately drawn upon his Jewish ancestry, save in this one work. The rhapsodic emanation, the declamation, cantillations, and shofar of the synagogue are stated overtly and by implication. Although any musical work keyed to idiomatic expression has certain limitations, this does not keep it from having formal unity. Nor are the biting dissonances stylistically incorrect in a composition in the Jewish manner, *circa* 1929.

Unfortunately, the University gentlemen never get the music off the ground and the sound engineering is not all one desires. While the intonation is good, the tone of the trio suffers from a checked sonority scale. The places that sound definitely out of tune are where Copland employs quarter-tones—a simulation (intended or not) of cantorial speech.

——University of Oklahoma Trio. UNIVERSITY RECORDINGS 1 (with Harris: Trio, and Kerr: Trio).

QUARTET FOR PIANO AND STRINGS

Although this work (composed in 1950) has precise formal elements, it is not austere, nor is it forbidding and introverted, or hedonistic and extroverted. It is difficult to play and asks almost as much from the listener as from the performers. Copland employs a modified tone-row technique and each movement derives from a single theme. He relishes color in this piano quartet; in fact, he employs more instrumental techniques here than in any of his other pieces. Though he makes no compromise, there is a judicious combination of melodic folk elements and the objective resources found in his other works. A significant addition to contemporary chamber music and performed by those who gave it its première. Excellent.

——New York Quartet. COLUMBIA ML-4421 (with Concerto for Clarinet and String Orchestra).

SEXTET FOR STRING QUARTET, CLARINET AND PIANO

Originally this was an orchestral work entitled "Short Symphony," composed in 1932 and 1933. Its exceedingly difficult rhythms were not (and still are not) attractive to most conductors, who so often deprive a new work of sufficient rehearsal time in order to polish and repolish their own interpretation of a hackneyed item in the orchestral repertory. The "Short Symphony" is one of Copland's consummate compositions and it is pitiful and frustrating that this work remains on the shelf, unperformed and unrecorded.

The arrangement for six players was made in 1937. In the transcription Copland produced his most cogent contribution to chamber-music literature. Germinal material is paramount in the construction. It is motivally synthesized from the start, not developed into strung-out thematic statements, or leading to associated themes. Quite often, the main impetus is rhythmic, the very opposite of grandiose. In the final part Copland exhibits jazz in long pants. Relentless rhythmic virtuosity stems from his study of this musical vernacular. Conclusive music of significance, projected magnificently by the performers. This is an important recording from every point of view.

——Juilliard String Quartet; David Oppenheim, clarinet; Leonid Hambro, piano. COLUMBIA ML-4492 (with Kohs: Chamber Concerto for Viola and String Nonet).

VOCAL

TWELVE POEMS OF EMILY DICKINSON

The ogre of the vocal world is present in this recording—the all-voice, no-words problem. Though Lipton sings with pitch precision and ideal intonation, she is guilty of dissolved diction. Why one must follow a text in order to understand a vocalist is beyond comprehension. Copland's exceedingly attractive song thesis, of earnestness and almost fragile beauty, becomes vague because of this. Aside from word-meaning the style is good (Copland's aid at the piano is not to be overlooked). One prophesies a long life for this cycle. Columbia is on the mark with the highest fidelity in this recording.

——Martha Lipton, mezzo-soprano; Aaron Copland, piano. COLUMBIA ML-5106 (with Weisgall: The Stronger).

CHORAL

IN THE BEGINNING

The creation of the world according to Copland. Although the music forms a single extended movement, each of the six days involved in the tale is marked by a different mood, introduced by a solo mezzo-soprano who serves as a singing narrator. The style is Coplandesque, including some light jazz touches, plus the integration of material from the old American school of hymnody. This is music of almost objective detachment; yet by its reticence it conveys a sense of religious belief, if not especially deep. This significance is read only fairly well into the performance. It has quality and a properly dignified style, but it is not totally integrated.

——San José State College A Cappella Choir; Gloria Surian, soprano; William J. Erlendson, cond. MUSIC LIBRARY RECORDINGS MLR-7007 (with Corsi: Adoramus Te, Christe; Handl (Gallus): Ascendit Deus; Tallis: O Nata Lux De Lumine; and Villa-Lobos: Ave Maria, No. 20).

BALLET

APPALACHIAN SPRING

Ormandy displaces all the available partial versions not only by superb performance, but by having the advantage of playing the complete score. The sections not heard in the suite (*see under* Orchestral) are compelling and should make *le tout ensemble* mandatory for any future recordings.

——Philadelphia Orchestra, Eugene Ormandy, cond. COLUMBIA ML-5157 (with Billy the Kid).

6. *Henry Cowell*
(1897—   )

Up until approximately 1940, Cowell was a tireless musical investigator, an intrepid experimentalist with the stubborn temperament of the real creator. Tone clusters—successive diatonic or chromatic scale-steps, sounded simultaneously—not employed in isolated instances, but as a full technique involving melody, harmony, polyphony, as well as color, were his invention; the transformation of the piano into a percussive stringed instrument, by beating, plucking, muting, or sweeping the strings, was his idea. Improvisational forms, new means of notation, co-invention with Leon Theremin of the Rhythmicon—all these and more were manifestations of Cowell's fertile talent. Since many of these have been adopted by composers of differing tendencies, one may lose sight of the man who was the originator.

Cowell, meanwhile, has abandoned this avidness for the musical search. Now he concentrates for the most part on folk materials—translating early American hymnody into orchestral structures, and the like. Though this means a more relaxed manner, his music is not mundane, nor is it hackneyed. In fact, Cowell's antipathy to sophisticated international musical speech poses a unique paradox. Because his music is in a special position in the contemporary scene it turns on itself and becomes sophisticated as well!

Though the recording catalogues contain only a few of Cowell's neoteric compositions, these are sufficient to appease the appetite. His later works are fairly well represented. Some enterprising company should take in hand the "Synchrony" for orchestra, the Piano Concerto, and some of the music for percussion instruments exclusively. Meanwhile, the listener has a good range of music from which to sample the inquisitive mind of this American composer.

ORCHESTRAL

Music 1957
"Music 1957" is informative in two ways—it not only gives the title but the year of composition. It was used by the Minneapolis Symphony Orchestra on its 1957 tour of the Far East.

This is a work of wit, good fun, and healthy devotion to treading lightly (with folk slippers) in the halls of orchestral composition. Not that an orchestral score must be "heavy," but the supposition that it should be remains in all too many minds. That it can be almost anything, including Cowell's semi-homespun product, is always refreshing.

Cowell's material is a jiggy tune, sometimes given a sophisticated touch by being surrounded with a dissonant, calliope effect; to this he contrasts a lyrical theme (a hybrid of Irish-Western U.S.A. culture), framed in sweetness or sourness. He has no inhibitions. The plentiful percussion (not only as rhythmic supports but as a solo group) is further evidence. Henry Cowell's "music made in America" is spirited art, the work of an extrovert composer.

——Japan Philharmonic Symphony Orchestra, Akeo Watanabe, cond. COMPOSERS RECORDINGS CRI-132 (with Kelly: Symphony No. 2).

PERSIAN SET

Cowell's latest musical investigation belongs in his long list of explorations. Overindulging in a cardinal point of technique may breed monotony and the "Persian Set" is almost a casualty of its overemphasis on the Iranian blueprint. There is no mistaking Cowell's honest preoccupation even though the work as a whole is an example of an isolated mannerism. Listeners will be stimulated by Stokowski's way with the music. This is his meat.

——Members of his Orchestra, Leopold Stokowski, cond. COMPOSERS RECORDINGS CRI-114 (with Harrison: Suite for Violin, Piano, and Small Orchestra).

SATURDAY NIGHT AT THE FIREHOUSE

A squint, through contemporary eyes, at country music—really a mixture. This four-and-one-half-minute piece is simply music for a square dance in a rural setting. Cowell is apparently also glancing at Ives's heterodox formulas, but the result just doesn't come off. Adler and his players seem to be struggling with the music. A bust.

——in "American Life," Vienna Philharmonia Orchestra, F. Charles Adler, cond. SPA RECORDS SPA-47.

SYMPHONY No. 4 (SHORT SYMPHONY)

Lyricism is predominant in the shifting moods of this opus, its American content stemming from hymn-proportioned tunes and the utilization of an eighteenth-century fuguing tune. Contrapuntalism, when it appears, is the type with rugged vitality and with as stern a disdain for so-called fugue rules. This is picturesque music that is not confined by a stated program; it is one of Cowell's best works. Hanson's performance is superbly intelligent and the sound of the orchestra is royal-robed.

——Eastman-Rochester Symphony Orchestra, Howard Hanson, cond. MERCURY 50078 (with Hovhaness: Concerto No. 1, and Riegger: New Dance).

SYMPHONY No. 7

Another prime example (providing one listens below the record's surface noise) of Cowell the integrator, in this instance using reel- and jig-styled melodies plus the plastic impress of fuguing tunes. Cowell's work is less a symphony than it is a compendium of the ingredients that go into the matrix of a symphony; it might be termed a huge suite. It does not contain the well-knit specific elements, nor exhibit the logical, unredundant growth that must take place in symphonic form. There are many tunes in this piece—for example: a "see-saw reel" in the opening movement, the nice ballad which appears in the slow section, and the country-dance melody utilized in the presto (third movement). But these are tunes, complete by themselves; they produce a symphonic shape but the patches show. The performance could be much better; it sounds as though it were recorded without much rehearsal time.

——Vienna Symphony Orchestra, William Strickland, cond. MGM E-3084 (with Ward; Adagio and Allegro; Jubilation, An Overture).

SYMPHONY No. 10

Tuned to the tuneful and with easily assimilated shapes plus mild dissonance, this is the kind of music one can expect from the Cowell of the '40's and '50's. The symphonies Cowell wrote during this period (especially numbers 4, 7, 9, and 10) feature ballads, dance melodies, and material based on the fuguing pieces of eighteenth-century New England composers. This method becomes almost routine: the contrapuntal freedom of hymn and fuguing tunes serves for the form of the outer movements, while song and dance themes occupy the slow and scherzo portions.

The Tenth Symphony is in six movements: a hymn and fuguing tune and another fugue are heard in the first, second, and last parts respectively; a "Comeallye" (an Irish-American ballad, its title pronounced "come-all-ye"), a jig, and an intermezzo form the inner sections. It is all clean and fresh, authentic and sufficient for pleasurable listening. The Vienna organization plays the score adequately, but the sound is lifeless.

——Vienna Orchestral Society, F. Charles Adler, cond. UNICORN UNLP-1045 (with Ballad; Fiddler's Jig; Hymn and Fuguing Tune No. 2; Hymn and Fuguing Tune No. 5).

SYMPHONY No. 11 (SEVEN RITUALS OF MUSIC)

Cowell's most constructive and individual symphony. The music's divisions describe man's progress from birth to death, making the opus not only diversified (which does not negate the symphonic title or its formality) but diverting. It combines set forms with downright good musical sense and a compendious use of orchestral colors, specifically the percussion. System and logic are all that are necessary for a work to register in whatever style, but in this case Cowell has gone beyond mere form and written a divertimento on a serious theme, which emerges as a profound symphonic dissertation. Highly imaginative playing by the Louisville group marks one of their finest releases, the proof being that Columbia has seen fit to issue the same version. There is little choice in terms of the different companion works. There is also no choice if one wishes to hear only a single section of Cowell's work, since no bands separate the seven movements on either disk.

——Louisville Orchestra, Robert Whitney, cond. COLUMBIA ML-5039 (with Creston: Invocation and Dance, and Ibert: A Louisville Concerto).

——Louisville Orchestra, Robert Whitney, cond. LOUISVILLE COMMISSIONING SERIES LOU-545-2 (with Tcherepnin: Suite, and Wagenaar: Concert Overture).

String Orchestra

BALLAD

An all-stringed-instrument conception of the same music that appears as the third movement of the violin and piano sonata (*see under* Chamber Music). It is lovely either way. Rich, semi-nostalgic song—American via Scotch-English musical inculcation. A more richly invested body of strings would do more for this concentrated slice of beauty.

——Vienna Orchestral Society, F. Charles Adler, cond. UNICORN UNLP-1045 (with Hymn and Fuguing Tune No. 2; Hymn and Fuguing Tune No. 5; Fiddler's Jig; Symphony No. 10).

——Vienna Orchestral Society, F. Charles Adler, cond. UNICORN UNLP-1011 (with Hymn and Fuguing Tune No. 2; Hymn and Fuguing Tune No. 5; and Mendelssohn: Symphony No. 2).

FIDDLER'S JIG

The "fiddler" is an incidental highlight within the "jig." Composed in 1952, Cowell's homespun music, welcome to the ear, is of the times only in the few measures that constitute a bridge passage; otherwise, this is music bred amongst the folk.

——Vienna Orchestral Society, F. Charles Adler, cond. UNICORN UNLP-1045 (with Ballad; Hymn and Fuguing Tune No. 2; Hymn and Fuguing Tune No. 5; Symphony No. 10).

HYMN AND FUGUING TUNE No. 2
HYMN AND FUGUING TUNE No. 5

Cowell has turned out a vast number of compositions in this form, for combinations ranging from a trio for two clarinets and a saxophone to full orchestra. Some of the hymn and fuguing tunes appear in more than one setting; others have been used as pieces in their own right in addition to forming portions of larger compositions (the two parts of the Hymn and Fuguing Tune No. 5 form two of the six movements in the Symphony No. 10 [*see under:* Orchestral]).

Cowell's fascination with the "fugues" of William Billings (1746-1800) results in a spiritual-historic link. Billings' music has interested a number of other contemporary American composers (William Schuman, Otto Luening, and Ross Lee Finney, among them). This New Englander's technique was rather crude but this did not nullify the forcefulness of his hymns and anthems. The freedom of part-writing in Billings' compositions has a kinship with the vigorousness of present-day musical thought.

In these compositions Cowell avoids mere fantasy, or paraphrase in an outlandish fashion. He retains the "up and at 'em," the "let's have a go at it" quality that inspired Billings. By keeping the improvisational contrapuntalistic style, he gives past formal consideration its present resolution.

The second of Cowell's series of hymns and fuguing tunes has a soaring sweet strength; it is scored to display the golden tone of a string orchestra. Adler's group plays the work with substantial quality.

The fifth hymn and fuguing tune is worshipful music cast in a broad, secular style. It is music of deep spirit, its harmonies cleanly and clearly diatonic, of modal formation. Its balance of primary elements is obtained by the continuum of horizontal motion—the music flows and the conductor, Adler, guides it well. The second portion is styled similarly, but with gingham starchiness. Cowell's method marks him as a composer who understands how to make trenchant use of the supply of early New England music. This is a musical result worth cultivating. Save for soprano edginess the recorded sound is worthy.

Either recording gives the buyer a pair of the hymns plus fuguing tunes, as well as the sensitive and haunting "Ballad," but Mendelssohn seems out of place as the companion composer.

——Vienna Orchestral Society, F. Charles Adler, cond. UNICORN UNLP-1045 (with Ballad; Fiddler's Jig; Symphony No. 10).

——Vienna Orchestral Society, F. Charles Adler, cond. UNICORN UNLP-1011 (with Ballad, and Mendelssohn: Symphony No. 2).

INSTRUMENTAL

Organ

PROCESSIONAL

Composing for the organ has defeated many musicians. Their idiom is affected and they become another person. The organ has plentiful resources to stimulate a composer as adventurous as Henry Cowell, but the "Processional"—the only work that Cowell has composed for the instrument—is certainly not exciting. In its total lack of identifying characteristics this work could be any church-choir director's effort. Cowell is also defeated.

——in "Organ Music by Modern Composers—Volume 1," Richard Ellsasser, MGM E-3064.

Piano

ADVERTISEMENT

A tone cluster is a set of compounded intervals, arranged dia-tonically, chromatically, or pentatonically. The more these tones are combined and the shorter the distances between them, the denser the sound. Cowell eases his clusters in this short piece by using them in small lots. Serious, yet amusing music.

——Henry Cowell. COMPOSERS RECORDINGS CRI-109 (with Piano Music; Prelude for Violin and Harpsichord; Hovhaness: Duet for Violin and Harpsichord; and Pinkham: Concerto for Celeste and Harpsichord Soli; Cantilena; Capriccio).

AEOLIAN HARP

In this the piano has a Jekyll-Hyde personality, changing into an amazing type of sustaining harp. The performer makes direct con-tact (via glissandi) with the strings, employing the pedal simul-taneously. (Cowell's "Aeolian Harp" was the first example of play-ing on the piano strings.)

The piece is included in the Folkways album without any per-former credited, though it is almost certain that Cowell himself is at the piano. However, to hear the full scope of his amazing piano discoveries, the CRI record should be chosen. The Folkways release is just as fascinating, but for other reasons, including tape-recorder compositions and "*Musique Concrète*."

——Henry Cowell. COMPOSERS RECORDINGS CRI-109 (with Piano Music; Prelude for Violin and Harpsichord; Hovhaness: Duet for Violin and Harpsichord; and Pinkham: Concerto for Celeste and Harpsichord Soli; Cantilena; Capriccio).

——in "Sounds of New Music." FOLKWAYS FX-6160.

THE BANSHEE

An extraordinary example of alluring sonorities, so organized as to depict the wailing of the legendary female who in this manner warns that death is approaching. All the sounds are drawn from the piano strings, with inferential polyphony created by overtones. Manifold color as well, obtained by string glides plus plucking and permitting the strings to vibrate. Not only for hi-fi fans but for the serious-minded listener. Cowell's performance has to be heard to be believed.

As is the case with Cowell's "Aeolian Harp," the Folkways disk gives no listing for the performer. Apparently this has been clipped from the old recording Cowell made of his piano music and on which he spoke about his work. In making the transfer the editor's scissors were not sharp—one hears Cowell's voice announcing the title of the piece! Both recordings are unique though for different reasons. Both are valuable acquisitions, despite the duplications of the "Aeolian Harp" and "The Banshee" on the Folkways disk.

——Henry Cowell. COMPOSERS RECORDINGS CRI-109 (with Piano Music; Prelude for Violin and Harpsichord; Hovhaness: Duet for Violin and Harpsichord; and Pinkham: Concerto for Celeste and Harpsichord Soli; Cantilena; Capriccio).

——in "Sounds of New Music." FOLKWAYS FX-6160.

THE IRISHMAN DANCES

Only a tidbit written with teaching purposes in mind, but with practically the same elements as Cowell's symphonic and chamber music. Short, sweet, and very Irish.

——in "Piano Music for Children by Modern American Composers," Marga Richter. MGM E-3147.

LILT OF THE REEL
SINISTER RESONANCE
THE TIDES OF MANAUNAUN

The first of these piano pieces is a Celtic evocation with spiced harmonies. Cowell does not believe in man-made divine laws insisting that music of folk quality requires a do-re-mi setting.

Music such as the "Sinister Resonance" was the forerunner of John Cage's compositions for "prepared" piano, in which the instrument's strings are muted with slats of bamboo, bolts, pennies, etc. Cowell uses the simple but powerful effect of choking the sonority via muting and adds delicate arpeggiated bits. Unique indeed are the sounds of this item—the sonorities of plucked and dampened strings are akin to a huge violin. Despite the title, the music is of pervading beauty.

Cowell's first use of tone clusters was in a composition with the very descriptive title of "Adventures in Harmony" (the manuscript was lost, unfortunately), written when he was but fourteen years of age. The following year Cowell composed "The Tides of Manaunaun," as a musical introduction to a pageant based on Irish legends. The invention of the tone cluster was put to excellent use as a strong sonorous resource to picture the sea god, Manaunaun, in this spectacle. The music consists of a folk tune embedded and surrounded with tone clusters that enhance and place the melody (a real tune!) in perspective. The "Tides" is one of the most-often played of Cowell's smaller pieces.

Better performances cannot be imagined. And, the required sensitivity of sound is accomplished by the CRI engineers.

——Henry Cowell. COMPOSERS RECORDINGS CRI-109 (with Piano Music; Prelude for Violin and Harpsichord; Hovhaness: Duet for Violin and Harpsichord; and Pinkham: Concerto for Celeste and Harpsichord Soli; Cantilena; Capriccio).

CHAMBER MUSIC

DUET FOR VIOLIN AND HARPSICHORD

Nothing characteristic, nothing important, merely a melody with accompaniment. The harpsichord instead of the usual piano is the only novelty.

——Robert Brink, violin; Daniel Pinkham, harpsichord. COMPOSERS RECORDINGS CRI-109 (with Piano Music; Hovhaness: Duet for Violin and Harpsichord; and Pinkham: Concerto for Celeste and Harpsichord Soli; Cantilena; Capriccio).

SONATA No. 1 FOR VIOLIN AND PIANO

Cowell's most recent style is elucidated in this five-movement sonata. Although it has certain suite-like connotations, rather than the more absolute outlines of a sonata, the work has cohesive style and there is even thematic transformation in the two outer movements. Melodicism is paramount, without odd twists or furbelows. This can be considered a kind of "homey" music, but is far short of being banal. The folksy quality is highlighted by the "Ballad," a type of American "Londonderry Air." As a preliminary to the coda of the last movement, Cowell employs one of his "percussion" ideas for the piano, resulting in an effect akin to muted gongs. An independent, artistic mind, we realize gratefully, is never reformed. The violin plays close-up and some extraneous sounds mar the performance.

——Joseph Szigeti, violin; Carlo Bussotti, piano. COLUMBIA ML-4841 (with Shapero: Sonata for Piano Four Hands).

SET OF FIVE

A trio for twenty instruments! But one does not need Martian performers. The set-up consists of piano, violin, and eighteen percussion—the last performed by one player. This is chamber music, though not generally "as she is spoken." (Nonetheless, how recently was Dussek's work for bass drum and piano trio written? As long ago as the eighteenth century!) The ear is treated to a cosmic conception of color, aided, in no small part, by the exotica of the percussion. In the final movement tone clusters and plucked piano strings form a secondary percussion type to match the normal percussion group.

When Cowell is formally new for artistic purposes his music turns out to be anything but formalistic. The "Set of Five" is a haunting work and a real achievement. It was a request by the Ajemian sister team that led to the composition of this work and they give it a beautiful performance.

——Anahid Ajemian, violin; Maro Ajemian, piano; Elden Bailey, percussion. MGM E-3454 (with Hovhaness: Kirghiz Suite, and Ives: Sonata No. 4).

TOCCANTA

Cowell of the past, when he was the unquenched and unquestioned composer-liberator of the '20's and '30's, with tone clusters, mathematically promulgated ideas, odd instruments, and other devices girdling the sounds he conceived. This is pure Cowell plunging into the uncharted seas of musical creation. His "Toccanta" is neither a toccata nor a cantata, but a Thorne Smith turnabout; the instruments play vocally and the voice sings instrumentally, without words. The performance is one of absolute truth.

——Carleton Sprague Smith, flute; Helen Boatwright, soprano; Aldo Parisot, cello; John Kirkpatrick, piano. COLUMBIA ML-4986 (with Ruggles: Lilacs; Portals; Evocations).

SUITE FOR WOODWIND QUINTET

Early Cowell (composed in 1933) and evidence of his predilection at that time for the stability of dissonantal language. Just as fresh today when harmonic frictions (aptly balanced by the performers) do not make audiences wince. Pithy expressions are employed throughout: mixed major and minor arpeggios float through the "Prelude," then a "Jig" with the clarinet and oboe colors oscillated against a fricative background, followed by a "Chorale" well-squared to the root of dissonance. The music ends with a movement in fugal style, its terminal chord expressing in one sound the suite's premise and aesthetic: C and E major in a cluster-clutch pivoting on the common sound of E.

The dry sound of the instruments is the proper flavor for this work. A well-engineered recording and the album of which it is a part is highly recommended.

——in "An American Woodwind Symposium," New Art Wind Quintet. CLASSIC EDITIONS CE-2003.

7. Paul Creston
(1906—   )

COMPOSERS CAN BE DIVIDED INTO FOUR CLASSES: FIRST, THE ACADEMI-
cians, who work according to the textbook, are generally concerned
with specific past periods, and never adopt new techniques, no
matter how valid. Second, the eclectics, who slavishly model their
creations on proven examples, drawn from the work of an individual or group—thereby becoming almost academicians. Third,
the experimenters; these delight in trying to discover new combinations, new forms and the like. Fourth, the "individual" composers,
cognizant of all past work, yet striving constantly to speak in their
own fashion without recourse to tight rules or the exact spirit of
another (past or present) style. In a way, their work is also experimental. While the experimental composer moves from one laboratory test to the next, the "individual" composer solidifies the
precepts he has made for himself.

Paul Creston is a composer who has moved through eclecticism
to his own brand of individualism. He steers clear of blatant mannerisms. His musical memory is sharp, but he does not simply
commemorate the achievements of the past. Present in Creston's
work are impressionistic dabs, rhapsodic plus mystical ramifications,
lush romanticism; at times, even the naughtiness of the French
style of the 1920's makes its appearance. Yet it is to the credit of
this self-made composer (he studied piano and organ but not composition) that though he chooses to be eclectic, he shapes his
materials in such fashion as to make them hold together.

The main features of his output are an unfailing melodic gift
and an assured hand at interweaving instrumental voices. In other
words, Creston's scoring is sure-fire, well sounding, proportioned,
and brilliantly logical. He avoids the specialized trends of the day,
but it does not follow that this makes him a minor figure in the
creative arena. It requires a forthright personality to compose attractive and informed music.

Creston has fared well in the recorded music catalogue. Two
debits are the deletion of his substantial string quartet (once on
Capitol 8260), and the short orchestral piece "A Rumor," which

was on the defunct Allegro label. These are compensated for by the recent release of two orchestral works ("Lydian Ode" and "Walt Whitman Suite") by RCA Victor.

ORCHESTRAL

DANCE OVERTURE

Creston's "overture," rather than following the prescribed academic form, is a four-ply set of variations on a theme. In uninterrupted continuity profiles of national dances are projected: a bolero from Spain, a country dance from England, followed by a French *loure*, and concluding with an American square dance. This is systematized music-making, but is incidental to the smooth, pleasant sounds that result. Written to specific scale and played accordingly.

——Oslo Philharmonic Orchestra, Alfredo Antonini, cond. COMPOSERS RECORDINGS CRI-14 (with Haufrecht: Square Set; Hively: Summer Holiday; and Sanjuan: La Macumba).

INVOCATION AND DANCE, OP. 58

Musical blueprints may seem well-organized on paper, but actual sound and aural reception are still required for complete substantiation. Creston here proposes a study in rhythmic technique (he emphasizes this principle in his music to a point just short of becoming a burdensome cliché). It works. But it works in spite of the metric ratiocination. If the listener cannot follow the composer's architectural-rhythmic plan, has the plan been successful? Perhaps Creston's disposition of meter is a logical device to defeat logicians. A well-informed, controlled piece of music, notwithstanding.

Fair performance; the Louisville group lacks string strength. As to choice of releases, the Columbia disk offers slightly better music to share the bill with Creston.

——Louisville Orchestra, Robert Whitney, cond. COLUMBIA ML-5039 (with Cowell: Symphony No. 11, and Ibert: Louisville Concerto).

——Louisville Orchestra, Robert Whitney, cond. LOUISVILLE COMMISSIONING SERIES LOU-545-1 (with Stevens: Triskelion, and Villa-Lobos: Dawn in a Tropical Forest).

LYDIAN ODE, Op. 67

The "Lydian Ode" was commissioned for the Wichita Symphony Orchestra by one of its patrons. Creston's music was to serve as a memorial to the donor's sister, who had shown promise of becoming a concert pianist. These facts explain the predominance of the piano in Creston's orchestral palette. Adhering to a single point, the music is nocturnal, sustained, neo-ecclesiastical. Not Creston with his best foot forward—the hymn overpraises itself.

——Academy Symphony Orchestra of Rome, Nicola Rescigno, cond. RCA VICTOR LM-2426 (with Walt Whitman Suite, and Kubik: Symphony Concertante).

SYMPHONY No. 2, OP. 35

A work of composite power, dealing with the "two foundations of all music: song and dance," as the composer explains it. Creston's composition (written in 1944) is neo-Franckian, minus the textural thickness of chromatic coloration. The entire symphony is like the relating of an odyssey, the initial themes forming the substance of the tale. Creston's music achieves coherence by interlocked and interconnective features. The symphony has only two movements, further concentration and formal interest resulting from this compounding of material. Creston has a magnificent sense for color; his orchestration needs no scoring thyroid.

This type of music requires a conductor who is not only an expressionistically minded musician, but who knows how to clarify a composer's formal plans. The National Symphony is led with firm ability and spontaneity by Mitchell. Westminster's sound is very good.

——National Symphony Orchestra, Howard Mitchell, cond. WESTMINSTER XWN-18456 (with Symphony No. 3).

SYMPHONY No. 3, OP. 48

Creston's Third Symphony is subtitled "Three Mysteries," these being "The Nativity," "The Crucifixion," and "The Resurrection." As in the composer's "Walt Whitman" music, the objective is a musical parallel, not an orchestral mural. Gregorian chant plays an important part, its quality enhanced by stylish and stylistically fitting orchestration. A neoreligious musical composition must draw on the storehouse of counterpoint; Creston's polyphony is masterful, especially in the variational material of the second movement and the fugue which concludes the previous section.

Any organist is influenced by the special instrument he plays when he sits at his creative work table. This is true of Creston, organist in a mid-town church in New York City. If his symphony is colorful it is also chorale-full and the resultant dignity clothes the work with a richness that reminds one of a modern César Franck. Like the Belgian master, Creston is not musically narrow-minded, sterile, or repetitive. This symphony has craftsmanship and unity. Its individuality has not only validity and logic, but expressive beauty.

——National Symphony Orchestra, Howard Mitchell, cond. WESTMINSTER XWN-18456 (with Symphony No. 2).

Two Choric Dances

Intelligibility of organization is the prime motive of musical form. When it functions thus it is not only proof of the composer's self-discipline, but, as in Creston's "Two Choric Dances," in the nature of a discovery. Both dances are abstract regardless of the title's descriptive adjective. Creston indicates that his orchestral ideas could well be choreographed, and indeed, should. Rhythmical richness is an exciting feature. Creston is a master of this facet of musical language, has written a text covering its techniques. It has been said often that only those that can't, teach. Creston can.

——in "Contemporary American Music," Concert Arts Orchestra, Vladimir Golschmann, cond. CAPITOL P-8245.

Walt Whitman Suite, Op. 53

A set of four aspects of Whitmaniana, derived from his *Leaves of Grass*. Creston does not take on the role of a present-day Richard Strauss, but analyzes musically the general meaning of Whitman in movements depicting the poet's "celebration of the individual," his "love of nature," "glorification of the challenge," and "serenity toward death." It is especially in the latter part that the music echoes the strange beauty found in Whitman. In the earlier sections the affinity is less apparent; the structures are classic, the textures romantically stitched, the dissonances discreet, the aesthetic tone expressive. For music of such make-up no other description need be attached.

——Academy Symphony Orchestra of Rome, Nicola Rescigno, cond. RCA VICTOR LM-2426 (with Lydian Ode, and Kubik: Symphony Concertante).

CHAMBER MUSIC

SONATA FOR SAXOPHONE AND PIANO, Op. 19

There are those who still feel the saxophone is not a legitimate instrument, and that if it is to be accepted it should not be permitted in the domain of chamber music. The saxophone is only illegitimate in the hands of the badly tutored; the whining tone produced by the semi-professional is not real saxophone playing.

Creston's sonata is one of several works written which will ultimately form an imposing and important saxophone literature. There are certain Parisian influences in the sonata, but its forthrightness makes it matter little where its ancestral deposits lie. Melodic spontaneity and jazz-strapped rhythms give life to the music, especially in the metrical subtleties that color the final movement.

Two versions are available (a third, with Marcel Mule as the saxophonist, was on the London label, catalogued LL-1479, but has been deleted). Both are worthwhile, but that by Rascher displays more verve. Nonetheless, Abato's playing is sensitive and supple. The Rascher disk offers a variety of music for the saxophone, including an excellent sonata by the Hindemithian, Bernhard Heiden. Persichetti's work is an admirable conception and makes the Columbia disk a desirable acquisition. The vote from this end is a tie—get both records!

——in "Sigurd Rascher Plays the Saxophone—Volume 2 (Advanced)," Sigurd Rascher, saxophone; Russell Sherman, piano. AWARD ARTISTS SERIES AAS-708.

——Vincent J. Abato, saxophone; Paul Creston, piano. COLUMBIA ML-4989 (with Persichetti: Concerto for Piano—Four Hands).

8. Norman Dello Joio
(1913—   )

THE MUSIC OF DELLO JOIO IS ANOTHER EXAMPLE OF TWENTIETH-century classicism as practiced in America. The stylized tonal function is that of Hindemithian diatonicism, in which the key feeling of the classical school is maintained (minus the overbearing chromaticism brought into play by the romantics) but with the chordal combinations of a specified key freed from rigidity of classification. Chords combine, therefore, within the scope of one key, freeing the tonality, yet, while unlimbering it, not permitting it to fall into pantonality (the opposite means, wherein all sounds are used freely).

Dello Joio illustrates the multitudinous differences that exist among composers of the American school. Listening to his music one realizes that an American composer must seize on a functional viewpoint, since there is little native tradition on which to build. These objectives differ widely, from the early experimentation of Cowell to the sonic structures of Varèse, from the egoistic nationalism of Ives to the cowboyisms that trademark some of Copland's music. Though conforming to the general idiom of international musical speech (we have no sanctioned methods as in the days of Handel, for example) and influenced by his study with Paul Hindemith, Dello Joio has never suppressed his Italian ancestral heritage. The inclusion of Gregorian and liturgical elements in his music stems from this background.

While one speaks of "internationalism" in music in the sense that the aesthetic is not concerned with a particular art climate, or with the manner of speech of a particular locale, actually there is no truly international music level, no musical Esperanto. Contemporary composers have ground down many of the ridges marking the varied and colorful landscape of national music, retained a few; but at the same time, they have scrupulously avoided touching certain characteristic landmarks fully surveyed in past historical periods.

The immediate and summed-up concentration of Dello Joio's work is not limited to any particular country. It joins craftsmanship with a modern outlook. Dello Joio's music is neoclassic in purity, Hindemithian in its dynamic energy, and, to complete this odd triple analogy, neoliturgical as well.

ORCHESTRAL

AIR POWER (SYMPHONIC SUITE)

Though in the music for "Air Power" Dello Joio's creative sins are as scarlet, the score (background music!) has been recorded. Why? This omnibus suite of twelve numbers from the music written for the CBS television series "Air Power" (covering 26 productions) has no personality; the music could have been written by any competent staff composer, resident in radio row or Hollywood. It has every cliché that has been dry nursed by composers of "The Library of Background Music" school. And the great Philly Orchestra plays it! Corn at very high prices.

——Philadelphia Orchestra, Eugene Ormandy, cond. COLUMBIA ML-5214 (MS-6019).

THE TRIUMPH OF ST. JOAN SYMPHONY

One cannot type Dello Joio either as a pure classicist or as a through-and-through disciple of Paul Hindemith. Either definition might point to a composer of the pastiche. Yet Dello Joio forms his three-part symphony on the classic tradition, and with the implications of the looking glass through which all Hindemith's music is seen. The influence of the first is seen in the dynamic development of expressive thematic ideas, the method which builds a structure from small materials, rather than fully stated melodies; the Hindemith parallel is in the series of sounds generated by free-tonal harmony together with chunky, choired orchestration. But it is Dello Joio's spontaneous creative imagination that makes his symphony a successful opus, not a shallow imitative show of technique. Though the "Saint Joan" music displays both classic and Hindemithian influences (and the two are not as divergent as many believe) the symbolism is not derivative. In this sense Dello Joio is a "new" traditionalist.

The movements are designated "The Maid," wherein variational treatment covers the thoughts of the girl of Domremy and the hearing of voices that summon her to fight the English; "The War-

rior," music of emotional force and drive; and "The Saint," a perorative section. This symphonic debate achieves classic form in its three-part contrasts. Both performance and recording are good.
——Louisville Orchestra, Robert Whitney, cond. COLUMBIA ML-4615 (with Villa-Lobos: Erosion).

VARIATIONS, CHACONNE AND FINALE

This work was composed in 1947 and given its initial performance by the Pittsburgh Symphony Orchestra, conducted by Fritz Reiner, the year following. Originally it was called "Three Symphonic Dances," but Dello Joio thought this title inappropriate and changed it after the première. It was accorded the New York Music Critics' Circle Award in 1949.

Dello Joio's formal objective in this three-movement opus is predicated on a liturgical theme. Although not completely dominant, a modal influence spreads through the piece. The working plan consists of a prelude followed by a half-dozen variants. From these a segment furnishes the fundament for the chaconne, and thematic interlocution is again found in the finale. This reincarnative method is a means of imparting freshness, in Dello Joio's hands; it is the system by which he controls and drives his musical vehicle. Style is maintained and personality emerges.

Ormandy's orchestra has seldom sounded better. Its tonal glow is akin to the spirit of the music. A cleanly recorded and balanced production.
——Philadelphia Orchestra, Eugene Ormandy, cond. COLUMBIA ML-5263 (with Vincent: Symphony in D).

String Orchestra

MEDITATIONS ON ECCLESIASTES

Variation form is a favorite device of this composer. To survey only Dello Joio's recorded compositions, this technique will be found employed in the Variations and Capriccio for violin and piano, the first movement of the third piano sonata, in the orchestral Variations, Chaconne and Finale, as well as in the opening part of the "St. Joan Symphony." But Dello Joio's employment of variation does not lead him to survey melodic dimensions braced by filigrees and patterns. In this set of ten "meditations" the variations develop the subject in a type of cumulative design; it is apparent where each portion begins and ends, and what its texture weighs.

The music can be considered in the absolute classification or heard as an affirmation of the Biblical verses, each beginning with the words "A time to. . . ." Accordingly, the music delineates the varied acts and emotions of weeping, dancing, embracing, of hate and war, of love and peace, and so forth. Perhaps a bit long, but sufficiently interesting to hold the attention. Antonini does a professional job and the Oslo group plays with good sound and ensemble.

——Oslo Philharmonic Orchestra, Alfredo Antonini, cond. COMPOSERS RECORDINGS CRI-110 (with Wigglesworth: Symphony No. 1).

INSTRUMENTAL

Piano

SONATA NO. 3

Classical procedures hold first place in this meaningful work, composed in 1948. The sonata opens with a set of recognizable variations, five in number; each successive variation undergoes changes of shade and shape, but the subject's core remains. The remaining movements are symmetrical in their arrangement: a scherzo, an adagio, and a vigorous end part. No dichotomy exists in regard to formal clarity.

This sonata has enjoyed countless concert-hall performances. Though this recorded performance is worthy, it is not noteworthy. Dello Joio's excellent sonata deserves new representation in the record lists.

——Del Purves. MUSIC LIBRARY RECORDINGS MLR-7021 (with Griffes: Sonata).

Violin

VARIATIONS AND CAPRICCIO FOR VIOLIN AND PIANO

This music is arranged with simplicity, evidence of the craft found in Dello Joio's art. In a way, this composer gives the lie to the view that a composition requires big lush sounds. The formula here is a set of variations that do not overburden the theme (the ear is permitted its chance to understand all moves), plus a neat final part, minus instrumental blood-letting. Dello Joio explains his work as "charming intellectually unproblematical." Touché. The performance is gentle, sweet, of high quality. ——Patricia Travers, violin; Norman Dello Joio, piano. COLUMBIA ML-4845 (with Bowles: Music for a Farce; Scènes d'Anabase).

9. Irving Fine
(1914—   )

FINE IS A COMPOSER WHO WORKS SLOWLY AND HAS THEREFORE produced only a small number of compositions. But these have significance—as much as four times the same number by others. At first Fine's creative course was that of twentieth-century classicism. The prosody and development plans, the essential tonal clarity of his music had its roots in Igor Stravinsky. The latter's neoclassical attitude precluded all posturing, and Fine was as true a disciple as one could find. That a young composer finds stimulus in the successful efforts of an older colleague is not to be regretted, but rather commended. While strict academicism may sometimes result, the inherent freshness of triadal language cannot be over-emphasized. In such style one observes Viennese concepts of the eighteenth century, merely translated into more nervous diction and unsymmetrical rhythms that prod the flow rather than halting it.

But there can never be a *reductio ad absurdum* in any artistic endeavor. Creativity depends simply on whether within the technical practice the product has total consonance and individual definition. It is generally understood that what exists is not "a music," but rather various species of music. Overpedanticism is as horrible on the part of the neoclassic Stravinsky disciples and the strict dodecaphonists as it is on the part of the academic graybeards. It results only in creative atrophy.

It is not surprising that a resourceful talent should have been sensitive to this theorem. Fine turned from the excellent music he had written in the neoclassic vein to serial technique—a system that has been adopted by so many composers of different countries that it proves a complete victory for the method. Row manipulation, in Fine's case, is just as successful as the avoidance of it in his earlier compositions. Twelve-tone music, however, must not be considered as a *modus operandi* that sits quietly, coldly, mundanely in repose. Being glued to an ordained technical method has no validity; genuine composers do not pivot on their sounds and all mime the same way.

92

Fine's serial music is clear, diatonically settled; he subjects the wilfullness of the system to his system of arbitration. It proves that dodecaphonic life can exist without turgid reliance on the philosophy of the Abstract. Fine's latest work is not dictated by outside controls; it is neither academically artificial nor in the twelve-tone straitjacket; all its particulars are clearly framed in artistic, emotional music.

The record catalogues contain only a few of Fine's compositions. In proportion to his concentrated output, however, he has fair representation. The most important recordings are of his chamber music.

ORCHESTRAL

String Orchestra

SERIOUS SONG: A LAMENT FOR STRING ORCHESTRA

Conventions are not smashed in Fine's works; yet the works are not conventional. This piece is termed by the composer "an extended aria." Its flexible lyricism and warm severity, plus a mood of demanding asceticism, mark it as a miniature symphonic poem for strings. Fine's music is devoid of flamboyancy. It carries the broadest sense of string-sonority meaning, minus overscaled color or instrumental trickery. It is possible, as proved here, to compress one's viewpoint in a small form.

The astute David Hall, in an article concerning the Louisville Commissions, calls the "Serious Song" "one of the best achievements of the entire Louisville series." No argument. The Kentucky orchestra plays Fine's music with warmth and Whitney shapes the phrases neatly.

——Louisville Orchestra, Robert Whitney, cond. LOUISVILLE COMMISSIONING SERIES LOU-57-6 (with Morris: Passacaglia, Adagio and Finale, and Rubbra: Improvisation for Violin and Orchestra).

INSTRUMENTAL

Piano

MUSIC FOR PIANO (EXCERPTS)

Movements three and two (recorded in that order) of the total of four, played with the authority of the composer's own interpretation. First on the disk is a set of three variations on a theme that moves around Stravinskian curves. The music is superbly educated. A Waltz-Gavotte follows and is twice a hybrid. The gavotte which gives the requisite contrast is demonstrated with uneven dance steps, and Prokofievian sarcasm blends with Stravinskian neatness of thought. But Fine's music is no mere carbon copy; it is filtered through a lighter cloth.

——Irving Fine. COMPOSERS RECORDINGS CRI-106 (with Mutability, and Brant: Angels and Devils).

CHAMBER MUSIC

FANTASIA FOR STRING TRIO

Aside from the fact that it adds to the scant literature of worthy trios for violin, viola, and cello, Fine's "Fantasia" is a refreshing inventive work. In being at first a classically objective composer, Fine was paying creative courtship to Stravinsky. His dynamic here is as different from Stravinsky as the score of "Pulcinella" is from "*Le Sacre.*" Analysis of Fine's score shows a textbook of possibilities for tone-row technique applied to the paradoxical relationship of tonal diatonicism. This is not mere distortion of technical direction. The exterior is beautiful, but the interior of this trio structure is just as exciting. We can safely say that twelve-tone music now has its national *characteristica*. The melos of Dallapiccola can be recognized as of an almost sensuous kind; Valen's austerity is not drawn from rules of use, but from his Northern heritage; Fine's impeccable clarity shows still another facet.

The three members of the Walden Quartet, however, do not master this work as it has been mastered by others. Their performance follows the symbols, is simply top-surface.

——Homer Schmitt, violin; John Garvey, viola; Robert Swenson, cello. UNIVERSITY OF ILLINOIS CUSTOM RECORDING SERIES CRS-5.

STRING QUARTET

Twelve-tone technique is not essentially so far removed from the architectural soundness that marks Beethoven's towering musical structures. The motival enfoldment of the classic master is matched at its analytical peak (no emotional premise is being considered) by the unity and variety of serial procedure. Fine's quartet furnishes important evidence to support this statement.

Fine, a new member of the dodecaphonic school, writes as though to the twelve-tone manner born. His use of this technique takes on new meaning, for his twelve tones are clothed with the royal purple of classic design. And within his music there is the necessary freedom that must be enjoyed by good art, unless it is to be a mere laboratory report. On top of all this the quartet has a tonal center. The twain have certainly met and embraced each other! Fine's heady rhythms are not bounded by serial blueprint; they hammer the spikes into the quadruple lines, strengthening and thereby clarifying the work as a whole. And in this way the Bartók heritage makes its presence felt.

Though these formal purposes would seem to be served by eclectic choice as distinguished from true serial technique, the facts are the opposite. Fine's quartet has clear positiveness; it is his own music, exhibiting a codification of rare sensibility and sensitivity. It is therefore a newer-than-new music. The Juilliard's performance is magnificent, styled with minute scrupulousness.

——Juilliard String Quartet. Columbia ML-4843 (with Kirchner: String Quartet No. 1).

Partita for Wind Quintet

Fine's Partita tends mainly to use this generic title in its truest meaning; although the word "partita" is used frequently to identify a miscellaneous group of movements in suite form and of that character, it means actually a set of variations. The first three and the last sections of this work are definitely in the variation category, while the penultimate is only subconsciously related to the variation principle. Regardless, the five movements establish a specific unit in one stylistic groove, essentially in the neoclassic manner, refined (if one may be permitted the pun) with crystal-clear workmanship and a neutral (black-white) viewpoint of instrumental colors. There is no attempt at establishing a basic timbre design; the instruments share equally in promulgating the essentials of the music. The organic instrumentation of the music's eighteenth-century ancestry is in direct opposition to any pictorial or decorative luxuriance.

This is one of the best of the many wind-instrument chamber pieces that have appeared within the last years. It is played by one of the best groups devoted to such literature.

——New Art Wind Quintet. CLASSIC EDITIONS CE-1003 (with Berezowsky: Suite for Wind Quintet, and Milhaud: Two Sketches).

VOCAL

MUTABILITY

Fine does not embellish or prettify his six songs, set to poems by Irene Orgel. Each one is concerned with sensitive musical essence rather than suave, vocalized delicacy. The music illustrates the prime consideration of equality between keyboard instrument and voice, in addition to scrupulous regard for the poetry. Alberts' voice has a good timbre—her diction is not memorable. No text is provided. This is always valuable, but so rarely available when needed.

——Eunice Alberts, contralto; Irving Fine, piano. COMPOSERS RECORDINGS CRI-106 (with Music for Piano—Excerpts, and Brant: Angels and Devils).

10. Lukas Foss
(1922—   )

Foss was one of the school of *Wunderkinder* composing at an age when most youngsters hardly know the alphabet; later he was a pupil of Hindemith, still later the pianist of the Boston Symphony Orchestra under Serge Koussevitzky, a man who did more for Foss than anyone by introducing his music. His career has been meteoric; awards star-stud his career (a Pulitzer Prize at the age of nineteen, a Guggenheim Fellowship when he was twenty-three; also, a Fulbright fellowship, Prix de Rome award, and many more). Foss has not only had his works performed by many major organizations, he has conducted them as well. He is an extraordinary pianist; if he had so chosen he would have been one of the world's great virtuosi.

Aside from a healthy amount of stage (opera and ballet) works, Foss's output has been mainly concentrated in vocal and choral compositions—prose material gives rise to his best music. A fair amount of piano works and music for orchestra has been produced, but little chamber music, by comparison. After the initial influence of Hindemith, he next entered the orbit of Copland. He has since become a more independent composer; there is a rhythmic incisiveness that parlays his music into healthy, assertive qualities. There is also freshness in his works without the need for utilizing an arbitrary, boundaried system.

Though Foss's career is very active—he teaches, conducts, lectures—its major focus is composition. There is no mistaking his importance in American music. Yet, despite a large number of performances by top-ranking conductors this composer is represented on records with only a paltry number of works. The absence from the catalogue of such emotional works as the "Song of Songs" (performed by the Boston Symphony eight times within a single tour, after its first hearing) and "Song of Anguish" remains one of the mysteries of record-making. Bernstein has prepared the former work but there is no indication as to when it will be issued. The one-act opera *The Jumping Frog of Calaveras County*, based on the Mark Twain story, was at one time available on Lyrichord (catalogue number 11) but it is difficult to obtain.

Lukas Foss's individuality is only partially exhibited in the available recordings discussed below. His creative ideals are matched by as splendid a technique. His compositions furnish examples of salutary advice for young composers, and music of discernment for contemporary audiences.

SOLO INSTRUMENT WITH ORCHESTRA
Concertos

PIANO CONCERTO No. 2

Music of romantic casing with some barbed hooks. Foss's concerto is made to order for a virtuoso, but has no Rachmaninovian music-for-the-keyboard characteristics; rather it is of tighter cast. No tiny dimensions are considered. The music has brilliance, is almost overdramatic in its manners. It can be considered as a written-down, fantastic improvisation. Throughout, the writing exemplifies a skilled contemporary composer's way of displaying a solo piano without imitating the crisp regulations of the traditional concerto. Decca's sound is below average and the balances are capricious, but Foss overrides this by the force and artistry of his performance.

——Los Angeles Festival Orchestra; Lukas Foss, piano; Franz Waxman, cond. DECCA DL-9889 (with Waxman: Sinfonietta for Strings and Timpani).

INSTRUMENTAL
Cello

CAPRICCIO FOR CELLO AND PIANO

A frothy work, making the piano almost a subsidiary voice to the mosaic virtuosity of the stringed instrument. Foss does not peep into the salon; his music is of concert-hall variety, informally glancing at Coplandesque Westernese and New England square-dancing. A fancy as light-hearted as a Haydn finale, superbly tossed-off by this pair of creative performers.

——Gregor Piatigorsky, cello; Lukas Foss, piano. RCA VICTOR

LM-2293 (with Busoni: Espressivo Lamentoso from "Kleine Suite"; Debussy: Sonata; and Stravinsky: Suite Italienne).

CHORAL

BEHOLD! I BUILD AN HOUSE

This is an example of Foss's favorite practice of using a Biblical text. This choral composition points up the fact that he has removed the national *characteristica* (splinters from Copland's composition work chest) that marked some of his early output, and has also disowned the Hindemith influence. Because of the fluid writing it will be observed that the composer's objective does not mark a full retreat into strict formalism. Foss is a present-day romanticist, regardless of his classic adaptations. This work is given a much better reading than the companion piece on the recording, "Psalms."

——Roger Wagner Chorale; James MacInnes and Lukas Foss, pianists; Roger Wagner, cond. COMPOSERS RECORDINGS CRI-123 (123-SD) (with Psalms, and Shifrin: Serenade for Five Instruments).

PSALMS

One of Foss's many commissions—this one was received from the Stockbridge (Massachusetts) Bowl Association in 1955. Although the texts of four psalms are utilized, the parts are not isolated; the forceful idea of contrast within continuity guides the conception.

There is less significant temper in the version recorded, which employs two pianos in place of a symphonic background, with its stimulating plectral and pungent orchestration. It may be that the author is prejudiced by having discussed the work with Foss during its scoring stages, or because he recalls the effect when the New York Philharmonic performed it, under the direction of Dmitri Mitropoulos. Whatever the reason the record lacks some of the power that is sonorously within the work.

——Roger Wagner Chorale; Claire Gordon, Richard Levitt, Keith Wyatt, vocalists; James MacInnes and Lukas Foss, pianists; Roger Wagner, cond. COMPOSERS RECORDINGS CRI-123 (123-SD) (with Behold! I Build an House, and Shifrin: Serenade for Five Instruments).

Choral with Orchestra

A Parable of Death

One of Foss's most powerful and individual pieces. The influence of the Rilke text is felt so strongly that rather than a personal musical narrative one hears a commentary, a musical paraphrase of the text. Foss's narrative with music comes by the grace of Rilke, his god.

This is not servility—it is rather a moving musical drama. If a composer has such a strong central point his goal becomes easier to achieve. Notwithstanding the individual differences that exist between the sections of the work, there is categorical unity.

The "Parable" was commissioned by the Louisville Orchestra. The chorus sings beautifully in this release (though the words cannot be distinguished very well, and there is no text to guide the listener). Vera Zorina's narration is perfect; no text is required to understand her beautiful reading. The orchestra is sensitive and conveys the exciting tone of Foss's music expertly.

A later version (it does not supplant the one recorded) replaces the orchestra by a few strings, organ, piano, and percussion. (This was recorded on Educo ECM-4002; not heard by this writer.)
——Louisville Orchestra; Vera Zorina, narrator; Farrold Stevens, tenor; Choir of the Southern Baptist Theological Seminary; Robert Whitney, cond. Columbia ML-4859 (with Martinu: Intermezzo, and Milhaud: Kentuckiana).

11. Alberto Ginastera
(1916—   )

OF ALL THE CONTEMPORARY ARGENTINIAN COMPOSERS, GINASTERA has achieved the highest reputation, has the honor of a goodly number of American performances, and the rare distinction of American publication.

At the start of his career Ginastera's compositions were conceived along impressionistic lines, but different assimilations soon changed this creative policy. Folkloristic properties became paramount in his work and it is with this strain that most of his important compositions, up to about 1956, are identified. Latterly, however, the elements of non-national material and international techniques have entered his music. The newest works may well be an amalgam—a subjectively intense, Argentinian-flavored method, guided by an objective naturalization (or neutralizing?) process stemming especially from the twelve-tone system. Ginastera's second string quartet (commissioned by the Coolidge Foundation of the Library of Congress) clearly proclaims this fact. The remarkable ingenuity of this quartet should be available on records, especially since a number of Ginastera's most representative compositions have now been recorded.

ORCHESTRAL

ESTANCIA—BALLET SUITE
An exciting reading of the very essence of folk *materia*. "Estancia" was commissioned by an American ballet company and depicts "scenes of Argentine rural life." Ginastera does not hold back his sonorities. The final dance is a thriller—designed for popularity, it is indeed odd that it has not been picked up by conductors, it outthrusts the "Sabre Dance," ten times over. These excerpted four dances represent Ginastera in his most characteristic creative stance.

The pairing on the second record makes available two Ginastera works (with a Villa-Lobos tidbit) on one disk; it also results in monotony, both Ginastera compositions being in the same style. The disk pairing the suite with Antheil's *echt*-Shostakovich symphony would seem to be preferable. In order to have both Ginastera suites one might select the 6013 record with Everest's 6003; the latter includes an interesting contemporary Australian work, which is well worth owning, with the "Panambi" ballet music (*see below*).

——London Symphony Orchestra, Eugene Goossens, cond. EVEREST LPBR-6013 (SDBR-3013) (with Antheil: Symphony No. 4).

——London Symphony Orchestra, Eugene Goossens, cond. EVEREST LPBR-6041 (SDBR-3041) (with Suite from the Ballet "Panambi," and Villa-Lobos: Little Train of the Caipira).

PAMPEANA No. 3—A PASTORAL SYMPHONY

Despite the picturesque title this work is held together logically by the subjective inspiration of the Argentine pampas and by its formal unity. But the scope of the music is more symphonic than anything else. And, as such, it needs a little musical stimulant. There is redundance in too large a measure—basic to the use of rondo and ternary forms in the end movements. Ginastera's ballet suites serve him far better. No criticism of Whitney's performance or the sonics, which have all the brightness required.

——Louisville Orchestra, Robert Whitney, cond. LOUISVILLE COMMISSIONING SERIES LOU-545-10 (with Bergsma: A Carol on Twelfth Night; Sauguet: Les Frois Lys—Symphonic Movements; and Ward: Euphony for Orchestra).

SUITE FROM THE BALLET "PANAMBI"

Ginastera composed his one-act ballet, "Panambi" (subtitled "a choreographic legend"), at the early age of twenty. A suite drawn from the ballet was made three years before the first performance of the complete stage work (presented at the Teatro Colón, in Buenos Aires, in July of 1940).

The profile of Argentinian melos is very strong in this music, based on a story about the Indians of northern Argentina; the composer permits it to be so. Ginastera's thematic material never departs from its basic spirit or native identity. Goossens' performance is not glib nor super-powerful, but a just portrayal of an interesting score.

——London Symphony Orchestra, Eugene Goossens, cond. EVEREST LPBR-6003 (SDBR-3003) (with Antill: Corroboree).

——London Symphony Orchestra, Eugene Goossens, cond. EVER-EST LPBR-6041 (SDBR-3041) (with Estancia—Ballet Suite, and Villa-Lobos: Little Train of the Caipira).

VARIACIONES CONCERTANTES

A novel plan, with the music just as enticing. Each of the eleven variants employs a different instrumental scheme, the orchestra, as an entity, being reserved for the end. Mercury's pairing is clever; both works are based on a variation scheme, and both are guides to the orchestra, the Britten presumably didactic but turning out to be the opposite, and the Ginastera a serious work of kaleidoscopic color, from which the auditor learns just as much about the orchestral palette. The performance is no less successful.

——Minneapolis Symphony Orchestra, Antal Dorati, cond. MERCURY 50047 (with Britten: The Young Person's Guide to the Orchestra).

INSTRUMENTAL

Organ

TOCCATA, VILLANCICO Y FUGA

Bach becomes Ginastera and the disguise is becoming. The initial and terminal portions will remind many of J.S.B.'s similarly formed works, though the Toccata is more restrained than Bach's would have been. No national characteristics are reflected in the piece. Bachian musical discipline makes the recording first-rate. Ellsasser's articulation and phrasing are aided by good registration and above-the-average sound.

——in "Organ Music by Modern Composers—Volume 2," Richard Ellsasser. MGM E-3585.

CHAMBER MUSIC

QUARTET No. 1

This gives a vigorous view of the norms of Ginastera's art as applied to the field of chamber music. The composer's interest and cultivation of folkloric musical style are illustrated here by two main facets: dance rhythms and contemplative, somewhat brooding song. The open-air quality of the finale and the wild initial movement represent the first; the deep-throated, extremely moving slow movement, the other. The scherzo suggests an Argentinian's thoughts while considering the conception of outer space and is illustrative of the composer's acute color intuition.

The Paganini foursome give what is probably their best recorded performance; intonation and ensemble—especially in the scherzo—are exceptional. Laszlo Lajtha's string quartet (his name is misspelled on label, cover, and liner copy) is an excellent companion piece and enters a brand-new personality in the literature of recordings.

——Paganini Quartet. DECCA DL-9823 (with Lajtha: Quartet No. 7).

CHORAL

LAMENTATIONS OF JEREMIAH

Since the only recording of this piece gives no liner data it would be well to indicate that Ginastera's "Lamentations" consist of a set of three motets for *a cappella* mixed chorus, were composed in 1946, and first performed in Buenos Aires, in 1947. The "Lamentations" could be by any composer; they are neutral, un-nationalistic, ninety-nine and ninety-nine one hundredths per cent pure, academically well-made.

The cover of the album does not list any of the works included on the recording but the Randall Thompson, hence the reader is directed to the data below. (Music Library Recordings is quite often most haphazard about notifying its potential customers that more than one work is included on a record.) The recording itself is marred by poor diction and rather unsonorous sonics. There are no bands if one wishes to hear any one of the three pieces.

——San José State College A Cappella Choir, William Erlendson, cond. MUSIC LIBRARY RECORDINGS MLR-7065 (with Berger: Brazilian Psalm; Lotti: Crucifixus; Thompson: The Peaceable Kingdom; Vaughan Williams: Prayer to the Father in Heaven; and Willan: The Three Kings).

12. *Howard Hanson*
(1896—   )

THE FACTS SPEAK FOR THIS MAN: THE GREATEST PROTAGONIST FOR American music—past or present. Pioneering efforts require a hardy soul and Hanson has proven his courage and strength. Composers in this country owe much to him for his efforts and constant work on their behalf. And in this unselfish spirit he continues to give concerts, festivals, and reading sessions devoted to American music, plus making a large number of recordings.

There is no part of musical life in which Hanson has not participated. He is that rare combination: an educator, writer, composer, conductor, lecturer, organizer, and warrior-at-large for all matters pertaining to the good of musical art. His own work proves the simple dictum that in music American nationalism is nothing more than music on any subject written by American composers. We have outgrown the fashion that required music identified as "American" to be based on Indian, Negro, ragtime, or jazz sources. It is fusion, not a dogmatic use of folk materials peculiar to the United States, or the dependence on a special technique, that makes music "American." There are no restrictions, whatever the force of association, to the definition. If Hanson is typed as a supreme romanticist, he remains as American as those who follow more abstract or less conservative tenets. Real music has no technical laws. Hanson composes accordingly.

Practically all of his recorded music was made under his own baton. Regardless of the music he directs one can be assured of a faithfulness of intent and a brilliance of conception. It follows that Hanson the conductor lives up to the responsibilities imposed by Hanson the composer.

ORCHESTRAL

ELEGY IN MEMORY OF MY FRIEND, SERGE KOUSSEVITZKY, OP. 44
Eloquent testimony of Hanson's ability to write emotional music that retains a dignified expression. The *long* line in music, not a simple matter for any composer, is not only moving and exciting, but sustains interest. It is not that the short, motival idea

is less efficient; it is more that the long subject generates emotional content by its maintenance of thematic constancy. Hanson's music communicates a radiant, threnodic quality as it rises to a huge climax and then subsides into quiescence. Sensory clarity in the performance marks this as one of the magnificent Hanson recordings and one of his noblest orchestral pieces.

——Eastman-Rochester Symphony Orchestra, Howard Hanson, cond. MERCURY 50150 (with Song of Democracy, and Lane: Four Songs).

MERRY MOUNT SUITE

Hanson's *Merry Mount* was given a full-scale production by the Met in 1934. Unfortunately it did not survive, despite its native subject matter, dealing with New England witchcraft. This recording of the suite from the opera is part of a novel release (*see under* Special). The last four bands on the second side consist of the "Overture," "Children's Dance," "Love Duet," plus "Prelude to Act II," and "Maypole Dances." All of it is lushly charged music and quite enjoyable.

Previous to the performance of the four sections, the role the orchestra and its scoring techniques play within the total construction is discussed, with illustrations, by the composer. Accordingly, if one wishes, he can listen to a number of examples from each of the movements, analyzed separately, before hearing the complete movement. For example, there are four separate discussions of the "Overture," eight of the "Love Duet," etc. Whether one is interested in pure music or music being dissected, the recording is of prime importance. Mercury's sound is a recommendation in itself.

——Eastman-Rochester Orchestra, Howard Hanson, cond. MERCURY 50175 (SR-90175) (with The Composer and His Orchestra).

SYMPHONY NO. 1 IN E MINOR ("THE NORDIC"), OP. 21

Hanson's three-movement symphony was composed when he was twenty-five. It had the unusual honor of being given its première in Rome, by the famed Augusteo Orchestra, conducted by the composer. The music of the opening is, in Hanson's words, "strongly Nordic in character." Movement two is gentle in mood, while the last section is the opposite.

The MGM recording has little quality, lacks subtle modifications, is an example of negative playing and sound. The composer is not represented properly. A pity, for in its youthful fervor and massive concentration this symphony exemplifies Hanson at his most rugged best. Perhaps Hanson will add the work to his Mercury list. If so, 'tis better to wait.

——Philharmonia Orchestra of Hamburg, Hans-Jürgen Walther, cond. MGM E-3141 (with Siegmeister: Ozark Set, and Skilton: Deer Dance and War Dance from "Suite Primeval").

SYMPHONY No. 2 ("ROMANTIC"), OP. 30

Hanson's own credo is important to the listener to this symphony. "I recognize, of course, that romanticism is . . . the poor stepchild. . . . Nevertheless, I embrace her all the more fervently, believing, as I do, that romanticism will find in this country rich soil for a . . . vigorous growth." This philosophy is deliberately espoused in the work Serge Koussevitzky commissioned in 1930 for the Boston Symphony's fiftieth anniversary, and which he introduced in November of that year.

One must not mind some of the Hollywoodisms—they appeared first in Hanson (and others) *circa* the late 1920's. The orchestration is both powerful and lush. Hanson knows how to arrange a huge sound; he wears the full romantic crown and is not ashamed of it.

Only the more representative sound gives the Mercury version the edge in consideration; otherwise there is no difference in the pair of performances.

——Eastman-Rochester Orchestra, Howard Hanson, cond. MERCURY 50192 (SR-90192) (with The Lament for Beowulf).

——Eastman-Rochester Symphony Orchestra, Howard Hanson, cond. COLUMBIA ML-4638 (with MacDowell: Piano Concerto No. 2 in D Minor).

SYMPHONY No. 3, OP. 33

This composition had a partial première when three of its four movements were broadcast by the CBS Symphony Orchestra, conducted by Hanson, in September, 1937. The finale was composed later and the complete symphony received its baptism, also on the radio, in March, 1938, when it was played by the NBC Symphony Orchestra; Hanson again was the conductor. (He also directed the initial concert performance when it was given by the Boston Symphony on November 3, 1959.)

Hanson's excellent craft is employed in a stern (though warm) elucidation of Sibelian dialect in this symphony. Hanson may be influenced but it matters little when the melodic curves, the dynamic thrusts, and the ripeness of color yield a music of discernment and craftsmanship. The soloistic use of the timpani in the scherzo movement is especially entrancing. The Bostonians' rendition is impressive; the sound is not.

——Boston Symphony Orchestra, Serge Koussevitzky, cond. RCA VICTOR LVT-1016 (with Harris: Symphony No. 3).

SYMPHONY No. 4 ("THE REQUIEM"), OP. 34

Hanson achieves a type of Gothic musical architecture in this strongly blended symphony (dedicated to the memory of the composer's father) wherein flowing sounds are contrasted with granite-leveled lines. The counterpoints represent decorative projections while block writing and rhythms symbolize geometric arches, the sternness and span of the total work justifying such terms. There is nothing mechanical in the score; the music is thrillingly alive. And so performed.

——Eastman-Rochester Symphony Orchestra, Howard Hanson, cond. MERCURY 50077 (with Harris: Symphony No. 3).

SYMPHONY No. 5 ("SINFONIA SACRA")

As Hanson's first two symphonies were related through their subtitles ("Nordic" and "Romantic"), so his Fifth Symphony relates to the Fourth ("Requiem") Symphony. Classical ideology, romantic enlargement of harmony, and a broad mural-like sweep of sound characterize this work. This is an example of a free yet controlled voice in the sophisticated welter of musical styles of the current century. Engineering is superb.

——Eastman-Rochester Symphony Orchestra, Howard Hanson, cond. MERCURY 50087 (with The Cherubic Hymn, and Barber: Symphony No. 1).

Band

CHORALE AND ALLELUIA

Simplicity is difficult to achieve; creative people spend their lives chasing it. But simplicity must not be confused with the trivial soporifics of light music. Simplicity has order, design, and functional magic. It requires as much of the intellect as does complexity. This engaging, brief piece that Hanson composed for band belongs to this uncomplex artistic order. Fennell's "chamber" band (for that is what it is, minus doublings and massed similar instruments) performs it with gusto, sonorous balance, and all the flavor necessary. Mercury's album of American band compositions is a refreshing musical totality.

——Eastman Symphonic Wind Ensemble, Frederick Fennell, cond. MERCURY 50084 (with Mennin: Canzona; Persichetti: Psalm; Reed: La Fiesta Mexicana; and Thomson: A Solemn Music).

MARCH CARILLON, OP. 19, No. 2

After Sousa, writing a right good march became a difficult procedure. Hanson's march is of the concert (not two-step, pit-a-pat) variety; replete with bells and some polyphony. Worth listening to occasionally.

——in "Marches," Eastman Symphonic Wind Ensemble, Frederick Fennell, cond. MERCURY 50080.

SOLO INSTRUMENT WITH ORCHESTRA

Concertos

CONCERTO FOR ORGAN, STRINGS AND HARP

Should auld acquaintance come to mind—much melodic resemblance to Hanson's symphony themes here. Notwithstanding a dramatic cadenza, the organ material does not seem to be conceived in terms of solo-instrument importance. The concerto is in one multi-sectioned movement, and rhapsodic in mood. On the whole a contrived work.

——Philharmonia Orchestra of Hamburg; Richard Ellsasser, organ; Arthur Winograd, cond. MGM E-3361 (with Poulenc: Concerto for Organ, Strings and Timpani).

Solo Piano with Orchestra

FANTASY VARIATIONS ON A THEME OF YOUTH, FOR PIANO AND
STRING ORCHESTRA

Inadequate definition and a prosaic quality are rare in Hanson's output. One has the feeling that this music was considered, formed, and then left snugly alone. It falls short of the convincing mark, perhaps due to the fact that variation design fits this man's lyrical and dramatic style rather uneasily. Though the piano part is well played, its sound is not advantageously balanced—surprising for Mercury.

——Eastman-Rochester Symphony Orchestra; David Burge, piano; Howard Hanson, cond. MERCURY 50114 (with Rogers: Leaves from the Tale of Pinocchio, and Triggs: The Bright Land).

Solo Wind with Orchestra

PASTORALE FOR OBOE, STRINGS AND HARP

An oboe equals a pastoral and rustic setting: thus precedents create unilateral rules. Hanson follows the dictum with a fluent and concentrated work, particular as to the color of the woodwind voice. The "Pastorale" was originally conceived for oboe with piano accompaniment; in the bowed and plucked stringed instrumental setting the solo oboe is enriched by a warmer background. All parties play beautifully in the single recording available.

——in "American Music for Solo Winds and String Orchestra," Eastman-Rochester Symphony Orchestra; Robert Sprenkle, oboe; Howard Hanson, cond. MERCURY 50076.

SERENADE FOR FLUTE, STRINGS AND HARP

In its most common form a "serenade" is a song to a lover's lady. But the term also applies to instrumental music associated with entertainment and happy events (an example: Mozart's "Haffner Serenade," written to celebrate the wedding of a friend's daughter). Hanson's "Serenade" is a romantic outpouring that fits both categories; it was written in 1946, as a wedding present to his bride.

The artistry of the soloist, Joseph Mariano, and the high level of insight this flutist shows in making his instrument one of multicolor sensitivity are accomplishments worth hearing. Mercury's sound is magnificent.

——in "American Music for Solo Winds and String Orchestra," Eastman-Rochester Symphony Orchestra; Joseph Mariano, flute; Howard Hanson, cond. MERCURY 50076.

CHORAL

How Excellent Thy Name

Quietly emotional music for four-part women's chorus, composed in 1953. Hanson's text is taken from Psalm VIII; his music is plastic, never governed by academic formula. It is sung with appropriate style and tidy diction.

——Jenny Lind Chorus (The Augustana Choir), Henry Veld, cond. WORD RECORDS W-4012 (with Brahms: Mary Magdalene; Fryxell: Christmas Wish; Schubert: Widerspruch; La Pastorella; Stenhammer: Sverige; and Vaughan Williams: Mass in G Minor; The Souls of the Righteous).

Choral with Orchestra

The Cherubic Hymn

The text is taken from the Liturgy of St. John Chrysostom. There is no better force for projecting a choral-orchestral work than a composer's ability to create sustained lines. This factor is present here, and illustrates Hanson's compelling strength as a writer of dynamic choral music, but color differentials are not thereby eliminated. A recording of exultant sound and sensitive performance.

——Eastman-Rochester Symphony Orchestra; Eastman School of Music Chorus; Howard Hanson, cond. MERCURY 50087 (with Symphony No. 5, and Barber: Symphony No. 1).

The Lament for Beowulf, Op. 25

A distinctive Northern element is found in many of Hanson's works. Influential in this early composition are the darker sides of Elgar and Vaughan Williams, aids in achieving the austere quality required for the Anglo-Saxon text. The author does not consider the work to be overly inspired; its effect is due chiefly to Hanson's control of dynamic contrast and relationship—the mark of the expert conductor as well as the professional composer.

——Eastman-Rochester Orchestra; Eastman School of Music Chorus; Howard Hanson, cond. MERCURY 50192 (SR-90192) (with Symphony No. 2—"Romantic").

Song of Democracy

One of the most representative of Hanson's works; definite Northern atmosphere, line-scoring which defines the orchestral compounds, and beautiful vocal writing make a massive, sonorous production. The music is moving, it registers, it is extremely worthwhile. Postscript: a portion of the slow movement theme from the composer's "Romantic" Symphony is apparently quoted.

The Eastman forces are welded into a unified group and the rafters will ring if the room-space is small. And, a non sequitur— the harp sounds extremely tinny.

——Eastman-Rochester Symphony Orchestra; Eastman School of Music Chorus; Howard Hanson, cond. Mercury 50150 (with Elegy in Memory of My Friend, Serge Koussevitzky, and Lane: Four Songs).

Songs from "Drum Taps"

Eloquent, warm-blooded music is Hanson's composition of three settings from Walt Whitman for mixed chorus, baritone solo, and orchestra, composed in 1935. It illustrates the cleanly romantic school of composition with nary a false step.

The performance standards of the Eastman Chorus are always very high; in this case they must be classed as superlative. Their tone is magnificently full and resonant; precise and meaningful enunciation enhances the patriotic feeling of this work. The clarity of diction makes the following of the text on the liner unnecessary. The recording is a choral joy; a brilliant achievement of a stunning work.

——Eastman-Rochester Orchestra; Eastman School of Music Chorus; David Meyers, baritone; Howard Hanson, cond. Mercury 50073 (with Thompson: The Testament of Freedom).

SPECIAL

The Composer and His Orchestra

It is to Mercury's credit that it has produced the first attempt to codify the science of orchestration via the dissection of a composition (Hanson's *Merry Mount* Suite—*see above, under:* Orchestral), from the working tools (the individual instruments) through a consideration of the effects these produce (combination of sound qualities) on to the final structure (the musical composition itself). While it is rather easy to report one's own practices, it is difficult to show how these will serve others. What Hanson proves, however, is valid no matter what technique is involved, for his presentation is based on solid sonoric facts without considering orchestration in terms of its ever-changing role within the creative aesthetic. The listener has the enjoyment of being a sidewalk engineer watching the musical structure arise. This is a truly successful project for Hanson, as he fills the quadruple role of composer, conductor, script writer, and narrator.

——Eastman-Rochester Orchestra; Howard Hanson, narrator; Howard Hanson, cond. MERCURY 50175 (SR-90175) (with Merry Mount Suite).

13. Roy Harris
(1898—   )

A PECULIAR STATE OF AFFAIRS PREVAILS IN REGARD TO THIS ONCE most-publicized composer. In the 78 r.p.m. days he led all the American and most of the European composers in total recorded performances; today he is far down on the list. The major chamber works—the sextet, piano quintet, and third string quartet—were all represented on 78's; now only the piano trio is available and then on an off-the-beaten-track label. The large choral-orchestral works could once be heard—not a one presently graces the catalogue. As for the symphonies, only three can be obtained; the important fifth and sixth works in this form have yet to be recorded. As with most public figures, Harris has those that are for him and those against him, but this does not solve the mystery of why his music remains unnoticed by the record companies. Being the low man on the totem pole is not the proper role for this individual musical mind. Harris has an important place in American musical history; this neglect is artistic crucifixion.

Like his own physical shape, Harris' music is lean and angular. His contemporary native music avoids folk tunes, jazz, or any specific part of the popular American current. Folk ingredients are present, but not in their raw state; they have been fully polished as Harris uses them. His melting pot is a spiritual mixture that defines Americanism objectively, in terms of breadth and scope, not by the subjective use of material from any group or locale of the country —from its Negroes, its Indians, its Lower East Side or Upper West Side. Harris' melodicism is most individual; it does not tread the path of "tunes" but of the architectonic line that has more probity than "melody." The fact that Harris' themes are not easily whistled does not make them any the less perfect. The functional, architectural means of his music are precisely tabulated but they never interfere with its total creative beauty.

The output of a composer of such striking individuality must be reckoned with. As far as Roy Harris is concerned the matter is a closed issue. Harris believes in every note he writes as the most important ever conceived. In fact, a more open, enthusiastic propa-

gandist for his own music cannot be found. Regardless of this im-
modesty there is little doubt that time will reflect the final judgment that the music of Roy Harris is honest, valid, and original.
But we must cease venerating this composer in silence. He deserves
hearing.

ORCHESTRAL

SYMPHONY 1933

Harris' initial symphony, first performed by the Bostonians in
1934. It is doubtless the recording made in that year that is now
heard on an LP transfer; the sound is pretty bad, stilted, wavy, and
annoying. It is arguable how much of a good turn is done the
composer, and the auditor, by such a poor example. The moods of
exuberance, pathos, and the will to power and action (descriptions
by the composer) are vaguely recognizable. The "1933" work was
never quite such a success as Harris' later symphonies; the composer's grasp of form was too studied, the orchestration somewhat
dull. However, the very roughness (crudeness) of Harris' unpol-
ished musical speech has an individual appeal and is worth anyone's listening time. Further, the seed of the later symphonies can
be recognized in this work.

In this instance we have history being served and music merely
being noticed. The reverse side of the disk offers the Seventh
Symphony, which provides a reason for purchasing this record.
——Boston Symphony Orchestra, Serge Koussevitzky, cond. Co-
LUMBIA ML-5095 (with Symphony No. 7).

SYMPHONY No. 3

The great contribution of the composer. There is unanimous
opinion that this symphony will be one of the works that will last
through the centuries. Depth of meaning, expressive power, glowing orchestration, all are contained in musical discourse that has a
completely individual sound. And yet the music is of such con-
sequence that very few listeners will remain unmoved. Make no
mistake—Harris does not seek the popular path in this one-movement composition; no unconditional surrender to academic rules
is made, nor any other concession. The symphony passes through
specific moods (tragic, lyric, pastoral, dramatic) and in this way
the composer combines expression and form in a synthesis which

makes the work a personal and a prophetic document—prophetic in the sense that it brought success to Harris and that the success has proven to be just and lasting.

Hanson takes the symphony in virile stride, but Koussevitzky displays a better understanding of the work by granting it more scope, and thereby gives it strength. Hanson's vigor is not misplaced; it gives the work a more active character. His version also has more telling sound, because the Boston version is a remastering from the original 78 r.p.m. release. However, sound can take second place to power of performance in this case.

——Boston Symphony Orchestra, Serge Koussevitzky, cond. RCA VICTOR LVT-1016 (with Hanson: Symphony No. 3).

——Eastman-Rochester Symphony Orchestra, Howard Hanson, cond. MERCURY 50077 (with Hanson: Symphony No. 4).

SYMPHONY No. 7

Harris' consistent concern for the polyphonic stimulant may be heard in this huge one-movement work. The initial passacaglia subject displays the melodic scope peculiar to this composer—continual thematic growth is as natural to him as the precise, easily recognizable, eight-measure length of a Haydn minuet theme. As the permutations of this generator are displayed they reflect the polyphonic devices common to all the centuries in which composers have utilized this form. Here, the sound is new and daring. Harris' orchestration disproves the criticism that he scores with gray neutrality. The brass and percussion color the virtuoso declaration of the symphony. Ormandy's performance, with its clean depiction of the lean score, stands as the definitive version, as did Koussevitzky's initial recording of the same composer's third symphony.

——Philadelphia Orchestra, Eugene Ormandy, cond. COLUMBIA ML-5095 (with Symphony 1933).

SOLO INSTRUMENT WITH ORCHESTRA

FANTASY FOR PIANO AND ORCHESTRA

Folk materials have always fascinated Harris, from his early-career success with "When Johnny Comes Marching Home," an overture. Three tunes are here run through the creative wringer and come out very much Harris. All of the composer's marks are here and here too is one of the most important champions of Roy Harris—Mrs. Harris, a fine pianist, to whom he owes so much. (Johana Harris, in addition to being the mother of a large family, has introduced or participated in more first performances of her husband's works than anyone else.)

Postscript: a characteristic, but not overly important work.

——MGM Symphony Orchestra; Johana Harris, piano; Izler Solomon, cond. MGM E-3210 (with Abraham Lincoln Walks at Midnight).

CHAMBER MUSIC

SONATA FOR VIOLIN AND PIANO

One of Harris' most inspired works. Spontaneity is difficult to achieve in set forms, yet each of the four movements gives the impression of complete freedom, an outpouring of noble themes, and a balance between lyricism and virtuosity (without negating proper chamber music instrumental equality). A splendid performance by Gingold and the composer's wife.

——Josef Gingold, violin; Johana Harris, piano. COLUMBIA ML-4842 (with Palmer: Quartet for Piano and Strings).

TRIO FOR PIANO, VIOLIN, AND CELLO

Harris' excursions into chamber music are few. The only trio he has composed makes one wish he had written more small-framed works. Sonata form, per se, does not govern the opening movement, but rather, thematic engenderment by rhythm, expansion, turns, and twists. This essence of continuity is found in both the slow movement and the finale. In the former Harris illustrates the principle of sustained form, without considering recapitulation even in a semiliteral sense. The latter is a fugue, and no design gives more voluminous opportunity for expansion upon a basic generative idea.

Unfortunately, the playing is cool-hearted, and never catches fire; the strength of the fugue is diminished by a chaste performance.

——University of Oklahoma Trio. UNIVERSITY RECORDINGS 1 (with Copland: Vitebsk, and Kerr: Trio).

VOCAL

ABRAHAM LINCOLN WALKS AT MIDNIGHT

A cantata ("of lamentation") for mezzo-soprano, two stringed instruments, and piano, written to a Vachel Lindsay text. This is pure, long-line Harris music, with a depth and quiet strength peculiar to his methods. The performance is blended beautifully and the mixed quartet has a warm sound. No text is provided.

——Nell Tangeman, mezzo-soprano; Johana Harris, piano; Samuel Thaviu, violin; Theo Salzman, cello. MGM E-3210 (with Fantasy for Piano and Orchestra).

14. *Alan Hovhaness*
(1911—   )

HOVHANESS HAS A UNIQUE STATUS AMONG ALL AMERICAN COMPOSERS, past and present. No other person has identified himself so fully with Eastern music, especially that of Armenia (where the composer's ancestors originated). Along with this, his music has an interlineation of medieval plus pre-Christian mannerisms. His picturesque ideas call for odd combinations and severely drawn forms. Modalism and Gregorianism are often present in his music; a tremendous number of reiterated figures and cross-rhythms are also used in setting forth his esoteric Eastern materials. Ascetic in sound, to some, with others a bit of Hovhaness goes a very long way. His music is of such quality that it often makes heavy the concert-hall atmosphere, titillating and stimulating but somewhat enervating the listener; hearing it is rather like visiting a Chinese theater, eating an egg buried for a hundred years, or making a trip through a strange house where words are uttered in a tongue which one has dimly heard and yet not really heard before. (Music is not always so international a language as one thinks.)

Nonetheless, Hovhaness' music shows the mark of a craftsman— one need not know the history of Coptic music or the Syrian modes to realize this. This knowledge and the ability to convey it is his chief strength, whether one accepts or protests against his unusual music.

The place he holds in the record catalogues is as odd as his work. The number of his recordings is impressive (as is not the case with many important contemporary composers) although Hovhaness is not yet a fully known, accepted international figure. No propaganda need be made for this solitary creator in present-day music life; he has succeeded quite well, both in the concert hall and in recorded performances.

ORCHESTRAL

CONCERTO NO. 1 "AREVAKAL"

Modal, churchly feeling marks a large segment of Hovhaness' music, and such is the case with this six-movement piece. (In this case the term "concerto" is as far removed from its usual meaning as Hovhaness' harmony is from dodecaphonicism.) The quietness of mood is fitting: "Arevakal" means the Lenten season of the Armenian church. Hanson plays this music with proper sensitivity to style.

——Eastman-Rochester Symphony Orchestra, Howard Hanson, cond. MERCURY 50078 (with Cowell: Symphony No. 4, and Rieger: New Dance).

CONCERTO NO. 7, OP. 116

Repetitive figures, odd timbre combinations, and forthright Eastern melos set partially in Western-style techniques distinguish this beautifully sensitive music. Hovhaness' polyphonic mixtures result in unburdened, intoxicating sonorities. And he can be very zealous: a Hindustanian scherzo and a final double fugue lead to an epilogue in the form of a hymn. The last is for the citizens of Louisville, Kentucky, in acknowledgment of the Louisville Orchestra's commission for this work. Incidentally, this is one of the best of the many Louisville commissions and it is played with complete understanding, matched by full-scale recording and plenty of fidelity. If Hovhaness is your taste, this disk could well be your best choice.

——Louisville Orchestra, Robert Whitney, cond. LOUISVILLE COMMISSIONING SERIES LOU-545-4 (with Castelnuovo-Tedesco: Overture to *Much Ado About Nothing,* and Surinach: Sinfonietta Flamenca).

MYSTERIOUS MOUNTAIN, OP. 132

In terms of performance by the major-league orchestras, this is the composer's most successful symphonic piece. Again, most of the music represents Hovhaness intoning the descant of bygone centuries, but in one portion of this work there are reflections which indicate that despite the composer's renunciation of his early music (that written prior to 1940, which, for the most part, he destroyed) something of it has remained with him. These are to be heard in the middle section, which has the Sibelian dash and defined Northern climate of the early work. No harm done: it provides relief from the persistent triadic neo-sacred sound that otherwise permeates the work. Reiner's performance is sensitive and the recorded sound is beautiful.

——Chicago Symphony Orchestra, Fritz Reiner, cond. RCA VICTOR LM-2251 (LSC-2251) (with Stravinsky: Divertimento from "The Fairy's Kiss").

PRELUDE AND QUADRUPLE FUGUE

Precisely balanced equations of tempi and style make this a composition that ranks extremely high in Hovhaness' catalogue. Since contrapuntal methods seep into the prelude and beyond, the fugal portion has divisions of varying type. One is offered compactness, stylistic affinity, plus the major premise of variety. Organizing cogent fugal material is not an easy task; to combine four such subjects is sheer contrapuntal black magic. Hovhaness is superbly capable. Hanson's performance is stunning, so is Mercury's sound.

——Eastman-Rochester Symphony Orchestra, Howard Hanson, cond. MERCURY 50106 (with Lo Presti: The Masks, and Sessions: The Black Maskers).

Chamber Orchestra

ANAHID, FANTASY FOR ORCHESTRA, OP. 57

Anahid was a goddess of pre-Christian Armenia and Hovhaness' music pictures the festivals honoring her mainly through chants and dances. The most fascinating element in the score is the use of opposed rhythms and meters. Although the polyphony is complex it is convincing and offers no aural problems. One finds Hovhaness' convictions persuasive, even though overemphasized.

——MGM Orchestra, Carlos Surinach, cond. MGM E-3504 (with Alleluia and Fugue; Tower Music).

"IS THERE SURVIVAL"—BALLET SUITE

This bears an alternate title: "King Vahaken," but the choice of appellations doesn't change this static conception. There must be more to music than automatic, rigid behavior. The interrelations in this work may be symbolic, but the similarity among the parts hardly breeds variety. Verdict: exceedingly constructional, but not constructive. The "Flowering Peach" suite with which this is paired is much better music and will not disappoint the listener.

——Alan Hovhaness, cond. MGM E-3164 (with Suite "The Flowering Peach"; Orbit No. 1).

ORBIT No. 1

Hovhaness patterns his "Orbit No. 1" (originally written as music for a dance composition entitled "Song") after astronomical movements. He proposes a musical work conceived "in the forms of the motion of the spheres—the strangeness of a body in space with ever-shifting relationships to its solar neighbors." The result is a study of a revolving chant-like line for a solo flute, with percussive (mainly a gong), tintinnabular (a gentle celeste), and plectral (the harp) saltings. An unwavering, Oriental demeanor is thus illustrated musically, and the effect is hypnotic, if nothing else.

——Alan Hovhaness, cond. MGM E-3164 (with Suite "The Flowering Peach"; "Is There Survival").

SAINT VARTAN SYMPHONY, OP. 80

A huge work in 24 sections, these grouped in five major parts; it is named for a fifth-century Armenian national hero. This music is symphonic in scope; in form it is rather a mural of canonical description. In presenting his picture of Armenian religion via chants and dances, Hovhaness' attitude is sectarian. Despite a large variety of instrumental colors not once does he depart from his apostolic music-making. This is a work of originality, but its scope can tax the listener. However, one can hear a single section or sections without disturbing the unity, for Hovhaness' symphony is organized in a multi-insular way. This music sounds unlike any other composer's. Hovhaness' so-called unsophistication is actually a new sophistication.

——MGM Chamber Orchestra, Carlos Surinach, cond. MGM E-3453.

SUITE FROM THE INCIDENTAL MUSIC FOR "THE FLOWERING PEACH"

Music originally written for the play by Clifford Odets, concerning the Noah's Ark legend, and in some parts slightly expanded for concert use. The texture is fragile, the sounds extremely sweet. Hovhaness' complete unpretentiousness makes his work almost forceful in effect, despite the restricted and exceedingly rarefied instrumentation of a clarinet, saxophone, harp, glockenspiel, ce-

leste, timpani, vibraphone, and tamtam. But listen in small doses.
——Alan Hovhaness, cond. MGM E-3164 (with "Is There Survival"; Orbit No. 1).

TOWER MUSIC, OP. 129

Six movements of archaic music, scored for four woodwinds (flute, oboe, clarinet, and bassoon) and six brass instruments (two horns, two trumpets, trombone, and tuba). Modal harmonic style prevails throughout—Hovhaness' solemn, ceremonial suite is an affirmation of the tonal language of sixteenth-century sacred music. The forms are of a simple nature: a prelude, fugue, and aria, followed by an antiphonal, a pair of hymns, and a postlude. The alternate performing of groups within the ensemble, like the responsorial singing in Gregorian chant, prevails in the last pair of movements as well as in the antiphonal. Only its pithiness saves the work from being monotonous.
——MGM Orchestra, Carlos Surinach, cond. MGM E-3504 (with Alleluia and Fugue; Anahid).

UPON ENCHANTED GROUND, OP. 90A

Four men do not a chamber quartet make; this is a minuscule orchestral piece and the many combined rhythmic patterns demand a conductor. The music, though of fairly enchanting character, makes no thematic gestures, avoids harmony as we know it, and diffuses its rhythms. Thus, with gentle-pulsed motility, Hovhaness defines his personal idea of Hindu music.
——Samuel Baron, flute; Lucile Lawrence, harp; Claus Adam, cello; Elden Bailey, tamtam; Alan Hovhaness, cond. COLUMBIA ML-5179 (with Suite for Violin, Piano and Percussion, and Wolpe: Ten Songs from the Hebrew).

String Orchestra

ALLELUIA AND FUGUE, OP. 40B

Intense concentration on incessant modal harmonic contours is displayed in this very sonorous outpouring of religious atmosphere. The short fugue offers the requisite contrast.
——MGM Orchestra, Carlos Surinach, cond. MGM E-3504 (with Anahid; Tower Music).

ARMENIAN RHAPSODY, OP. 51, NO. 2

Music catalogues are crammed with so-called Oriental music, Chinese music, Hindu music, and the like, making a great deal of ordered confusion, for in most cases the music is strictly sham exotica, an imitation made from an imitation. Hovhaness did not compose from rote-observation in this case. Though he is not an Easterner, his Eastern-designed music is stated with authority; it is the real thing, the result of study, research, orientation, as well as conviction of purpose.

Armenian folk material is drawn on for the themes of this stringed-instrument rhapsody. The design of the work is two-fold —corresponding to sacred and profane moods. The first half of the piece is based on a feast-day melody (a liturgical *dagh*); the second utilizes two dance tunes, exceedingly Oriental in sound. The MGM Orchestra's performance is indeed exhilarating and provides a splendid introduction to the composer's output.

——in "Music by Alan Hovhaness," MGM String Orchestra, Carlos Surinach, cond. MGM E-3517.

CELESTIAL FANTASY, OP. 44

Hovhaness was born in Massachusetts and in his early works one can perceive in his aesthetic demeanor the staid New England background. This is not to be found in his mature compositions. Hovhaness' first-period work showed him to be quite polyphonically minded (preludes and fugues, canons, and the like, are very numerous). This contrapuntal attitude has never been abandoned. Although Opus 44 has a "heavenly" title, it turns out to be a prelude and fugue in Eastern musical style, dressed in modal fashion. It has a warmth of sound that is engaging and is projected beautifully.

——in "Music by Alan Hovhaness," MGM String Orchestra, Carlos Surinach, cond. MGM E-3517.

Brass Instruments

SHARAGAN AND FUGUE, OP. 61, NO. 1

Hovhaness' penchant for a baroque quality of sound is expertly set forth in this hymn (the meaning of "Sharagan") and fugue. Modalism is the technique, fully utilized, with hardly any exotic overhang. The playing of the anonymous ensemble is a magnificent example of brass virtuosity; these performers have the subtlety and sensitivity of superfine string players.

——in "Music by Alan Hovhaness," MGM Brass Ensemble, Carlos Surinach, cond. MGM E-3517.

Percussion

OCTOBER MOUNTAIN

The emotional tone of Hovhaness' music is directly related to percussion equations. This work for marimba, glockenspiel, timpani, tenor and bass drums, gong, plus tamtam, has the exotic colors, the patterned conformations he favors. All the performances in the compilation are exemplary.

——in "Percussion!," Manhattan Percussion Ensemble, Paul Price, cond. URANIA UX-134 (USD-1034).

SOLO INSTRUMENT WITH ORCHESTRA

Concertos

CONCERTO No. 2 FOR VIOLIN AND STRING ORCHESTRA

Apart from its exorbitant length and an emphasis on rhythmic passiveness, this composition has the inherent beauty of stabilized style plus true use of the string spectrum. The solo violin is employed as a vocal-type instrument, while the string orchestra simulates unearthly and earth-bound timbres: pizzicato or tone-clustered, glissando, or secco-designed. The effects are entrancing and the performance, though recorded with dulled resonance, makes a direct impact. One of the best of Hovhaness' works. Miss Ajemian might have sweetened or schmaltzed her tone—the opportunity was available, but she obtains her soloistic appeal by musical truth, not showmanship. She is a highly skilled artist. If you wish only a representative example from Hovhaness' huge recorded catalogue you can do no better than to choose this disk.

——MGM String Orchestra; Anahid Ajemian, violin; Carlos Surinach, cond. MGM E-3674 (with "Lousadzak"—Concerto No. 1 for Piano and String Orchestra).

"KHALDIS"—CONCERTO FOR PIANO, FOUR TRUMPETS AND PERCUSSION

A unique instrumentated concerto (the colorful forces of triple percussion and quadruple trumpets opposing the piano). Formally as well, the composition is off the beaten path. Its basic *modus operandi* is that of polyphonic style set forth in block ostinati, each of the seven movements containing a set of particulars which lead to further premises (not developments, but rather enlargements). By way of seeming improvisation on a basic idea, Hovhaness successfully negotiates an important creative problem—the engendering of informative substance of an individual character. "Khaldis." is certainly a positively new contribution, not even slightly imitative. Beautifully recorded.

——Chamber Ensemble; William Masselos, piano; Izler Solomon, cond. MGM E-3160 (with Piano Music).

"Lousadzak"—Concerto No. 1 for Piano and String Orchestra

Doubtless the most unusual concerto ever written for the instrument. It is a singular event when the piano (especially in a concerto) is heard homophonically, minus its usual chordal and polytextural cast. Hovhaness indicates that he is imitating various Armenian instruments. Melisma and sound curves revolving around themselves are the main features. The piano ripples, and is in practically constant use. This is a concerto of hothouse chants and exotica, with orchestral color that is particularly un-Western. Hovhaness is at his best in the pair of concertos that comprise this recording.

——MGM String Orchestra; Maro Ajemian, piano; Carlos Surinach, cond. MGM E-3674 (with Concerto No. 2 for Violin and String Orchestra).

Talin—Concerto for Viola and String Orchestra, Op. 93

Hovhaness' idiom is drenched with the philosophical melos that stems directly from his Armenian heritage. Those who like modality will find more than enough of it in this haunting three-movement work, idiomatically written for the burnished timbre of the viola. It is enticingly delivered by Vardi, with excellent string support. No pyrotechnics; the middle section is fast-paced, but "Talin" is not a display piece.

——MGM String Orchestra; Emanuel Vardi, viola; Izler Solomon, cond. MGM E-3432 (with Hindemith: Trauermusik, and Partos: Yiskor).

INSTRUMENTAL

Harmonica

SIX GREEK FOLK DANCES

Conventions are not smashed when a harmonica player appears on stage, yet no recital of harmonica music, nor any work written for the instrument, can be called conventional. To persuade with this elusive music-maker (one must ignore the entertainment world's name "mouth organ") is a task few performers have managed, and similarly, there are few compositions for the instrument. Some important composers have tried their hands, however, with the realization that they were writing for a handful of harmonica virtuosi numbering less than a half-dozen. Hovhaness joins Ralph Vaughan Williams, Darius Milhaud, Gordon Jacob, Malcolm Arnold, Alexander Tcherepnin, and a few others, by the composition of this suite.

As usual with this singular composer, the effects are gained by the use of patterns and ornamentations that give color but are not florid embellishments. These are worked in the folkloric manner chosen by this exotic pilgrim to the past. The subtitles intrigue: "The Selybrian Syrtos," "Sweet-Basil Green," "Karagouna," a "Tsaconian Dance," followed by a "Pastoral," and "Sousta."

One owes it to himself to hear the harmonica as played by Sebastian, a master of the instrument, and magnificently recorded, to boot. (The record includes transcriptions of sonatas by Veracini and Telemann, a Bach *"Bourrée"* with harpsichord accompaniment, the Ravel *"Pavane"* arranged with piano support, and originals by Milhaud and Sebastian—the last for harmonica alone.) ——in "John Sebastian—a Harmonica Recital," John Sebastian, harmonica; Renato Josi, piano. DEUTSCHE GRAMMOPHON DGM-12015 (DGS-712015).

Piano

ACHTAMAR

Program music for the piano, Oriental in character; curious in sound, characteristic of the composer. Too long, except for the dedicated Hovhaness fan.

——William Masselos. MGM E-3160 (with Piano Music; "Khaldis"—Concerto for Piano, Four Trumpets and Percussion).

FANTASY ON AN OSSETIN TUNE

An example of Hovhaness' creative handling of a primitive folk theme. Interesting, yet uncomplex, and of much more variety than usual with this composer.

——William Masselos. MGM E-3160 (with Piano Music; "Khaldis"—Concerto for Piano, Four Trumpets and Percussion).

HYMN TO A CELESTIAL MUSICIAN

Virtuosity dominates this highly individual conception. Hovhaness enlarges the piano palette by string contacts made with a mandolin plectrum; the zephyr-like timbres are esoteric, but refreshing.

——William Masselos. MGM E-3160 (with Piano Music; "Khaldis"—Concerto for Piano, Four Trumpets and Percussion).

JHALA

Hovhaness regards the piano as a single, super-concentrated substitute for a diverse instrumental combination, in this piece inspired by a Japanese poetic form. The piano becomes a hybrid, melodic-pulsatile instrument by keyboard manipulation plus striking directly on the strings with a beater.

——William Masselos. MGM E-3160 (with Piano Music; "Khaldis"—Concerto for Piano, Four Trumpets and Percussion).

LULLABY

Effective music, despite its simplicity. This short piece has real mood and the collection in which it is found is not intended only for young listeners.

——in "Piano Music for Children by Modern American Composers," Marga Richter. MGM E-3147.

MOUNTAIN IDYLLS, OP. 39, NOS. 1, 2, AND 3

Rather monotonous conceptions in a quasi-Eastern vein. The two end pieces are lullabies, with a "Moon Dance" in between. The dance is the best of the lot, but it lasts only about 25 seconds. It is the poorest example on the children's music record and, in the all-Hovhaness compilation where it also appears, it is certainly tenth-rate as compared with the other compositions.

——in "Music by Alan Hovhaness," Marga Richter, piano. MGM E-3517.

——in "Piano Music for Children by Modern Composers," Marga Richter. MGM E-3181.

ORBIT NO. 2

Free in form, but anchored and held in balance by a central theme set into perspective by colorful, "off-beat" piano sonorities. Music of this type is not the bread and butter of the average concert pianist. Masselos has the know-how and the necessary devotion.

——William Masselos. MGM E-3160 (with Piano Music; "Khaldis"—Concerto for Piano, Four Trumpets and Percussion).

PASTORALE NO. 1

Despite the use of the piano as a percussive medium (mallets on the strings of the instrument producing sweeping sounds, etc.), plus its normal melodic role, there are no acrid sounds in Hovhaness' little invention.

——William Masselos. MGM E-3160 (with Piano Music; "Khaldis"—Concerto for Piano, Four Trumpets and Percussion).

SLUMBER SONG AND SIRIS DANCE, OP. 39, NOS. 4 AND 5

No complexities: the first of this pair of pieces is a rather sweet, but nice, folkish tune, and the dance is an exceedingly short item —so short it doesn't register.

——in "Music by Alan Hovhaness," Marga Richter. MGM E-3517.

——in "Piano Music for Children by Modern American Composers," Marga Richter. MGM E-3147.

Piano Ensemble

MACEDONIAN MOUNTAIN DANCE, OP. 39, No. 6

A folk piece, but not based on folk resources. Result: a good imitation of the real thing. Multi-piano performance doesn't help much in amplification of the design.

——in "Music by Alan Hovhaness," Manhattan Piano Quartet. MGM E-3517.

CHAMBER MUSIC

DUET FOR VIOLIN AND HARPSICHORD

Pretty poor stuff. I read the liner note after listening three times and didn't wonder why I found the music puerile, without a trace of invention and perversely boring. (Hovhaness composed the duo the very next day after it was commissioned, and two weeks later it was first performed!) The other works on the disk are, for the most part (Cowell's especially), deserving of ownership by anyone interested in matters contemporary, but don't go after the Hovhaness by itself. Though extremely short, that is not the reason for this warning. Its unworthiness is.

——Robert Brink, violin; Daniel Pinkham, harpsichord. COMPOSERS RECORDINGS CRI-109 (with Cowell: Piano Music; Prelude for Violin and Harpsichord; and Pinkham: Concerto for Celeste and Harpsichord Soli; Cantilena; Capriccio).

KIRGHIZ SUITE FOR VIOLIN AND PIANO, OP. 93

A work of inexhaustible patterns. Consider the opening Variations—based on a C major scale plus F sharp, maintained until the last section, when the piano shifts among three sounds. No bar lines are employed; the music walks within itself, rooted in and yet free of the tyranny of metrical measurement. The second movement, "A Kirghiz Tala" (a "tala" is a metrical plan in Hindu music), is set in bare harmonic intervals while the violin chants. The same constant intervallic base supports the short final movement. Of such are Hovhaness' technical ecstasies. His music requires a listener's willingness to meet it on its very pertinent Eastern terms.

MGM (a label very favorably disposed toward Hovhaness) offers two different disks for the above work. The record listed first below gives samplings of three important composers; the other record's concentrated objective is self-evident.

——Anahid Ajemian, violin; Maro Ajemian, piano. MGM E-3454 (with Cowell: Set of Five, and Ives: Sonata No. 4).

——in "Music by Alan Hovhaness," Anahid Ajemian, violin; Maro Ajemian, piano. MGM E-3517.

SUITE FOR VIOLIN, PIANO AND PERCUSSION, OP. 99

Repetitive oscillative patterns plus the effect of unending improvisation on and around the same sound-course typify this Eastern music in Western instrumental translation (save for the micro-toned violin, which occasionally plays sixth tones; but these are not clearly defined on the recording).

The six movements of Hovhaness' suite contain many other devices: improvisatory and meterless designs, plus rhythmic patterns which range in cycles from as few as six beats to as many as fifty-nine. Color is paramount; the pianist simulates a gong by striking the bass strings inside the piano with a timpani stick, and in the fifth movement (a canon) an effective sonorous impact is made by utilizing tri-tonality.

There is an oft-used instruction in the score which, at first glance, makes no sense; however, its meaning is disclosed upon hearing the music. This "hold pedal *forever*" (my italics) indication to the pianist does much to explain the static quality of Hovhaness' music and the effect it gives—the monotonous retracing over and over again of carbon-copied sounds, even though of original construction. (This writer does not pretend to understand the meanings that the composer gives for this suite—". . . ancient religious concept of form in three arcs: supplication, revelation, and ascension into praise.")

——Anahid Ajemian, violin; Maro Ajemian, piano; Elden Bailey, percussion. COLUMBIA ML-5179 (with Upon Enchanted Ground, and Wolpe: Ten Songs from the Hebrew).

QUARTET FOR FLUTE, OBOE, CELLO AND HARPSICHORD

Several years ago the well-known harpsichordist Sylvia Marlowe had the happy thought of requesting composers to write works for her to perform either solo or with a chamber group. For this purpose she organized a quartet and it was for her group that Hovhaness conceived this opus in 1952. (The four solo works on this recording were all written for Miss Marlowe—others who composed for her included Elliott Carter and Ben Weber.)

Though only the initial movement is titled "Ostinato," all three divisions display this repetitive device in the keyboard instrument. The string and wind voices express the melodic force, confined within small areas, as Hovhaness likes to do. There is a skillful play of textural weights: solo, duet, and tutti combinations are utilized. As unusual as the color of the ancient instrument in contemporary music are the asymmetrical proportions of Hovhaness' music. Interesting note: each movement ends as if incomplete. Hovhaness' keen sense of arrested motion is disarming. Strictly music for special listening; a music that must be probed if one is to find its meaning.

——Harpsichord Quartet. New Editions 3 (with Lessard: Toccata in Four Movements; Rieti: Sonata All'Antica; and Thomson: Sonata No. 4 [Guggenheim Jeune]).

Quartet No. 2 for Flute, Oboe, Cello and Piano, Op. 112

Coherence is obtained by the divertissement aspect of this opus. Usually one expects four movements, or at least three, in a "quartet." Hovhaness' use of the word applies strictly to the number of players participating. From the formal viewpoint the many movements are akin to musical aphorisms. They contain sensitive use of color, though the complete work tends to be overlong. At least one or two of the sections have a sardonic, humor-fed cast.

——in "Music by Alan Hovhaness," MGM Chamber Ensemble. MGM E-3517.

CHORAL

To the God Who Is in the Fire, Op. 146

Once again the monotonous retelling of the modal-styled tale, set here in a sea of "noodling" ostinati. Nor does the effect of the work gain from the weighty (actually overheavy) percussion. The performance is well-nigh perfect. (The three records in the album include some magnificent examples of contemporary music, especially Gunther Schuller's String Quartet, Irving Fine's Fantasia for String Trio, and Burrill Phillips' "The Return of Odysseus.")

——The University of Illinois School of Music, Varsity Men's Glee Club and Percussion Ensemble; William Miller, tenor; Robert Shaw, cond. University of Illinois Custom Recording Series CRS-5.

15. Charles Ives
(1874—1954)

AT ONE TIME, IVES WAS CONSIDERED AN ICONOCLAST, A COMPOSER who, together with other individualists (such as Ruggles and Varèse—both of whom, incidentally, are now "accepted," having scored in the late innings, as it were), provided the very pungent flavor of ultramodernism in the stew of contemporary music. But Ives has come into his own. He has now been recognized; the Pulitzer Prize was awarded him; he is called a great composer; forgiveness for critical sins is being asked. One cannot accept Ives totally, at least in strict honesty, for there are aspects of his work that confound one with their musical illiteracy. Yet these were part of the man and his music; accept the friend, and you must take with such friendship the quirks and foibles of a human being. It was part of Ives's method to be a finger painter, one who drew with original strength and the individuality of the primitive, yet lapsed into doodling from time to time. Yet, even though endorsement of him is not total, the Ives cult is ten thousand times the size of the small band that supported him in the early 1920's.

This man was a creative crossbreed—a Joycean as well as a Proustian composer, with elements of the folk singer, the mountaineer, the revivalist. He combined with seeming casualness all known compositional techniques, from four-part elementary harmony to a partial employment of the twelve-tone system, use of microtones, double orchestras, athematicism, and other "isms" as well. Yet he was no musical pirate. All these techniques were natural to him, were so years before Messrs. Schoenberg, Stravinsky, Haba, Stockhausen, and the like "discovered" them! One can find them all in his works, plus pantonality, pandiatonicism, polytonality, and polyrhythms. The engineering facility of the man was staggering. Ives was more *creative* than any composer one would find among a hundred names picked at random, for most composers imitate rather than create. He was one of the most daring and original of visionaries, a composer who ran far in front of the pack. If the facts are analyzed coldly, regardless of

133

personal tastes, it must be admitted that some of his music is the most individual of all time.

To the credit of the recording companies, we are able to hear on records a good portion of Ives's compositions. These include a pair of symphonies, the complete violin and piano sonatas, songs, and so on. The question can therefore be asked: when will Ives's music be admitted to the polite society of our string quartet organizations and our conductors?

ORCHESTRAL

SYMPHONY No. 2

Ives's Second Symphony links the nineteenth and twentieth centuries in several ways. It was composed between 1897 and 1902; it was first performed just one year short of a half-century later—in 1951—by the New York Philharmonic, under Leonard Bernstein.

Ives's unconventionality led him to rescore his compositions for different media, take sections from one work and place them with those from another, retitle and fully mix his output. The Second Symphony is in five movements; with the exception of the second of these all were originally part of, or the complete scores of, other works. Movement one was a portion of an organ sonata, movement three was a prelude for organ. The fourth movement was a section of a revival service for string quartet, afterward revised and amplified, while the final movement was "partly from an early overture, 'American Woods.' "

Ives's music is truly a mixed bag, but with what fascinating contents! Orchestral hymnody plays an important part, as do patriotic and college songs. Some of the themes sound like gospel hymns and others suggest (as Ives described them) "Steve Foster." These are displayed in a nineteenth-century showcase of austere romanticism. But wait—Ives's daring contrapuntalism (the use of "Columbia, the Gem of the Ocean" with a Brahms-like tune is but one example) is the opposite of mid-Victorian musical sanctimony.

One hopes for a new recording since the only available one is poorly done, played imperfectly and the engineering rather on the dead side. How about it, Mr. Bernstein?

——Vienna Philharmonic Orchestra, F. Charles Adler, cond. SPA RECORDS SPA-39.

SYMPHONY No. 3

A composer transcribing his own music is illustrated in Ives's Third Symphony. The middle movement (the fast section of the work) is an orchestral version of a "Children's Day Parade," originally for string quartet and organ, while the outer movements (both in slow tempo) were at first organ pieces. Ives composed the symphony between 1901 and 1904, and revised it in 1911.

From first note to last the spirit of a church service of bygone days is nostalgically implied and reflected in this work (secularly speaking; there is no programmatic definition whatsoever). It is as though Ives were writing a huge anthem for small orchestra. Though the tonality range is restricted and the sounds are based on memories of hymn singing and tent meetings held in New England, there is no academic constraint and thereby nullified effect. But nullification of another kind comes to mind—the 1947 Pulitzer Prize was awarded Ives for this work 36 years after its composition!

Stewart's performance is properly grained, states the quaint spiritual essence with sympathetic style, while Hanson's conducting is of an extrovert nature, which makes the symphony less effective.
——Baltimore Little Symphony, Reginald Stewart, cond. VAN-GUARD VRS-468 (with Donovan: Suite for String Orchestra and Oboe).
——Eastman-Rochester Symphony Orchestra, Howard Hanson, cond. MERCURY 50149 (SR-90149) (with Three Places in New England).

THREE PLACES IN NEW ENGLAND

The prime ingredient of this work is its insistent refusal to consider consonance or dissonance as fixed alternatives. There are no technical hierarchies in Ives's music, no commitment to a specific system. All the sounds in the "Three Places in New England" are valid by themselves, none are dependent on previous models. Thus magnificent orchestral polyphony and delicate use of timbres mingle in this remarkable example of music written in 1914.

The most audacious part is the second movement, "Putnam Park, Redding, Connecticut." This is a sonorous juxtaposition of two groups, each playing in a different tempo, a reminder of Ives's youth when he was fascinated by the effect of the approach into town of a pair of bands, each playing a different tune. The opening movement "The St. Gaudens in Boston Common," describes the "Moving—Marching—Faces of Souls!" In the final section, "The Housatonic at Stockbridge," the swirl of water is sensitively illustrated by polyrhythms. The music is so different it defies classification; yet there is no inconsistency in style, despite the varied treatment. It remains as new music, difficult to forget, once heard.

Credit Howard Hanson with still another major contribution. He is due special thanks for ungrudgingly preparing music as unrelated to his own as the work of Charles Ives. To put in order the complexities of this score, with its polyrhythmic paired groups, was no mean task. In this suite the formal scheme becomes as free as any round-table talk or the town hall meetings held in any village. Here and there sharper outlining might have made Ives's discussions clearer, but this is very minor in relation to the genuineness of the whole.

This jumbo polyphony is made to order for stereo. While it will not make the aural effect less biting and dissonant, it will clarify the polyrhythmical condition.

——Eastman-Rochester Symphony Orchestra, Howard Hanson, cond. MERCURY 50149 (SR-90149) (with Symphony No. 3).

Chamber Orchestra

CENTRAL PARK IN THE DARK SOME FORTY YEARS AGO

A very original example of orchestral picture-painting of quiet nocturnal sounds and active night noises. Ives combines melodies, harmonies, keys, and rhythms in a dazzling array. What is arrived at is sensitive and poetic music, a polydimensional montage. Ives described this piece (with some others of similar content) as "cartoons or take-offs of undergraduate and other events, academic, anthropic (*sic*), urban, athletic and tragic." To be listened to for the totality of its effect, not for its specific ingredients.

Polymusic Records is no more, but anyone wishing to own a disk of Ivesiana which includes a number of works otherwise unrecorded, should not mind the pains it will take to uncover a copy. (The other works on the record are discussed in this section in their proper places.)

——in "The Music of Charles Ives—Volume 1," Polymusic Chamber Orchestra, Vladimir Cherniavsky, cond. POLYMUSIC RECORDS PRLP-1001.

HALLOWE'EN

This is no gambol on the green! The sensations are direct, obtained by meaningful cacophony. Its 14 measures are played several times around, progressing from slow to fast to faster still, from soft to loud to louder still, each instrument—piano and strings—in a different key. Hail music, well met (and meant). There is room for such raw musical caricature.

——in "The Music of Charles Ives—Volume 1," Polymusic Chamber Orchestra, Vladimir Cherniavsky, cond. POLYMUSIC RECORDS PRLP-1001.

OVER THE PAVEMENTS

A scherzo design utilizing flavorsome polyrhythms, suggested to Ives by the hurry of city dwellers. The jazzy, nervous accents convey a Shavian-Ivesian humor. Well played and with good sound.

——in "The Music of Charles Ives—Volume 1," Polymusic Chamber Orchestra, Vladimir Cherniavsky, cond. POLYMUSIC RECORDS PRLP-1001.

THE UNANSWERED QUESTION

More and more performances are being given of this program music, based on a philosophical essay of the composer. In fact, it has become *the* Ives piece of the present day. The strings play out of sight and a wind group plus solo trumpet are on stage. The strings represent silence, the trumpet propounds the "perennial question of existence," and the winds attempt to give the answer, but never succeed. As Ives conceived the piece it is not to be performed with exactitude; tempi and meters are in opposition to one another. Therefore, the conductor must regard one group, playing in extremely slow tempo, and another, at ever faster speed, as separate entities, meeting only by happenstance.

The closer the conjunction the wider of the mark. This is neither a joke nor a trick. With three different levels at work simultaneously it is amazing how easily the tri-dimensional facts are followed by the ear. This is the criticism of the Foss performance, which one suspects has been carefully regulated to avoid disparity. The old (difficult to obtain) Polymusic version is better in this respect; it has more of the non-coincidence, less crystallization of the three instrumental components, though it cannot compare soundwise with the Unicorn release.

——in "The Music of Charles Ives—Volume 1," Polymusic Chamber Orchestra, Vladimir Cherniavsky, cond. POLYMUSIC RECORDS PRLP-1001.

——Zimbler Sinfonietta, Lukas Foss, cond. UNICORN UNLP-1037 (with Bartók: Divertimento for String Orchestra; Milhaud: Symphony No. 4 for Strings; and Skalkottas: Little Suite for Strings).

INSTRUMENTAL

Piano

SONATA NO. 2 ("CONCORD")

Lawrence Gilman termed this sonata, composed in the years 1909 to 1915, "the greatest music composed by an American, and the most deeply and essentially American in impulse and implication." In technical difficulty of performance and in the scope of its concentrated expressiveness plus forcefulness, the "Concord" is the equal of the greatest of the late Beethoven piano sonatas. Ives intended in his sonata to express the spirit of transcendentalism as represented by Emerson, Hawthorne, the Alcotts, and Thoreau. The sonata contains such an immense amount of detail that it can be regarded as objective music, paradoxically composed subjectively. It is a work that demands repeated hearings. Then, and only then, do the tumultuous intensities of its music register.

While there are a number of pianists who could master this work, it needs more than technical proficiency; it requires a religious faith in Charles Ives, the composer. However, the function of the average *good* concert pianist is to be a captive artist for his audience; the music he performs is for lazy ears blissfully closed to brave new sounds. John Kirkpatrick is an exception.

He understands the spiritual climate of this huge art work. He understands how to play the piano. He has recorded a remarkable presentation.

——John Kirkpatrick. COLUMBIA ML-4250.

CHAMBER MUSIC

SONATA NO. 1 FOR VIOLIN AND PIANO

Ives is neither short-winded nor for the person who wishes his music in apple-pie order. He offers a feast of techniques that paradoxically hold his music in place. This is in direct opposition to the creative law that style must be integrated. Because of the many national backdrops that color this music thematically, it can be classified as American. Truly this man is a Connecticut Yankee serving in nobody's court! The part of the sonata that throws together sacred (hymn-tempered) items with profane (ragtime-rhymed) material makes this an unconventional opus of impressive power.

The performance of any Ives duo-sonata is a test for a fiddler and a pianist. Druian's insight and Simms's fabulous knowledge combine in a performance that is as rare as snow in summer. And Mercury's sound is radiant. The other recorded performance is far below this. Field and Mittman try their best, but there is no comparison either individually or as a team.

——Rafael Druian, violin; John Simms, piano. MERCURY 50096 (with Porter: Sonata No. 2).

——Joan Field, violin; Leopold Mittman, piano. LYRICHORD LL-17 (with Sonata No. 3).

SONATA NO. 2 FOR VIOLIN AND PIANO

Ives's Second Violin and Piano Sonata depicts his true creative spirit, his full ripeness, the scope of his thoughts from the very intimate to the most rollicking type of musical horseplay. It is real sport to listen to this fantastic musical mural, to identify snatches of "Old Zip Coon," variations on it, "Dixie," counterpoint drawn, borrowed, and quartered from Strauss's "Till Eulenspiegel" motive, et al. It is touching to hear the last movement, "The Revival," and realize that Ives could produce such an amazing type of finished art as early as 1903. And, that we had to wait 43 years before hearing it for the first time!

When a violinist will shape his playing to the true intent of the music, when he will gladly whine, or imitate the dips and scrapings of a country fiddler, make syncopation sound authentic and integral rather than a mere part of rhythmic property, it is time to doff one's hat and give the fullest credit. Druian's consideration of the middle movement of this sonata, especially, is a high point in his recording career. He and his partner are a major team that interpret the contemporary literature for violin and piano in superb style.

Mention must also be made of a performance which displays radiant understanding and magnificence in every sense. Despite dated engineering, the Second Sonata is played even better on the Polymusic disk than the so much newer Mercury release. Why doesn't the team of Magaziner and Glazer re-record this sonata and others?

——Rafael Druian, violin; John Simms, piano. MERCURY 50097 (with Sonatas Nos. 3 and 4).

——in "The Music of Charles Ives—Volume 1," Elliot Magaziner, violin; Frank Glazer, piano. POLYMUSIC RECORDS PRLP-1001.

SONATA NO. 3 FOR VIOLIN AND PIANO

A mood of vital seriousness persists throughout Ives's Third Violin and Piano Sonata. Together with long lines brought over from classic-romantic models, there are crossed arrow-points of rhythms that move together and apart, as well as against each other, indicating Ives's affinity for national speech.

Despite the sonata's complexity Druian and Simms express the music fervently, while Field and Mittman present it in a carefully organized manner. The latter pair give this piece much more coloration than the other Ives sonata they play. Still, the far better sound on the Mercury recording greatly aids enjoyment, as does the stylistic mastery of the all-male twosome.

——Rafael Druian, violin; John Simms, piano. MERCURY 50097 (with Sonatas Nos. 2 and 4).

——Joan Field, violin; Leopold Mittman, piano. LYRICHORD LL-17 (with Sonata No. 1).

SONATA NO. 4 ("CHILDREN'S DAY AT THE CAMP MEETING") FOR VIOLIN AND PIANO

Hymn inspiration and hymnodic extraction salted and peppered by Ives are the chief strains in this gentle, somewhat ecstatic work. Ives had great personal integrity and it is to be observed in his unencumbered music-making—a matter of what might be called sonoric slang. Quite often the music is out of joint, even impure; yet, even "incorrect," it is in its purport as artistically pure as any music from the rule book and therefore just as correct. It would have to be, since what Ives has done is not a matter of outward development but of inward divestment, of breaking down the "tune," and bringing to light its skeletal make-up. Rare indeed, this type of technique—with everyone but Charles Ives. That is what gives this music its original quality of being sacred, though without dogma.

Though the artistic sense of the performers in the MGM issue registers, the playing in the first movement is too sharply etched and the sound is hard, whereas the Mercury disk is just as clearly performed, but with a far greater warmth of sonority. (A word must be said for the magnificent liner notes by Lou Harrison, supplied with the Mercury set of four Ives violin and piano sonatas— this is a bonus not to be overlooked.)

——Rafael Druian, violin; John Simms, piano. MERCURY 50097 (with Sonatas Nos. 2 and 3).

——Anahid Ajemian, violin; Maro Ajemian, piano. MGM E-3454 (with Cowell: Set of Five, and Hovhaness: Kirghiz Suite).

LARGO FOR VIOLIN, CLARINET AND PIANO

Ives's music in almost a stark-naked state—no hymn tunes, no march snippets, nothing but the sounds of strange voices, formed from mixed tonalities. This pithy work of 62 measures grows upon repeated hearings. The performance is splendid.

——in "The Music of Charles Ives—Volume 1," Elliot Magaziner, violin; Frank Glazer, piano; David Weber, clarinet. POLYMUSIC RECORDS PRLP-1001.

SECOND STRING QUARTET

Ives's heterodox formulas are not cramped by the limitations of four stringed instruments. His musical intensity and fervor (notwithstanding the fact that the basic reasoning may well seem that of madness, to some) belong to no fanatical school. One may call this quartet atonal, polyrhythmic, of linear counterpoint, built partly of folk materials, sarcastic, happy, moody, or even skeptical.

It is all these. The resultant combination is his, *his* style; and in that manner he writes purely.

Though all three movements have titles, the work is not programmatic. The "themes" of this quartet are those of conversation, expressed in the give-and-take of free counterpoint. But the music is of diabolic origin. It is no sham, however; rather, prophetic art displayed in the pantheistic visions of this composer.

The Walden four are master performers and toss off the pyrotechnics with ease. This record will not be easy to obtain; still, it can be purchased in out-of-way shops. Look for it. Buy it.
——Walden String Quartet. PERIOD SPLP-501.

VOCAL

There are only two recordings of Ives's compositions for voice: Overtone's "24 Songs," and a collection issued by Spa, titled simply "Songs" (with a group of vocal works by Revueltas). The song "At the River" is the only duplication on the two disks.

The complete list of titles is given below, the songs collected on the Spa disk being indicated with asterisks (**). The two collections are discussed separately, the songs being treated alphabetically within each.

Abide With Me
A Night Thought**
Ann Street
At Parting**
At Sea**
At the River (*in both*)
Autumn
Berceuse
The Children's Hour
Christmas Carol**
Disclosure
Evening
General William Booth Enters
    into Heaven
The Greatest Man
Harpalus
He Is There!
I'll Not Complain**

In Flanders Field
In Summer Fields**
Maple Leaves
Mists**
1, 2, 3
The Seer
Serenity
The Swimmers
Tarrant Moss
Tolerance**
Tom Sails Away
Two Little Flowers
Walking
Walt Whitman**
When Stars Are in the Quiet
    Skies**
Where the Eagle
The White Gulls

Ives's songs (which total more than 140) cover a huge range, from satire to electioneering, from musical doggerel to expressive art pieces. These compositions contain all of the typical Ivesian stylistic touches; some are primitive, others are exceedingly complex. No other composer in American musical history has equaled the output or matched the diversity and originality of this vast song collection. Ives's songs represent every phase of his creative character, and one can trace his career through these vocal works.

Ives recognized no restrictions as to text. The authors whose lines he chose to set include Emerson, Longfellow, and Whittier; other texts are by Ives himself or his wife, and a number are by unknowns. Some of the poems he found in newspapers, merely signed by initials; a number of the songs were set to newspaper clippings, and others to political tracts, lecture notes, and aphorisms. The freedom in choice of text was echoed in the music; the songs illustrate Ives's violent Yankeeism (but without any sham), his rough and ready humor, his brilliance and his gentleness. The most remarkable feature of the songs is their graphic portrayal of the texts.

The initial publication of the songs was by Ives himself. He selected 114 numbers and distributed the volume without cost to anyone who wanted it. In a note that appeared with the songs Ives asserted that some of the pieces "cannot be sung," and that others were merely "trial balloons" with "little musical value." Ives was a belligerent smasher of conventions—he was also exceedingly modest. His songs *can* be sung and have artistic value. There is little argument that the vocal compositions of Charles Ives are both an inspiration and a challenge to performer and listener.

At the River

"At the River" is still another illustration of the composer's penchant for musical interchange. The song was fashioned from the end portion of a movement of the Fourth Violin and Piano Sonata. At that, the tune is an old one; it is chordally refurbished and modernized here.

This is the only Ives song that exists, at the present time, in two recorded versions. Boatwright shows greater ability than Greissle. In addition, Overtone has better sound than Spa, so no problem exists in making one's choice.

——in "24 Songs," Helen Boatwright, soprano; John Kirkpatrick, piano. OVERTONE 7.
——Jacqueline Greissle, soprano; Josef Wolman, piano. SPA RECORDS SPA-9 (with Ives: Songs, and Revueltas: Songs).

SONGS

Nothing is ventured in "A Night Thought." This is ordinary, unexciting music, with none of Ives's communicative creativeness. He didn't think much of this song. Agreed.

"At Parting" is a split-personality song, composed in 1889, when Ives was merely fifteen. The first half is in rigid G major, the second swamped with accidentals.

"At Sea" illustrates the role of chromaticism in embellishing tonal solidity. The song is quiet, simple, and with neat, pungent effect, though the performance is rather uninteresting.

Ives termed his "Christmas Carol" a "traditional" piece. It certainly is, beginning with the words "Little Star of Bethlehem." Sung with correct conventionality, it adds up to one of the better performances on the disk.

Among Ives's vocal compositions are settings of texts by French, German, and Italian poets. Some listeners may recognize the Heine text in "I'll Not Complain." This is an Americanized "*Ich Grolle Nicht.*" The song is a dated item.

"In Summer Fields" is one of a set of four "German" songs. Not important; Ives considered it one of his weaker efforts. (The dull accompaniment bears him out.)

"Mists" is an average vocal work, set in ternary form. There is little to recommend in the fitful chromaticism.

Ives drew the contents of "Tolerance" from an early (unidentified as to date) orchestral piece. He then used a text taken from a university lecture! Unorthodoxy is an undeviating tenet in this composer's career. This song is one of the better examples in the Spa release.

"Walt Whitman" is actually an excerpt from the twentieth stanza of Whitman's "Leaves of Grass." The forceful quintal harmony shows how carefully Ives organized his material. Despite some critics' opinions Ives was no harum-scarum, cigar-ash-on-the-paper composer. This song is of sensitive sonorescence and Greissle is inspired to do her very best work as a result.

"When Stars Are in the Quiet Skies" is only moderately interesting. Ives writes in G major, with an undeviating three-four meter. And two verses with no change!

Many of the eleven songs in the Spa compilation are not of Ives's best; those in the Overtone recording are measurably better. Why neither vocalist chose some of the striking examples such as "An Election" or "Majority" (both displaying keen use of tone clusters), or "December," a song that shows Ives at his very best, or the lusty "Charlie Rutledge," is difficult to understand.

Generally speaking, Greissle is distinctly not at ease in this type of music. Her style is rather uninteresting and prosaic. (She doesn't do much better with the Revueltas songs.) Restraint has no place in the singing of Ives's songs—rather a willingness to "let go" is needed. Nor can Wolman match Kirkpatrick's masterful pianism, on the Overtone recording.

——Jacqueline Greissle, soprano; Josef Wolman, piano. Spa Records SPA-9 (with Revueltas: Songs).

24 Songs

"Abide With Me" was composed when Ives was fifteen, soon after he had been hired as the organist for the First Baptist Church in Danbury, Connecticut. Harmonically, the hymn is an example of simmering rebellion on the part of the young composer. The sureness of touch in this song is not that of a neophyte, however.

Charles Ives never took anything for granted. He rewrote his music if he felt it could fit elsewhere; he rearranged a composition after seeing it in a different light, or if he felt it could serve more than its original purpose. Many of the songs were transformed into chamber works and vice versa. "Ann Street," a short vocal item (to a text found in the New York *Herald Tribune* of January 12, 1921), turns up as the third part of a "set" scored for four instruments. It is one of the finest songs in the album; it is also one of the best sung.

"Autumn" is an example of conventional song composition. But it has a tender sentiment, as enchanting in its way as the songs composed in a more fanciful, extroverted manner. This is set to a text by Ives's wife, who has the apt name of Harmony.

The "Berceuse" is especially compelling. Although the music was composed originally to the same poem that Brahms used for his famous "*Wiegenlied*," Ives substituted his own text. It is not a lullaby in the usual sense, but lyrical and warm.

"The Children's Hour" is one of the most exquisite songs Ives composed. He saw the Longfellow poem in a newspaper and utilized a fragment of it (twelve lines). A great many of Ives's songs are quite unorthodox, but in this case orthodoxy rules, with subtle beauty marking the styled clarity.

Another text by Ives himself is used in "Disclosure." The song has a craggy line and the lyrics are rather mundane. Boatwright gives an artistic performance with good shading in this instance.

"Evening" is a segment (Book 4, line 598) from Milton's "Paradise Lost." The tonal prospectus is as usual with Ives; the dynamic range is not—ranging from piano to triple piano.

"General William Booth Enters into Heaven" is lusty, a block-buster conception. Usually this song is noted as a setting of the poem by Vachel Lindsay, but actually it is not the complete poem. Ives's rip-snorting song deals with the general whose reforming zeal went on under the very eyes of Jesus. It is a real inspiration, based in part on the Salvation Army hymn "Are You Washed in the Blood of the Lamb." Though Boatwright sings with womanly pep one would rather hear a male voice in this virile piece.

A poem found in a newspaper (written by Anne Collins and published in the New York *Evening Sun*, sometime in 1921) forms the text of "The Greatest Man." This piece represents declamation set to song with amusing results. Ives's creative scrapbook comes in handy as he writes in a semi-vernacular way. Like a blackout on the burlesque stage, this song has a "tag" ending ("There're lots o' great men, George Washington 'n Lee,/ but Dad's got 'em all beat holler, seems to me!"). Boatwright adapts her style perfectly to suit.

"Harpalus" is a pastoral song. It illustrates a sensitive portrayal of the text without mimicry.

"He Is There!" is uncompromising Ivesiana. Real Yankee spirit is illustrated by this marching song, composed during the First World War. Some patriotic airs are intertwined with the syncopative rhythm, including "Columbia, the Gem of the Ocean," and "Battle Cry of Freedom." Can anyone think of a serious composer today writing a true-blooded hunk of chauvinistic music?

"In Flanders Field" represents an unusual idea, that of setting John McCrae's well-known poem. Like "He Is There!" this is a war song and includes an integrated snatch of "America," as well as a larger segment of "Columbia, the Gem of the Ocean," the quotation of the "Marseillaise" is very moving. Morbidity is absent—proper dissonance and optimism are present.

Chromatic tonal chemistry makes the song "Maple Leaves" of a beauty rare in the Ives corpus. The half-tone descent that marks the last of the four lines of Thomas Bailey Aldrich's poem is vivid musical illustration. And the whole song is only eleven measures in length.

"1, 2, 3" is almost as short as the title and a real vocal quip. Ives's words merely ask the question why a Yankee prefers "one, two" to "one, two, three." The answer is not sung:—because he'd rather walk than waltz! One cannot find such a vocal delight in any other composer's song stock.

Initially (in 1913) "The Seer" was a "Scherzo" for clarinet, cornet (or another brass instrument), alto horn (or saxophone, French horn, or even trombone), plus piano and drums. Some seven years later Ives synthesized this piece into a song. Dissonances cling to the music; the dynamic intensity shifts very little, but the sonorous twist at the end suggests an O. Henry conclusion.

"Serenity" was originally composed for unison chanting, then changed to solo form. The repetitive idea in the piano is old hat but in this song it is creatively refreshing—as is the slow, syncopative rhythm which gives power to the song. Sung with a nice sense of style.

Ives indulges in "Mickey-Mousing" word meanings into their musical equivalents in "The Swimmers." The song is music of impassioned declaration, despite the sounds' clinging to the precise descriptive meaning of the words (by Louis Untermeyer). The exceedingly difficult piano part is played with technical perfection by Kirkpatrick.

"Tarrant Moss" is an oddity. For a long time the text was presumed to be by Rudyard Kipling, but the true facts were disclosed in Henry and Sidney Cowell's excellent book *Charles Ives and His Music*. Ives had set music to the Kipling poem but could not get proper permission to use the words. He therefore published the song, using only Kipling's title and the first four words of the poem. As Ives put it, ". . . the nice poetry . . . was written (not by Mr. Kipling)." In this song Kipling-Ives is represented by a real ballade.

Like a refrain hidden within, the spiritual "Deep River" is implied and the war tune "Over There" is defined in "Tom Sails Away," one of three First World War songs. No subtle disguise—"Over There" is employed when the words appear in Ives's own text. Boatwright's delivery is very compelling.

"Two Little Flowers" is in a tender mood—a rare emotion for Ives. The text is by Harmony Ives.

There are two lines of semi-song, which can be described as Ives's version of "*sprechstimme*," in "Walking." The harmonies are rather simple, but their use in relation to the text shows true invention. A song of moving sentiment, free of banality.

"Where the Eagle" is expressive vocal music. But for Ives, rather conventional.

The very close reflection of the text fundamental to Ives's songs is seen in "The White Gulls" (on a Russian text translated by Maurice Morris)—an excellent illustration of poetry conveyed by song.

Boatwright has made her reputation on the music of past eras, but she can certainly sing Ives with conviction and understanding. This vocalist possesses the ability to phrase, her voice is warm and pure, and her diction a joy to hear. Her singing in this album of two-dozen songs deserves the highest praise. Kirkpatrick matches her achievements. A distinguished release in all respects.

——Helen Boatwright, soprano; John Kirkpatrick, piano. OVER-TONE 7.

CHORAL

HARVEST HOME CHORALE III

A contrapuntally designed hymn, short in duration, long in effect. It is not performed with organ and brass, as Ives scored it; only the organ is used in this case.

——Concert Choir of Teachers College, Columbia University; Harry R. Wilson, cond. MUSIC LIBRARY RECORDINGS MLR-7071 (with 67th Psalm; Rozsa: To Everything There Is a Season; and Wilson: A Thing of Beauty; Finger of God).

67TH PSALM

Small wonder that in 1937 Ives wrote Lehman Engel, the conductor, that this work's success was something of a surprise to him as it "brought back the memory of the trouble it made, and the scowls it brought from some of the pews (but not the pulpit) about forty years ago." The chorus is divided into two groups and each sings in a different key. This duo-dimensional effect is enhancing, even in this not well-balanced recording.

——Concert Choir of Teachers College, Columbia University; Harry R. Wilson, cond. MUSIC LIBRARY RECORDINGS MLR-7071 (with Harvest Home Chorale III; Rozsa: To Everything There Is a Season; and Wilson: A Thing of Beauty; Finger of God).

16. Leon Kirchner
(1919—)

THE NATURAL EVOLUTION OF AN ART IN ITS CONSTANT OVERHAULING (first called "experimentation," "ugly," sometimes "nonsensical," "hysterical") leads critics (and listeners) into unknown, frequently uncomfortable territory. New ideas are considered and tested; some are retained, others discarded. In time the aggressive becomes the expressive; the new becomes the old; the language adds fresh words. It was thus with Stravinsky, with Beethoven; yes, also with Bach. Current trends show twelve-tone music (once radical) incorporating triadic constructions without deviating from the core of the system. Alban Berg is now considered a romantic, not a frenzied cacophonist; music by Anton Webern is encored.

But many young composers have begun sifting the materials used in the past half-century, and out of that group there doubtless will emerge in the next half-century one who will be able to take his place in the line of the important composers. Examples of this "new" music—of music a product of Schoenberg's, Berg's, Webern's, Sessions', Stravinsky's, and Bartók's findings—are seen in the work of Leon Kirchner. His compositions are not eclectic, any more than passages in any work can be related to previous (as well as present) composers. One writer calls Kirchner not the usual "talent," but the "real thing." In his case, the example of technical newness based on the old is rather remarkable, a matter to be watched.

This composer has a clarified creative horizon. Each new opus (he works slowly: he has produced but fifteen compositions, though more than half of these are of major size) proves him to be unconcerned with the enervating glorification of a system and fully devoted, rather, to the triumph of living music. Kirchner's works reveal the new outline of modern music knowledge. They are neoteric and personal, derived from and conjoined to the past as all important art must be, but free of bald imitation. Kirchner deserves his success; the creative tiara sits well on his head.

Considering Kirchner's small output, the availability of his music on records is quite satisfactory. Although three of the four recorded works are chamber pieces, they are illustrative of his most compelling work. One of his most recent compositions (a "Toccata for Strings, Winds, and Percussion") would be a marvelous addition to the stereophonic library.

SOLO INSTRUMENT WITH ORCHESTRA

Concertos

PIANO CONCERTO

Many forms have changed their shape in accordance with shifts of fashion in musical speech through the years. The concerto has not remained static; many variations have been tried. Yet the assorted contributions of the many composers who have cast their music in the concerto form have shown the form to be remarkably strong, perfectly adaptable to diversities of speech, changes of style, as varied as from Mozart to Kirchner.

Kirchner makes the piano both a solo and symphonic instrument in his concerto. Nor does the instrument discourse with frenzy when it takes the limelight. The motival development of the opening movement is a deterrent to unbridled soloism. There is no direct, impulsed theme; the music debates on specific points: a conjunct interval and a snapped-rhythmic idea. Movement two is restless: its frictions, rhapsody, and inner agitation might be termed super-romantic, but the décor is of the present. Violence marks the final section. Once again Kirchner has produced an important work. This concerto is not merely deserving of intellectual consideration; it is thrillingly alive.

——Philharmonic Symphony Orchestra of New York; Leon Kirchner, piano; Dimitri Mitropoulos, cond. COLUMBIA ML-5185 (with Schuman: Credendum).

CHAMBER MUSIC

SONATA CONCERTANTE FOR VIOLIN AND PIANO

In this work Kirchner casts off certain technical helps; the values are integrated, rather than arrived at eclectically. The interval of a third, triadic stimuli, and conjunct moves are the principal devices used in this duo. These occur as inlays and overlays, creating the matrix on which the music rests.

The sonata lives up to its title—concerted elements rival one another, though cooperation is fully at work. Integral cadenzas are given each of the instruments and contrast emerges from the breadth of the violin's lines and the sense of qualified violence in the piano, making the work in effect a concerto grosso with orchestral adjuncts eliminated.

The Sonata Concertante requires that rarely-found combine of artistic virtuosi; no others need apply—its cool fires will not appeal to lesser lights. No ordinary pianist himself, Kirchner teams with Eudice Shapiro, a violinist with extraordinary insight into contemporary music. The performance is truly masterful.

——Eudice Shapiro, violin; Leon Kirchner, piano. Epic LC-3306 (with Trio for Violin, Cello and Piano).

Trio for Violin, Cello and Piano

In certain respects, Kirchner's work brings to mind the sensitive comment Mozart wrote in a letter three years before his death; ". . . it is better to be short and good." This control is illustrated in Kirchner's trio. It is in only two movements. Warmth of technique and warmth of emotion make the trio a composition of classic-romantic simultaneity in a twentieth-century climate. The spirit and the rhythms are constantly free; the colors are related to Webern's pointillism and Bartók's *ruvido* means, but once again, with Kirchner this is a matter of assimilation and productivity, not imitation.

Kirchner's trio is a complete experience, the listener must realize that the important matter, beyond any technical explanation, is the emotional contact he will experience. In this work there are few musical carom shots; practically all are straight to the expressive mark.

——Nathan Rubin, violin; George Neikrug, cello; Leon Kirchner, piano. Epic LC-3306 (with Sonata Concertante).

String Quartet No. 1

Kirchner's quartet is derivative only in its nervous asymmetries; it is scarcely so as to form, or in its manner of painting colors and measuring sonorities. The first movement's rhythms are exceedingly plastic, the pulse rhapsodic, and the same emboldening of the rhythm applies to the form. In the slow movement the negotiation of the intervallic second is all-important—vertically, horizontally, embellishing, or gliding chromatically. The third movement, a Divertimento, is the only symmetrical one of the entire quartet. It has the graphic design of a large Beethoven scherzo (tempoed faster than that style, however). Though harmonies, inner rhythms, color, and vocabulary are a far cry from Beethoven, the aid of that composer's acute balances cannot be overlooked. The last part is like a cadenza in slow motion. Throughout, Kirchner's keen exploration of rhythm is paramount.

This quartet has strange power, communicated the moment one hears its sounds. It has irrepressible musical imagery and is an outstanding argument for contemporary art. The performance by the little-known American Art Quartet raises a question: Why doesn't this foursome tour the country and record as well? Their playing is the equal of any quartet on the concert scene.

——American Art Quartet. COLUMBIA ML-4843 (with Fine: String Quartet).

17. Gian-Carlo Menotti
(1911—   )

Despite the fact that he retains his Italian citizenship, Menotti is considered an American composer. His life in the United States began when he came, at seventeen, to the Curtis Institute of Music in Philadelphia to study with Rosario Scalero. Since that time he has been very much involved with musical life in America, including a period of teaching at his alma mater, supervising the filming of one of his works, and directing a number of productions of his operas. He is one of the most widely known composers in this country and abroad and a triple threat on the musical gridiron—as composer, librettist, and organizer.

Menotti's creative direction is chiefly toward the musical theater, despite some successful concert works. He is fortunate in having the ability to write his own opera libretti. These have ranged from the satirical *Amelia Goes to the Ball*, and the farcical *The Old Maid and the Thief*, to the tragic plots of *The Island God*, *The Consul*, and *The Medium*. Unique indeed is Menotti's record of operatic success on Broadway, with the long run of a double bill consisting of *The Medium* and the fun-piece *The Telephone*.

These attainments do not make the composer a creative chameleon, but rather an expert. Menotti's Italian origin may be the reason for his know-how in the musical theater. Whatever the factors one cannot deny the dramatic effect of his work, in which there is no loyalty to any of the "isms," save that of modern romanticism. In certain respects his music is sweet-toothed, fed so it will be a healthy success, but it is never over-rich. One cannot fool many people many times. Menotti has proven the right to his musical victories with Metropolitan Opera performances, and by becoming a top attraction on radio and television. His *Amahl and the Night Visitors* was written for the latter medium and has become a tradition on the TV calendar, presented annually on Christmas Eve.

The recording field confirms Menotti's success. It also proves his disavowal of an all-out modern idiom, for with the number of expensive releases to his credit (a number of the albums consist of more than one record) one can be assured the music was not recorded for the specialist-buyer. However, no one can deny the technical finish of Menotti's compositions or their general appeal. The collector has no quarrel with the record industry in this composer's case.

ORCHESTRAL

BALLET SUITE FROM "SEBASTIAN"

Menotti not only writes the libretti for his operas, he has written the scenario for this ballet, though in the case of this suite of seven extracts the story of "Sebastian" is of no importance to the listener. Menotti's vocal flair is exemplified instrumentally to a marked degree in this score, especially in the haunting and poignant "Barcarolle." Here is a tune to whistle. And Stokowski knows how to play this kind of music. He informs the music with particular taste.

——Members of the NBC Symphony Orchestra, Leopold Stokowski, cond. RCA VICTOR LM-1858 (with Gould: Dance Variations).

BARCAROLLE FROM "SEBASTIAN"

Only the other pieces in the album warrant the selection of this version rather than the performance by Stokowski as part of the suite. There are those who desire only a certain part of a score and are willing to purchase a record in order to obtain it. Fiedler's compilation is interesting enough, though the lead piece gives the record an odd title.

——in "Slaughter on 10th Avenue," Boston Pops Orchestra, Arthur Fiedler, cond. RCA VICTOR LM-1726.

SOLO INSTRUMENT WITH ORCHESTRA

Concertos

CONCERTO FOR VIOLIN AND ORCHESTRA

More than any other instrument, the fiddle is the proper vehicle for this composer's lyricism. In this violin concerto, Menotti fuses the elements of operatic song with the warmth of restrained, instrumental virtuosity. One has the feeling that the solo line is a renovated aria in three parts. The marvel of the recording is the transparent, spun-silk tone of the soloist. A listener can be confident that he will enjoy Menotti's concerted sounds, set forth in a glowing, integrated performance by violinist and orchestra.

——Boston Symphony Orchestra; Tossy Spivakovsky, violin; Charles Munch, cond. RCA Victor LM-1868 (with Honegger: Symphony No. 2 for String Orchestra).

INSTRUMENTAL

Piano

Ricercare and Toccata (on a Theme from the Opera "The Old Maid and the Thief")

If one is fortunate enough to have seen Menotti's wonderful light (it was termed comic) opera which furnished the source for this piano composition, he will understand the happy-go-lucky figurative transformation of one of its ideas. If not it will be immediately apparent that the "touch-and-go" of toccata style is handled in a very clear manner. Nothing involved in this piece, merely an excursion in piano kineticism. The "Ricercare" section is strictly a prospectus for the material that follows. A nod to Westminster for an excellent compilation of music in one form. The range of composers covers four centuries and some "sleepers" are included. The soloist is good, the sound likewise.

——in "Toccatas for Piano," Raymond Lewenthal. Westminster XWN-18362.

CHORAL-BALLET

The Unicorn, the Gorgon, and the Manticore, or The Three Sundays of a Poet

Menotti describes his three-quarter-hour work as "a madrigal fable." It is unique in having no solo parts, merely a chorus that relates the story in madrigal style, while all the action is choreographed and colored by a nine-piece instrumental group (four winds, a trumpet, two strings, percussion, and harp). The moral of this allegory, according to the composer, is: "Although the world may not suspect it,/All remains intact within/The Poet's heart." Menotti's tale discloses the stupid pretenses of affected respectability and the carefree adoption of the passing whims of fashion.

The entire work has the fragrance of very old wine, in bottles of much newer make. Menotti's musical suavity and humor make his fable a sensitive and genuine art piece. It need not be seen to be enjoyed. The Angel recording furnishes the means. It is beautifully made and executed.

——Chorus and Instrumental Ensemble, Thomas Schippers, cond. ANGEL 35437.

OPERA

AMAHL AND THE NIGHT VISITORS

There is no doubt that this one-act opera, the first ever composed expressly for television, is destined to become a classic, having rolled up a huge total of performances, and being repeated yearly around the Christmas season.

Menotti's sensitive tale was suggested by the Bosch painting *The Adoration of the Magi*. It relates a visit by the Three Kings on their way to Bethlehem to find the Christ Child. They meet the crippled shepherd boy, Amahl, and in return for his generosity the Kings perform a miracle and restore him to perfect health. Menotti's score is extremely moving, has unusual character in that every nuance and color fits the story. *Amahl* illustrates the composer's cardinal gift for setting words to music that can stir the senses without moving outside the frame of its chosen style.

The original (1951) cast of the opera made the Victor recording and this fact gives it extra value, especially since the important part of Amahl can no longer be sung by Chet Allen (a problem that arises when a lead role calls for a boy soprano). No one has ever bettered Allen's colorful treble. Rosemary Kuhlmann is superb, as are the three singers representing the Kings. A potent recording with superb sound. Get it.

——Orchestra and Chorus; Chet Allen, boy soprano; Rosemary Kuhlmann, mezzo-soprano; Andrew McKinley, tenor; David Aiken, baritone; Leon Lishner, bass; Francis Monachino, baritone; Thomas Schippers, cond. RCA VICTOR LM-1701.

AMELIA GOES TO THE BALL

Comedy and satire combined with a light touch make this early Menotti opus a worthwhile theater piece. There are sufficient influences to make the opera not of earth-shattering proportions, but it would be unprofitable to spend time in making comparisons with other composers; "theatrical" and "effective" are not separate words in Menotti's case. The result is an entertaining score, with a story of cute amorality.

Carosio has a nice, coquettish voice (the opera is given in Italian, the language employed for the 1937 Philadelphia prêmière) and portrays Amelia with skill. The lover (of course: lover, husband, friend, and police chief—the opera has the usual cast of characters) is sung by Panerai, a good baritone. All the others are just as capable. Though Angel's sound is good, there are some imbalances —this firm has done better. Worth owning as an introduction to Menotti's later works.

——Orchestra and Chorus of the Teatro alla Scala, Milan; Margherita Carosio, soprano; Rolando Panerai, baritone; Giacinto Prandelli, tenor; Maria Amadini, contralto; Enrico Campi, bass; and others; Nino Sanzogno, cond. ANGEL 35140.

THE CONSUL

The horrors of a police state and the agonies of political fugitives attempting to flee, but caught in a mesh of red tape as tortuous as barbed wire, are the themes of Menotti's "musical drama." Operatic law being an aggregate of steadfast customs and rules, it is rare to find an opera so crammed with action, excitement, and compelling music. When these are combined with an uncanny degree of originality in the treatment of dialogue, it is apparent Menotti has made a distinct contribution to artistic operatic coherence.

Menotti does not flog any dead horses in his plot. Louis Untermeyer has succinctly outlined the theme: ". . . a universal problem—the problem of the physically disrupted and geographically dispossessed. . . ." A man and his wife are being spied on by the police; the man escapes to a free country, while the wife attempts to obtain the necessary visa to leave. Despite daily visits to the consulate she is unsuccessful. The woman's tragedies multiply: her mother and her baby die; her husband, tormented by anxiety, returns and is captured by the police. She commits suicide.

Menotti knows his trade. He utilizes various techniques to heighten his story, combines styles without creating an aesthetic mishmash, since those used are proper for the points they delineate (examples: warm romanticism for a lullaby, pantonality for a stark situation). It is a creative blend that reinforces the plot.

The recording is by the original cast. Marie Powers, magnetic in the key role of Menotti's *The Medium*, is magnificent as the mother; Patricia Neway, the heroine, has become one of the big operatic names because of her portrayal of this role. Gloria Lane, in the part of the secretary, Cornell MacNeil as the hunted man, and the entire cast perform with chilling reality throughout the seven scenes.

——Orchestra; Marie Powers, contralto; Patricia Neway, soprano; Gloria Lane, contralto; Cornell MacNeil, tenor; Andrew McKinley, tenor; Leon Lishner, bass; George Johgeyans, baritone; Maria Marlo, soprano; Lydia Summers, soprano; Maria Andreassi, soprano; Francis Monachino, baritone; Lehman Engel, cond. DECCA DX-101.

MARIA GOLOVIN

Menotti's three-act opera was first presented at the Brussels International Exposition in 1958, had an extremely short New York run, then was given an excellent television performance, and has not been heard since. The plot centers around the clandestine love of Maria (waiting for the release of her husband from a war-prisoner's camp) and Donato, a blind young man; the latter's affliction makes him overly possessive. When Maria's husband returns she decides to fulfill her obligations as a wife; Donato pleads with her unsuccessfully and plans to shoot her. Being blind, he calls his mother to guide his aim; she complies and he thinks he has killed Maria. Donato's mother does not tell him the truth, that she caused his shot to go wild. Instead she says to him, "Now you will have peace, my son." Although the theme is old-fashioned, Menotti's treatment gives the Ibsenian-cum-Proustian tale a great deal of dramatic fire.

The subsidiary characters are excellently drawn, especially the tutor of Maria's son, an affected and precious fellow. Menotti places the music almost in a secondary position, permitting the story to unfold with its own impact; the vocal lines comprise an instrument for projecting the acting. The orchestral colors are sparse, intense, concentrated on framing rather than illuminating the problems on stage.

The recording is well-nigh perfect, especially so in the matter of diction. Duval, Neway, and Cross are stars in this respect. Every element is produced beautifully by RCA Victor; the notes include an article by Samuel Chotzinoff, as well as the libretto plus pictures.

——Orchestra and Chorus; Richard Cross, bass-baritone; Patricia Neway, contralto; Genia Las, mezzo-soprano; Franca Duval, soprano; Lorenzo Muti, boy soprano; Herbert Handt, tenor; William Chapman, baritone; Peter Herman Adler, cond. RCA Victor LM-6142 (LSC-6142).

The Medium

A powerful piece of theater. A fake medium (Madame Flora) has an assistant (Toby), a deaf-mute, in love with her daughter (Monica). During a séance Madame Flora feels a clammy hand at her throat. She believes Toby to have been the culprit, but of course cannot make him talk. The medium caught between the real and unreal is driven to near insanity. She beats her assistant and drives him out of the house. When Toby returns to be with Monica she shoots him. The story ends with Toby "the dead ghost" holding the answer to the riddle. Who was it?

Not for a moment does the tragic tale lapse from the macabre. It is steeped in gruesomeness despite the few bright moments called on for relief. Menotti writes with dramatic expertness though he styles his work on the *verismo*-Puccini school. It serves well despite having been served before.

No composer, however, has been better served than Menotti in the case of his star—Marie Powers, who takes the role of the tragic heroine, Madame Flora. Her singing on the recording matches her dramatic ability in the flesh. This does not mean the remaining roles are a minor contribution. Everyone in this Ballet Society production is an accomplished vocalist and with a perfectly paced performance under Balaban's baton, the result is a fascinating and exciting recording. The music speaks with substantial power and proves Menotti's dramaturgical talent.

——Orchestra; Evelyn Keller, soprano; Marie Powers, contralto; Beverly Dame, soprano; Frank Rogier, baritone; Catherine Mastice, soprano; Emanuel Balaban, cond. COLUMBIA SL-154 (with *The Telephone*).

THE SAINT OF BLEECKER STREET

All the ingredients in the recipe for proven (not original) Grand Opera are here. This is a logic all of its own, since opera with a capital "O" means the past has been summoned up in full. Yes, Menotti's *Saint*, with all of its cogent effectiveness, is eclectic to its Puccinian core. Menotti rarely alters his Italian stops; the idiom is quite familiar and intensely nondebatable, in the sense that one knows what to expect. The ending is pat theater—how else describe the heroine's taking the veil, to the background of choral counterpoint? The reproduced recipe turns out an excellent morsel—any dry eyes in the house? Let not this mixed metaphor confuse. Menotti sets out to trace a story of sacred-quasi-profane pattern and the music is cut to fit, from models no longer fashionable but still very serviceable.

The cast is excellent; in that one can find nothing to quibble about. This finds its just reward in an excellent recording, carefully and nicely produced by RCA Victor. Even if one doesn't care for Menotti's work he can still enjoy some beautiful voices in the persons of Lane, Poleri, and Ruggiero. Schippers keeps the entire score alive.

——Orchestra and Chorus; Catherine Akos, mezzo-soprano; Maria de Gerlando, soprano; Maria Marlo, soprano; Leon Lishner, bass; Gabrielle Ruggiero, soprano; David Poleri, tenor; Gloria Lane, mezzo-soprano; David Aiken, baritone; and others; Thomas Schippers, cond. RCA VICTOR LM-6032.

THE TELEPHONE

An amusing one-act opera, in form closer to a skit, with high-class, but unaffected music. Though calling for only two characters there is actually a third, the mechanical sound of a telephone. It is the latter that imperiously rings and constantly frustrates the man whenever he is ready to "pop the question." He finally uses the telephone himself, calling from the corner drugstore and asking the girl to marry him. And they probably lived happily ever after.

Perfectly performed and magnificently suited for mechanical reproduction, since no visual element is needed in order to follow the simple story line. *The Telephone* is part of a two-record set reproducing the double bill that enjoyed a long Broadway run.

——Orchestra; Marilyn Cotlow, soprano; Frank Rogier, baritone; Emanuel Balaban, cond. COLUMBIA SL-154 (with *The Medium*).

18. *Walter Piston*
(1894—   )

AMONG COMPOSERS WHO CULTIVATE THE NEOCLASSIC VIEWPOINT IN music, the most important in America is Walter Piston. Contrast though it may be to the drama and turmoil of the neo-Tchaikovskian manner, Piston's neoclassicism is neither dry nor academically mannered. Nonetheless, it has enough source-stuff within it for several treatises on how to compose music in the twentieth century. And there is humor and fantasy of a quasi-camouflaged type; the classicism of Piston is more elegant than that of the rougher Stravinsky.

But the mark he has already left on music by his own work and the magnificent successes of many of his pupils at Harvard (where he has been a member of the faculty since 1926) are but part of the Piston story. His compositions have demonstrated new ways of working within the tonal system, as well as of incorporating techniques formulated otherwise. Piston's music is quietly emotional, precise and graceful, almost matching the etched quality of his musical calligraphy. Expressiveness and design are the coefficients which make classical music great art. Piston honors these principles in every one of his compositions.

On records, Piston's music can be obtained in fair amount; three of the best of the symphonies and a smattering of chamber music are available, plus the well-known "Incredible Flutist," and some short pieces. It is regrettable that the piano quintet has disappeared with the discontinuing of the WCFM label. The same is true of the Perspective recording (2004) which included Piston's piano trio paired with Hindemith's vivid quartet for clarinet, violin, cello, and piano. However, the reorganized Westminster firm will soon be remastering and reissuing the very comprehensive catalogue of the American Recording Society. When this occurs we can look forward to Piston's Second Symphony, a representative work in a fairly happy mood. Since we have suffered untold artistic losses through the demise of the smaller companies, let the buyer beware —support must be given those that remain ere they, too, follow the path that leads into oblivion. Meanwhile, the high-water mark for Piston's music on records is one release per work, except for "The Incredible Flutist."

ORCHESTRAL

SERENATA

A cross between a short symphony and a suite, Piston's Serenata is influenced by the divertimento form. A "divertimento" should give pleasure, and this piece is not found wanting. The themes are gay (even in the *"con sentimento"* slow movement the serious-nesses are on the sweet side); the rhythms are refreshing and American in origin. This is one of the best of the many Louisville performances, especially stimulating in view of the fact that the rhythmic contours of a neoclassic work quite often are designed with an evenly articulated pulse but are uneven in accent. The sound is white-bright and clear.

——Louisville Orchestra, Robert Whitney, cond. LOUISVILLE COMMISSIONING SERIES LOU-58-6 (with Bentzon: Pezzi Sinfonici, and Van Vactor: Fantasia, Chaconne and Allegro).

SUITE FROM THE BALLET "THE INCREDIBLE FLUTIST"

It is certainly a pity that Piston has composed no program music other than this superb, jaunty score. Of course it is his prerogative, but it is our loss that such a master of roguish, frisky entertainment has seen fit otherwise to stay strictly within the bounds of serious, formal production. It is a rare gift that Piston displays in this single work that is diametrically opposed to his entire output of sym-phonies, suites, quartets, and other compositions.

"The Incredible Flutist" has a little of the midway atmosphere about it; changes occur in rapid succession—a tango (a haunting tune that will stay with the listener), a minuet, a waltz, a polka, and so on. And for dessert, a rousing circus march, accompanied, in all the recordings save that issued by Urania, with crowd noises, whistling, and so on, made by the orchestra players. This bit of extra-curricular fun will not be found in the printed score. It was improvised at the first performance and has become a traditional addition, awaited by those "in the know."

Despite Fiedler's having had the honor of giving the first ballet performance (May 30, 1938), his recording (available in single-record form with a pair of other works or as part of a three-record luxury album) is not the best, due to less than distinguished sound. Further, one is annoyed at the lack of banding (a production feature one expects for any suite or music in defined movements). Eliminating the bands permits another work to appear on the same side, but the bargain is hard-driven. Although all the other issues cover a complete record-side, only Epic's is banded. No economy is achieved, only a listener's irritation.

The Hanson version has a freshness and resoluteness that injects proper pep into the proceedings. To a smaller degree the same applies to Lane's performance. Hanson does more with the nostalgic swing of the quintuple-metered tango, however. Urania's is a very poor last. It is heavy-laden, has little style, and is a model of what the work is not.

——Eastman-Rochester Orchestra, Howard Hanson, cond. Mercury 50206 (SR-90206) (with Moore: The Pageant of P. T. Barnum).

——in "Pop Concert U.S.A.," Cleveland Pops Orchestra, Louis Lane, cond. Epic LC-3539 (BC-1013).

——Boston Pops Orchestra, Arthur Fiedler, cond. RCA Victor LM-2084 (with Ibert: Divertissement, and Rossini-Respighi: La Boutique Fantasque).

——in "The Ballet," Boston Pops Orchestra, Arthur Fiedler, cond. RCA Victor LM-6113.

——Symphony Orchestra of Radio Berlin, Arthur Rother, cond. Urania URLP-7092 (with Copland: Appalachian Spring).

Symphony No. 3

Intrinsic consonance of musical form can only be achieved when the composer attains a point in his work where his patterns become those of inevitability. Piston requires no novel devices in his music. He is a modern classicist. In this symphony the four movements are paced à la eighteenth century in their alternation of slow and fast tempi. The music's eloquence is spontaneous, not merely intellectually controlled (the method that prevails in too much creative work). The classical allegiance to form finds a contemporary parallel in Piston's handling of his materials; poetry and drama, repose and strife are the basic elements in this example of absolute

music. No novelty, no program to follow; only pure symphonic music, written with the clarity expected of a mature composer. The orchestration is crystalline and this gives a conductor a distinct advantage. Hanson demonstrates his appreciation of this by directing a fine performance; the sound is the full-bodied Mercury brand.
——Eastman-Rochester Symphony Orchestra, Howard Hanson, cond. MERCURY 50083.

SYMPHONY No. 4

This symphony was commissioned by the University of Minnesota, for its centennial celebration in 1951. It is an achievement of no small order, and a wonderful credit to American music. Piston rarely wears his heart on his sleeve, yet this work has no dryness about it whatsoever. In fact, it is almost refreshingly folksy at the start, vigorously red-blooded in the concluding movement. The inner divisions (a "Ballando" of dance-like nature and the very eloquent third part, marked "*Contemplativo*") have a freshness of concept and are as bracing in their effect as any music of sheer gusto. This does not mean a lessening in Piston's purity of technique. It is all there: smooth flowing lines, counterpoint that moves with confidence, plus the bite of dissonance. Ormandy's performance is expert and the tone of the orchestra is wondrous as only the Philadelphia group can achieve.
——Philadelphia Orchestra, Eugene Ormandy, cond. COLUMBIA ML-4992 (with Schuman: Symphony No. 6).

SYMPHONY No. 6

There is some obsession with pedantic mannerisms in this opus; it does not have the individuality and striking profile of Piston's earlier symphonies. The only exception is found in the pyrotechnical second movement, a veritable reincarnation of Mendelssohnian deftness and gossamer texture. The music demands virtuosi and the Boston men eat it up. Formally, the symphony runs its course as one expects, but Piston's imitation of himself is of rather negative value.
——Boston Symphony Orchestra, Charles Munch, cond. RCA VICTOR LM-2083 (with Martinu: Fantaisies Symphoniques).

Band

TUNBRIDGE FAIR—INTERMEZZO

Listening to this piece in the stimulating collection Fennell has assembled (all original band works, by Bennett, Barber, Schuman, Persichetti, and Gould) I thought of the title of Oscar Wilde's play, *The Importance of Being Earnest,* not only in reference to Fennell's determination to perform and record the best music, but in regard to Walter Piston's creative outlook. Whatever Piston does he does earnestly, and with meticulous craftsmanship. All too many composers compromise and write down when they come to grips with the band medium (how far behind the times is a composer permitted to be?). One group takes a snobbish attitude, while another honestly fears it has not had sufficient experience in writing for band. There is still another group, of third-rate composers who are quite willing, but their bandstrations sound like orchestral translations (screaming clarinets to equal the missing violins, etc.).

Band composition has not yet reached its artistic maturity—too few first-rank composers have dealt with this important creative problem. But, with the English school as an inspiration, plus some of the Russians, and a few Frenchmen, the time is not too distant when our American composers will produce the works one expects of them. An example of how they should go about this is furnished by Piston's piece. Here is a composer who in his one and only composition for band passes any acid test: of color, of balance, of proper stuff and substance for the medium. Piston's "Intermezzo" is bright, alive music, with a rhythmic tang and some jazzed spice to heighten the flavor. Try it.

——in "American Concert Band Masterpieces," Eastman Symphonic Wind Ensemble, Frederick Fennell, cond. MERCURY 50079.

INSTRUMENTAL

Organ

CHROMATIC STUDY ON THE NAME OF BACH

The thematic subject of this work is the musical equivalent of the letters that spell "Bach." Thus: in German, "B" equals B flat and "H" becomes B natural; these, with "A" and "C," all fall in the chromatic scale. This musical acrostic has been employed by a number of composers.

Piston's piece is tightly knit by polyphony, in keeping with the minute intervallic span between the sounds of his theme. It is almost *too* contrapuntal, save that polyphony is manna for the organ. The critical view of this work is divided—one can find in it in equal amounts both emotional content and the cool abstractions derived from a professional composer's counterpoint. The registration is accomplished and the playing is clear.

——Mildred Andrews. UNIVERSITY RECORDINGS 2 (with Krenek: Sonata, Op. 92; Luebeck: Complete Organ Preludes and Fugues; and Sessions: Chorale No. 1).

CHAMBER MUSIC

SONATINA FOR VIOLIN AND HARPSICHORD

If classicism is the generic term applied to seventeenth- and eighteenth-century music, then the use of the harpsichord is quite fitting in the work of a neoclassicist. What makes a composer choose the harpsichord is an understandable question; it is easily answered: either a desire for the link with tradition and sentient color of the instrument, or a wish to write for a special performer on the instrument. Probably both these factors led to Piston's choice of the piano's ancient relative, for the very clean writing (so cleanly played!) illustrates the harpsichord medium at its best.

When Piston's "Sonatina" was published it bore a dedication to the two musicians who later recorded it. The composer must have been as pleased with their magnificent performances as they were with the vivaciousness of the music he had written for them. This is a striking example of contemporary music in a brilliant recording. (Catch the companion work, a real "triple far-out" piece for strings.)

——Alexander Schneider, violin; Ralph Kirkpatrick, harpsichord. COLUMBIA ML-4495 (with Cage: String Quartet).

SONATA FOR VIOLIN AND PIANO

As usual with Piston, three movements (two outer fast ones and a slow central section) form the sonata's plan. Also as usual with him, the elements of contrapuntal jugglery are used.

The performance does the sonata artistic justice. Especially compelling is the presentation of the long-lined theme of the slow movement, and the fugue that is part of the final movement's rondo design. The players' conception is an overall one; the movements are not considered separately, as is so often the case. Musicians such as these clear the road for a more favorable view of contemporary music.

——Joseph Fuchs, violin; Artur Balsam, piano. DECCA DL-9541 (with Lopatnikoff: Sonata No. 2).

THREE PIECES FOR FLUTE, CLARINET, AND BASSOON

This is very early Piston, his second composition, written in 1926 (the first being a sonata for piano). The pieces are in squarely confined forms, and the symmetry of each is unmistakable, all three being cast in ternary style. One will recognize the dryness of wit, controlled by use of *ostinati* rhythmic figures, in the first piece; the foggy chromatic haze gives a nostalgic quality to the second one of the set; while the final portion also runs on *ostinati* feet. Piston has stated that these are like "concise pencil drawings." If so, the softer lead used by the Boston group is preferable to the harder employed by the New Art. Both organizations perform expertly.

——in "Modernists," Members of the Berkshire Woodwind Ensemble. UNICORN UNLP-1029.

——in "American Woodwind Symposium," Members of the New Art Wind Quintet. CLASSIC EDITIONS CE-2003.

WOODWIND QUINTET

The "pingy" quality that marks this neoclassicist's music remains unchanged as he moves from work to work. One wishes he would not ride so comfortably on his creative horse and would at times take chances. The texture in the quintet is thinner than in most of Piston's compositions, but this is doubtless due to instrumental accommodation, rather than to the music's plan per se.

The release marks the recording debut of the fine Boston Woodwind group, which duplicates here a concert given at the Library of Congress. It also marks the initial recording of the composition.

The disk illustrates a true beauty of sound, proper to the aural joy that one obtains from the work of this ensemble. The Bostonians make one wonder why so many wind groups sound as though their instruments were covered with thistles. This fivesome has a sweetness without being sonorously slick. It helps the Piston work considerably.

——Boston Woodwind Quintet. BOSTON RECORDS B-407 (1005) (with Reicha: Quintet; Ropartz: Quintet; and Telemann: Overture from "Suite in D").

19. *Silvestre Revueltas*
(1899—1940)

As the two greatest composers of the modern era in Hungary are Bartók and Kodály, so, in Mexico, they are Revueltas and Chávez (in both pairs, the first man is deceased). The analogy can go much further. Chávez is less (if only a little) a composer of the earth than was Revueltas; Kodály's music is less savage than was that of his fellow composer Bartók. To a certain degree, Revueltas can be called "the Bartók of Mexico." His music is nationalistic, springing from the life and soil of his country. Such pragmaticism did nothing, however, to inhibit his freedom and vigor in the unfolding of his music. The more freedom a creative intelligence displays, the more credit such music does its composer's nation.

Revueltas was an advocate of music for the masses, but he refused merely to imitate the popular idiom in his music. It was his opinion that the real character of native music was better conveyed by a stylized distillation, without slavish imitation or mere quotation. In his veins the Mexican musical blood flowed purely—he had played in cafés, drinking houses, and theaters of all types. This *musica méxicaña* is at the base of all his work: its primitive outlines, stripped of heavy, overladen romantic dress, convey not popular song, nor the general imitation of dances and popular songs, but Mexican music per se, in the raw. It is absolute nationalism.

The recording companies have almost completely ignored Revueltas, with the sole exception of MGM. Capitol has one work in a miscellany, Spa (which is now defunct) paired some Revueltas songs with a set by Ives, and Westminster made one dip into the composer's reservoir. MGM deserves more than a laurel wreath. When will the record firms realize that some alertness can mean money in the bank (often the equivalent of courage or enterprise), if not immediately, in time? Meanwhile the listener is urged to buy at least some of these recordings.

ORCHESTRAL

CUAUHNAHUAC

Starting softly and building to a tremendous climax, the rhythm of primitive Mexican life is in this piece. Revueltas' tone poem is not descriptive, despite its picturesque title (the ancient Indian name of the Mexican resort, Cuernavaca). No program music for Revueltas; he termed such "tourism music." This composition is made for the riches of high fidelity. It has orchestral brilliance of a dry-textured kind; it has been given "the works" in performance. The Lab version is quite expensive; the collection, which also contains the composer's "Sensemaya," is a better buy for the budget.

——in "Hi-Fi Feast," London Philharmonic Symphony Orchestra, Argeo Quadri, cond. WESTMINSTER XWN-18451.

——London Philharmonic Symphony Orchestra, Argeo Quadri, cond. WESTMINSTER LAB.-7004 (with Sensemaya; Chabrier: España; and Mossolov: Iron Foundry).

SENSEMAYA

The initial scoring of "Sensemaya" was for voice and small orchestra. Revueltas made his large-orchestra version a little less than a year later (March, 1938). This "chant to kill a snake" takes its inspiration from a work by Nicolás Guillén, an Afro-Cuban poet. There is no picture-painting, but the insistent rhythm engenders a sweat of excitement, far more earthily blunt than Ravel's "Bolero." Though Revueltas said he had not followed the poem, there is a quite conscious limning of the reiterative lines, "The snake has glossy eyes/The snake comes and coils itself around a tree./With its glossy eyes around a tree." The pulsatile presentation is constant, the barbaric orchestration a compendium of primitive, idiomatic style.

Although the strings are somewhat overpowered, Quadri's interpretation is of high order and the sound is Westminster's best. Top-drawer engineering is naturally found in the Lab series (plenty of groove room!), but the bargain buy is the other record.

——in "Hi-Fi Feast," London Philharmonic Symphony Orchestra, Argeo Quadri, cond. WESTMINSTER XWN-18451.

——London Philharmonic Symphony Orchestra, Argeo Quadri,

cond. WESTMINSTER LAB.-7004 (with Cuauhnahuac; Chabrier: España; and Mossolov: Iron Foundry).

Chamber Orchestra

HOMENAJE A GARCÍA LORCA ("HOMAGE TO GARCÍA LORCA")

Revueltas was proud of his heritage, considered himself of the people. As a lover of freedom, he went to Spain in 1937 to partici- pate in the musical activities of the Loyalist government, and there, in Barcelona, he conducted a concert sponsored by the Committee against War and Fascism. His admiration of the poet García Lorca was unlimited. It was in memory of García Lorca's death at the hands of the Spanish Fascists that Revueltas composed this moving three-movement composition, in October of 1936. Another bow to the poet was made in the set of songs, written in 1938 to his texts (*see under* Vocal). (An unrecorded memory of Revuel- tas' sojourn in Spain is his "War Song of the Loyalist Fronts," written for eight brass instruments, piano, and percussion.)

The "Homage" is considered one of the major pieces by Revuel- tas. It is activated by Indian and Hispanic rhythms, and all the thematic lines progress without being covered by a heaviness of texture. Severe colors are used to express all the ideas. Unfortu- nately the rarely incorrect Edward Cole has made several errors in his liner notes for this and other works in the MGM album. The "*Baile*" which opens the work is *not* a serious dance, but rather one of more popular (salon) type. The "*Duelo*" is actually a cradle song, not a funeral march; its music is among the most moving in the composer's catalogue. In the final "*Son*," Ivesian grotesquerie, the fun-faceted idiom of the vernacular mixed with dissonance, makes its appearance.

Although the MGM album is worth owning for all the works it contains, it is a bargain for the "*Homenaje*" alone. The De la Fuente performance is just a bit better (more refined recorded sound), but the music in "Viva Mexico!," though interesting as illustrating the work of three young Mexican composers, is not as exciting as that by Revueltas. One would do well to own both records, despite the duplication of the single Revueltas piece. At the risk of belaboring the suggestion, better obtain all the Revuel- tas to be found.

——in "The Music of Silvestre Revueltas," MGM Chamber Orchestra, Carlos Surinach, cond. MGM E-3496.

——in "Viva Mexico!," Orquesta Sinfónica Nacional Mexico, Luis Herrera de la Fuente, cond. CAPITOL T-10083.

OCHO POR RADIO

Prefatory explanation: The title used by the composer is "8 x Radio." This is simply Revueltas' quip. No mathematical monkeyshines are intended; it is merely music for eight players to perform on the radio. Reading the liner notes, however, one finds purple prose describing the piece as a "musical joke" (which it is not) and calling it a "phantasmagoric aural view of Mexican radio music—as heard . . . with a great deal of . . . interference," which it also is not.

Facts: The form is exceedingly free, its sections in severe contrast, broken and nervous in action; it reminds one of a variational digest without benefit of a principal theme. Within the definite Mexican atmosphere improvisatory elements ride herd on systematized standards of musical creation; with these snippets of popularisms are intermingled. All this makes one think of Charles Ives. Thus spake Revueltas.

Performance: Solomon keeps clear the juxtaposed voices which make up a polyphonic picnic, but in at least two places the score and the playing do not have the preciseness one expects from top performers and a first-class conductor. However, the articulateness of the music is sufficient to warrant overlooking these few, below-par points.

——in "Spanish and Latin-American Music for Unusual Combinations," MGM Chamber Orchestra, Izler Solomon, cond. MGM E-3155.

PLANOS, A GEOMETRIC DANCE

Despite the liner note no joke is implied by the title of this dissonant music. The essence of Revueltas' music is its nonconformity to formal standards; the outer surfaces are concisely primitive, drawn tight and sharp, driven together with sound that makes the most direct impact. Revueltas explained *"Planos"* by stating that the melodic fragments ". . . sing in persistent rhythms, ever in motion; they produce sonorities that may seem strange because they are not common." This is so, and the music makes the nine-piece group harsh, uncompromising, but exciting. This is the *pure* Revueltas.

MGM records an authoritative performance with very bright sound that nicely matches the music. (There is a version for large orchestra, but no recording exists. In a way the condensed scoring gives better effect.)

——in "The Music of Silvestre Revueltas," MGM Chamber Orchestra, Carlos Surinach, cond. MGM E-3496.

Toccata sin Fuga

Revueltas' music is a paradox, in that it sounds untutored, yet is supplied with a plenitude of architectural stability. But there are no formal preoccupations.

As Damon goes with Pythias, a toccata goes with a fugue, save for this composer, who presents his toccata "without fugue." But "*sin fuga*" does not signify "*sin* counterpoint." The dazzling and kaleidoscopic polyphony is in high gear throughout.

Revueltas' scoring method makes the recorded sound register with harshness. But this is as it should be, since the composer chooses tensile timbres: a high-pitched piccolo, three types of clarinets, a horn, trumpet, timpani, and a single violin. Still another example of the remarkable imagination and ingenuity of this first-rate composer.

——in "The Music of Silvestre Revueltas," MGM Chamber Orchestra, Carlos Surinach, cond. MGM E-3496.

Tres Sonetos

Each of these "sonnets" is short. None of the group have definite programs, but express the general temper of the uncredited sources: "I am coming back to you, lonely, empty water," "June gave me the voice, the delightful music of keeping a feeling quiet," and "My heart was a river stone." These word sketches are conveyed by dark-crayoned instrumentation, expertly assigned to the deeper gamut of the clarinets, bass clarinet, bassoon, tuba, and piano. A tamtam adds its threatening tone, and the horn and pair of trumpets give edge but not shrillness. No flashy coinage here, merely a visionary aspect of the composer's personality. The performances are singularly moving and the listener can rely on their authenticity.

——in "The Music of Silvestre Revueltas," MGM Chamber Orchestra, Carlos Surinach, cond. MGM E-3496.

TWO LITTLE SERIOUS PIECES
  The second piece of the pair mixes French salon atmosphere with Mexican night-air stuffiness in waltz tempo. A snide comparison is strongly hinted. Number one of the set is like a denuded capsule version of the "Rite of Spring." It is as serious as the companion piece is unserious. Rhythm and sonority are the techniques of the composer, with both items starkly primitive in conception. Revueltas is not casual with his ideas—note the scoring: a piccolo, oboe, trumpet, together with a clarinet and a tubby baritone saxophone. Clean and clear reproduction, clean and certified performance.
  ——in "The Music of Silvestre Revueltas," MGM Chamber Orchestra, Carlos Surinach, cond. MGM E-3496.

INSTRUMENTAL

Violin

THREE PIECES FOR VIOLIN AND PIANO
  Revueltas' earthy style is heard in the two outer pieces of the set. What is a beautiful surprise is the poignant expressiveness of the haunting, lullaby-like slow movement. This reveals a far different side of the composer from the rhythmic, ground-crushing dynamics present in most of Revueltas' other works. This music cries for transcription so that all types of audiences might share its folkloric beauty.
  The Ajemians play the slow movement with sensitive probity. The asymmetrical percussive richnesses of the other sections are also well done. Note: when the tone sounds like a scraping sculptor's tool it is Revueltas' wishes being carried out precisely. A rare gem in the contemporary literature for violin and piano.
  ——Anahid Ajemian, violin; Maro Ajemian, piano. MGM E-3180 (with Chávez: Sonatina for Violin and Piano, and Surinach: Doppio Concertino).

VOCAL

BULL FROGS
  "*Ranas*" (Bull Frogs) is the only song in which Revueltas fully

lets himself go. Potent music-making will be recognized before a single measure is completed. The piano is assigned a seemingly crude sound, via an extreme manner of part-spacing. This is typical of the composer and such brilliant sound-plotting is maintained. The musical ideas propel the prose thoughts: the frogs are "croaking pseudo-sirens," they "raise an endless row of empty fifths," et cetera. It is serious-popular-national music, without any reserve on the composer's part.

However, Revueltas' dry humor is not realized (understood?) by the performers. They sing-play it too straight. Spa's below-average sound must be accepted if one wishes this song and the others.

——Jacqueline Greissle, soprano; Josef Wolman, piano. SPA RECORDS SPA-9 (with Five Songs of Childhood; The Owl; Two Songs; and Ives: Songs).

FIVE SONGS OF CHILDHOOD

Despite the fact that Revueltas' songs are the least in importance, in his total output, they have sufficient segments of interest to warrant attention. With few exceptions Revueltas adopted a partly neutral, almost conservative viewpoint in his vocal compositions; only a few bear his creative trademark. One can criticize the almost casual, quasi-mechanical shape of the "Nonsense Song" in this cycle or the limited view in the last of the set, "Mr. and Mrs. Lizard." The titles of the songs would seem to signify many promises—but few of these materialize.

Part of this may be due to the English translations, which read very awkwardly (one example: "Birds are approaching the firmament"). Another reason may be the singer herself. Greissle makes no shift in her style; she is resistant and restricted, there is no consuming malleability of the vocal instrument. Neither is Wolman prone to let himself become involved. He accompanies; no more, no less. Spa's sound is hollow and not very responsive. Truly a negative report.

The texts are by García Lorca and are typical tales concerning the young: a small horse, an "hour" song, and a lullaby, in addition to the pair already mentioned. One might expect folksy tunes but Revueltas' essential Mexicanism bypassed the use of native material. The highlight of the set is the fourth song in the group—the doleful, plastically lyric *"Cancion de Cuna"* (to use the original title, though it is not given on the disk), translated as "Cradle Song." This has admirable simplicity and a real inspiration serving as the piano background. "The Four Hours" is a brightly neat song with a real "tag" ending.

——Jacqueline Greissle, soprano; Josef Wolman, piano. SPA RECORDS SPA-9 (with Bull Frogs; The Owl; Two Songs; and Ives: Songs).

THE OWL

A real *lied*, with "Bull Frogs" the peak of Revueltas' song composition.

There is an old Mexican superstition that whenever an owl sings an Indian will die. "The Owl" concerns a ranchero whose Creole has deserted him for a horseman. The man remembers the horseman is an Indian and with vengeance in mind hopes an owl "will soon be singing."

One critic has said Revueltas' songs are "post-Ravel French and occasionally Spanish." This can be argued. Minute particles from popular art fall into this song's measures without destroying its individuality. Every note receives distinct guidance from Revueltas, which means devotion to no other cause than the subtle suggestion of Mexican nationalism.

——Jacqueline Greissle, soprano; Josef Wolman, piano. SPA RECORDS SPA-9 (with Bull Frogs; Five Songs of Childhood; Two Songs; and Ives: Songs).

TWO SONGS

Another set composed to texts by García Lorca, consisting of a "Serenade" and "It Is True." Both songs are framed with *ostinato* patterns.

Revueltas' remark that "music that makes one think is intolerable" goes too far, perhaps, in its generalization. But he may have been thinking of his vocal pieces when he made this statement. The writing is fair to middlin'. Little thinking will be required. Sung with casualness. No runs, no hits, and two errors.

——Jacqueline Greissle, soprano; Josef Wolman, piano. SPA RECORDS SPA-9 (with Bull Frogs; Five Songs of Childhood; The Owl; and Ives: Songs).

20. Wallingford Riegger
(1885—   )

Riegger is the "grand old man" of American music, its dean, yet in spirit one of its youngest. No composer has been more compellingly clear in his work, nor more modest. His total lack of jealousy and his friendly, unselfish aid to younger composers is a lesson in creative humanitarianism.

After a long career of the most honest attention to his work, without the sham and conventional pose of making a "big noise," or working the social front so as to be in the spotlight, Riegger's achievement was finally recognized. It occurred belatedly, but it was with unanimous approval that he was given the New York Music Critics' Circle Award for the most significant new work in the 1947-48 season (his Third Symphony). He remains a composer who composes first and last; musical politics has never been an attraction.

While Riegger began as a super-romanticist, he turned to nontonal music rather suddenly in 1926, creating quite a storm with his "Study in Sonority" for violins divided into ten parts. From this point on Riegger evolved a very personal style, though it fully embodies the tenets of twelve-tone technique.

It is agreed that dodecaphonicism does not produce the simplest music and that it requires a sharp ear and acute concentration to find in it proper satisfactions. Many listeners persist in trying to hear all sounds in the same way, or in forcing one type of music into the orbit of a different one. When it will not fit into such a pattern, the music is dismissed summarily. But, in Riegger's case, his supreme belief in dodecaphony does not mean he puts intellectual practice above artistic application. His is a different twelve-tone music. He is the one individual in that entire school who can make his tone-serial production sound like a natural departure from traditional means, rather than an arbitrary technical method. For this the dogmatic members of this musical clique may criticize him (they have!)—unjustifiably.

To some it may seem sheer nonsense to say that twelve-tone music can be beautiful or enjoyable. But the quality of innateness,

179

of stylistic consistency sharpened by technical perfection (as in Schoenberg) is no small pleasure to an auditor. If a dodecaphonic composer has a sense of wit and of the fanciful—if his ideas are pertinent, the designs clear, the tensions regulated so that climaxes are pointed—it is not special pleading to state that his music has its own form of beauty and can be enjoyed. This is the magic Riegger performs in the twelve-tone style.

Technically, how is it done? Clear, formal shapes are utilized and the patterns within these produce the defined tones, chords, and characteristics of the diatonic system. These, plus the rhythms that clarify the progress of these elements, are all taken over bodily by the twelve-tone method. As a result the sound is fresh; the fragmentary objectives employed by most of the dodecaphonic composers are absent. The corresponsivities of the tonal and the twelve-tonal methods are made to jell, without Riegger's being false to the spirit or style of the latter system. Thus, as Beethoven "freed" tonality in his late works, so Riegger has "tonalized" dodecaphony.

The pernicious practice of deletion has resulted in none of Riegger's string quartets being obtainable in recorded performance. At best, the records discussed below are merely a sampling of his output. Where is the enterprising conductor who will make "Dichotomy," the "Study in Sonority," and many of the other powerful Riegger works available?

ORCHESTRAL

Dance Rhythms

An example of Riegger in a pose that does not reveal his true personality. This is in a class with the utilitarian music Riegger composed for dance groups and the like during the WPA days. The recipe consists of a light batter of jazzified rhythms, pops coloratives (such as mallet-played instruments), Kostelanetized fiddles, and seasoning taken from Morton Gould's cook book. No one will flee the music room when listening to it, but it is somewhat less than one has a right to expect from a work composed in the early 1950's. Acceptable performance, save that the sound is somewhat out of whack in places where the marimba is contrasted to the other orchestral sections.

——Oslo Philharmonic Orchestra, Alfredo Antonini, cond. Com-

POSERS RECORDINGS CRI-117 (with Music for Orchestra; Romanza; Avshalomov: The Taking of T'ung Kuan; and Cazden: Three Ballads from the Catskills).

MUSIC FOR ORCHESTRA

The formal title is the clue that we may expect to find Riegger wearing his twelve-tone clothes. However, his apparel is designed with convincing beauty. The pulsative consistency of driving, assembled rhythms plus the repetition of segments, forming units (there is little development of thematic material, as it is generally understood), do not conceal the important fact of the absence of a tonic-dominant tonal relationship. Rather, they make for a naturalness, which in someone else's hands would sound forced and contrived. This is writing free of tonality and at the same time free of twelve-tone rigidity; yet the music sounds healthy and correct— as it should. The other two Riegger works on the CRI disk are of dubious merit, in this reviewer's opinion; the reason should be apparent from listening to "Music for Orchestra" first.
——Oslo Philharmonic Orchestra, Alfredo Antonini, cond. COMPOSERS RECORDINGS CRI-117 (with Dance Rhythms; Romanza; Avshalomov: The Taking of T'ung Kuan; and Cazden: Three Ballads from the Catskills).

NEW DANCE

Riegger has done a considerable amount of composing for the modern dance, quite often writing his music *after* the choreography has been set—a matter of some difficulty, with little individual judgment permitted the composer. Nonetheless, he has conquered these restrictions and his scores for the dance have been some of the very best produced.

"New Dance" was originally for pianos and percussion. In fact, seven different versions exist. That heard on this disk is the best of the lot (an orchestral setting of the finale of the original work composed for the dancers, Doris Humphrey and Charles Weidman, in 1935). It is fresh music, outside the Schoenbergian camp in which Riegger holds an important post, cast in a conga-like rhythm that is very bold in its rhythmic ardor. Superbly played and with beautiful sound. It is one of three works in a fascinating compilation of American music.

——Eastman-Rochester Symphony Orchestra, Howard Hanson, cond. MERCURY 50078 (with Hovhaness: Concerto No. 1 for Orchestra—"Arevakal," and Cowell: Symphony No. 4).

SYMPHONY No. 3, OP. 42

Riegger's contact with both classical tradition and Schoenbergian freedom is beautifully realized in this trenchant, dramatic four-movement symphony. It is the most definitive work of the composer, probably his best, and proves conclusively the rightness of the place Riegger holds in the hierarchy of American music composition.

No dry, pedantic twelve-toner has the stuff to interest a listener throughout even a short piece, let alone a full-fledged symphony of close to twenty-five minutes. But Riegger is both free of tonality and aloof from the dodecaphonic science that can freeze a work into immobility. His music is rugged, direct, forceful. At the same time, it takes into account the need for balances that can be realized and understood without reference to the printed score. What Riegger has accomplished in this symphony is a perfectly styled rapport that in turn creates a new style. There is no eclectic throwing together of ingredients; there is control, aesthetic truth, and individual quality. This is obtained by a pithiness of generative material, striking rhythmic contours, brilliant orchestration, and, above all, the realization that formal logic needs emotional explanation. This is the perpetual renewal of art: logic extends into new spheres; emotion is a constant measuring rod. Only exceptional composers can achieve the fusion. In this symphony Riegger has. Hanson's belief in the composition is proven by his minute attention to detail and the clearest exposition. Columbia has given the record its best engineering attention.

——Eastman-Rochester Symphony Orchestra, Howard Hanson, cond. COLUMBIA ML-4902 (with Mennin: Symphony No. 3).

SYMPHONY No. 4

I find this symphony a little unbecoming to Riegger. It is dedicated to the memory of his wife, and it is this very occasion that causes a slight mixture of style. In the second movement Riegger has utilized material from a work he wrote in 1936 for Martha Graham, called "Chronicle." This dance piece pictured the suffering that took place in Spain during the war between the Loyalists and the followers of Franco. It is the Spanish cast of this music which seems out of place in the symphony, despite the threnodic tone desired by the composer. When compared with the unity and amazingly clear shapes of his Third Symphony, the latest symphonic creation of Riegger's must take a lesser place.

But it must be said that the initial part of the work is a reinforcement of the composer's very logical musical arguments for the artistic sense derivable from twelve-tone technique. Riegger's freedom is not a playing false to the system. His expositional clarity is convincing, since he avoids diffuseness or overagitated propaganda for the science and concentrates instead, in his compositions, on the art of dodecaphonicism. But in this symphony the music has less impact and continuity. Putting myself out on a flimsy critical limb, I do not see a long life for this work, whereas I think the Third Symphony will enjoy a solid old age.

The album in which Riegger's Fourth Symphony is contained is worthy of everyone's interest. There are important works by Schuller, Fine, and Phillips; the Riegger is worthy, and compositions by Hovhaness and Krenek are there if one is interested. Performance and engineering throughout are excellent—not one point of criticism can be raised. The University of Illinois has done itself proud.

——University of Illinois Symphony Orchestra, Bernard Goodman, cond. UNIVERSITY OF ILLINOIS CUSTOM RECORDING SERIES CRS-5.

String Orchestra

ROMANZA

The assorted release that includes this with two others of the composer's works is a mishmash that may well confuse the record buyer. It is all well and good to illustrate a composer's historical growth, but to record music that was written in 1953 but sounds like 1853 is nonsensical. Warning, therefore! This "Romanza" is not early Riegger at all. The cloyingness of the work sounds like Elgar's "Serenade" for strings; at best it is no better than mild Hugo Kaun or Paul Graener. A worthwhile early work would have been an honest choice and would have displayed the composer properly. For shame! And a shame that the performance is over-heated; simple music needs simple presentation—no more.

——Orchestra of the Accademia Nazionale di Santa Cecilia—Roma, Alfredo Antonini, cond. COMPOSERS RECORDINGS CRI-117 (with Dance Rhythms; Music for Orchestra; Avshalomov: The Taking of T'ung Kuan; and Cazden: Three Ballads from the Catskills).

SOLO INSTRUMENT WITH ORCHESTRA

VARIATIONS FOR PIANO AND ORCHESTRA, OP. 54

Classical décor rules this work; the theme is not dismembered but is strikingly recognizable even when the variation treatment is rather free. The dozen variants are connected, yet each is distinct; each portion of the whole is a fresh thought and acts as a developed confirmation of the generative idea. The theme may twitch but it never acts rowdy. Riegger employs a cumulative design with the completion of the twelve variations codified by a fugue as the postscript. In twelve-tone deployment this plan makes the structure twice as solid, with as clear a façade as one can imagine. The Louisville players are satisfactory, but one senses an instrumental reticence on their part quite the opposite of the top-quality work of the soloist.

——Louisville Orchestra; Benjamin Owen, piano; Robert Whitney, cond. LOUISVILLE COMMISSIONING SERIES LOU-545-3 (with Mennin: Symphony No. 6, and Toch: Notturno).

CHAMBER MUSIC

SONATINA FOR VIOLIN AND PIANO

Riegger's paradoxical manner of being a non-tonalist but plotting his music to make it sound convincingly tonal is exemplified in this work. The first movement is in two parts, all the material evolving out of the gentle motive announced at the start; all articulations can be traced to it.

The second movement, after a rhythmic introduction, is derived from a twelve-tone row. In this case the music is designed to make possible the following of the basic row. Intellectuality is not the deciding factor—emotional sensations are. Riegger's method is not a matter of merely juggling the row, but employing it as a motive.

From this come repeated tones, rhythmic cells, and all the means of making free use of the method without dogmaticism. The well-prepared and integrated developments make the twelve-tone technique as clear to the ear, in this work, as a Mozart sonata. Somewhat dry sound, a tendency of the MGM label, but not too harmful for enjoying the music plus the top quality performance.

——Anahid Ajemian, violin; Maro Ajemian, piano. MGM E-3218 (with Krenek: Double Concerto for Violin, Piano and Small Orchestra, and Sessions: From my Diary).

QUINTET FOR WINDS, OP. 51

Opposites attract each other, or are designed to attract each other in this one-movement work. The seriousness of a fugue is compounded with truly flippant treatment of the four woodwinds and horn. Each of the separate fugal subjects is tossed around and real pillow-throwing play ensues. And the proficiency of the New Art players clarifies each and every note of the whole. This is colorful twelve-tone music. It nullifies the argument that the dodecaphonic scheme of musical composition is neurotic, hysterical, and scratches the nerve ends.

——in "American Woodwind Symposium," New Art Wind Quintet. CLASSIC EDITIONS CE-2003.

CONCERTO FOR PIANO AND WOODWIND QUINTET

Though in the field of chamber music this title may seem self-contradictory, it is actually correct. Usually signifying a work for a solo instrument with orchestral accompaniment, the truest definition of a concerto is a relationship of equality, the pitting of one voice against others. Riegger follows the practice of many contemporary composers in using this classic form for a small combination.

The ingredients and methods of this composer's compositions are here displayed, plus a surprising and free technical shift in the last part. If the textbook of others does not govern Wallingford Riegger, neither does he follow his own manual. At the start the usual tone row is announced, it moves swiftly to a restatement in inverted form, and then is developed with proper associative resources. The twelve tones are used freely without making it inordinately complex to follow the composer's thoughts. After such unshackled writing it is stimulating (and not stylistically incorrect) to have diatonic representation dominate the final movement. This duality is tied together by bringing back the basic row for completion. Q.E.D: license within composition, albeit complete unity. The twain have met.

CRI's recordings have been progressively better—this, one of its latest, is very impressive. Ease and relaxation with sensitive and subtle consideration of highlighted material mark the teaming of this fine band of wind players and one of the best chamber-music pianists available.

——Harriet Wingreen, piano; New Art Wind Quintet. COMPOSERS RECORDINGS CRI-130 (with Laderman: Theme, Variations and Finale for Four Winds and Four Strings).

21. *William Schuman*
(1910—   )

SCHUMAN IS ONE OF THE BIG NAMES IN AMERICAN MUSIC, AND deservedly so, notwithstanding the fact that, having found his methods, he clings rather strongly to them. Formulas, even clichés, are, after all, the dominating characteristics of a man's style. Schuman's music, as a result, is recognizable as almost certainly his alone; there is but one close comparison and that is to the music of his onetime adviser, Roy Harris. (Schuman did not study formally with Harris, but had him go over his early works very carefully; the influence of an adviser can be as potent as a teacher's.) To cite two ways in which Harris and Schuman are dissimilar, the latter's rhythms are more those of motor traction; another difference is in Schuman's occasional smart jazz tone. But Harris and Schuman have an affinity as composers in their common adherence to and fondness for classical tactics set in the frame of neoromanticism (but without thickness). This mixture of musical metaphor arises through their use of classic devices, with the neoromantic chordal furbishings of polyharmonies, direct and implied bitonalities, and the like. Parallel to the relationship of Harris and Schuman is that of Schoenberg and Berg; in both cases, the second composer's technique was derived from the first, was influenced by it, but resulted in a completely individual artist.

The facets of Schuman's career make a fascinating outline. He began with the composing of popular songs; today he is the president of the Juilliard School of Music. In between he was a member of the faculty of Sarah Lawrence College and then director of publications at the well-established firm of G. Schirmer. Awards he has had galore, commissions as well; he received the first Pulitzer Prize ever given for music, for his secular cantata "A Free Song." The amazing postscript is that this work has not been recorded!

Schuman's music has a fair representation on records. Some major works are lacking, especially the four string quartets, none of which can now be secured, save an odd copy that one might turn up somewhere of the fourth quartet, once on Columbia (ML-4493). Although the selection of compositions that are available is not too large, this must be related to the fact that Schuman is not the most prolific of composers. However, most of his recorded catalogue is of topnotch quality and this must serve over quantity. (Mention should be made of two choral pieces this reviewer was unable to hear, though the albums in which they are included are presumably currently available. The first is a "Prelude for Voices," with text by Thomas Wolfe, completed in 1939. It is sung by the Concordia Choir on Concordia 6. The other is a "Te Deum," set for *a cappella* mixed voices and was originally part of the incidental music Schuman wrote for a production of *Henry VIII*. Performance of this is by the Washington University Choir on a little-known label—Aspen 1511.)

ORCHESTRAL

CREDENDUM

This "Article of Faith" was written between June 20 and September 6, 1955, in response to an unusual commission, received through the United States Department of State for UNESCO. Thus the American government, never a supporter of the arts, made a step in the right direction. If only because of this fact, Schuman's work is historic. Sensing the importance of his commission, Schuman has produced a composition of which he can well be proud. In so doing he has not sacrificed his personal style in the interests of popularization.

"Credendum" (first performed by the Cincinnati Symphony Orchestra, under Thor Johnson, in November, 1955) divides into three parts, played without pause: a "Declaration," followed by a Chorale, and Finale. The moods of these range widely, but are attuned to reciprocal balance. Schuman's music is both declamatory and serene, colored by grandeur and huge sonorities. (The orchestra is far from "normal," including four flutes, six horns, two tubas, and a large percussion section.) It has a tearing quality which suits the militant material set forth by the composer. In its way this is program music, but there is no line-by-line evidence of this, and no text is necessary for understanding it.

The Ormandy disk is magnificent, eloquently played, brilliantly recorded. This is a case where composer, orchestra, and conductor are in full agreement. Integrity is the word that describes everything.

——Philadelphia Orchestra, Eugene Ormandy, cond. Columbia ML-5185 (with Kirchner: Piano Concerto).

NEW ENGLAND TRIPTYCH (THREE PIECES FOR ORCHESTRA AFTER WILLIAM BILLINGS)

The music of William Billings, an eighteenth-century amateur, displays the divine gift, if not technical maturity. His views are as inflexible a statement of artistic faith for the present as they were in the late 1700's when he wrote: ". . . all the hard, dry, studied rules . . . will not enable any person to form an air. . . ." A primitive but a true composer, Billings has won a posthumous fame that is unique in American musical history. Schuman has based his three-piece set on themes of Billings: the anthem "Be Glad Then, America," an inspired melody which has a nobility that is quietly exciting; the pleading and sensitive "When Jesus Wept"; and a stirring march tune, "Chester," which became the American Revolutionary hymn.

Schuman's kinship with Billings seems to extend only to the latter's melodies; yet, paradoxically, it goes further. He retains Billings' style by synchronizing present-day techniques with the traditional past. It is as if Billings were alive and composing music, having had Schuman's training and experience. Though "Chester" is a bit brash and brassy, it concludes the triptych on the proper note. It is the center movement which is the high spot of the work—there the listener will obtain his greatest reward.

Kostelanetz commissioned this piece, gave the first performance with the University of Miami Symphony Orchestra, in October, 1956, and properly records it for the first time. The only criticism to be made is of some false unison playing, odd to hear and showing that carelessness attends some recording sessions.

——New York Philharmonic, Andre Kostelanetz, cond. Columbia ML-5347 (MS-6040) (with Barber: Intermezzo from Act IV of *Vanessa*, and Copland: A Lincoln Portrait).

SYMPHONY No. 3

Individuality of formal patterns, the flow of contrasting currents, and truly exciting orchestration mark this work, given the New

York Music Critics' Circle Award in 1942. Contiguity of design is joined with properly forceful disassociation as a passacaglia preludes a fugue, and a chorale flows into a stirring toccata. Thus the compelling way of a contemporary dealing with classical forms. Further, Schuman is freed linguistically by the tonal transiencies of the twentieth century. And all the structural components are highly colored by orchestral virtuosity (the reason why Schuman's symphonies can only be performed by the major-league organizations). In this symphonic essay one observes an orchestrational extrovert working with sound: an English horn is given fast, not rural-somnolent music to play; trumpets perform like acrobats; the timpani has solo lines; themes are exposed in their skeletal form, rhythmically outlined by a snare drum, melodically by a bass clarinet; on top of all this the brass form a band within an orchestra. These colors are cool or hot, but always clean, correctly chosen for the composition, and coincidentally made to order for recording.

Ormandy's orchestra plays impressively: the power of the work is felt and fully expressed. Columbia's sound is not as vibrant as one would desire, but this does not defeat Schuman's singular symphony.

——Philadelphia Orchestra, Eugene Ormandy, cond. COLUMBIA ML-4413.

SYMPHONY No. 6 (IN ONE MOVEMENT)

It is not necessary to follow old dictates with the use of old devices. The fusion of new elements with earlier ones is more than a new look, it is the avoidance of academicism. This symphony does not whistle its tunes; Schuman is not a composer of whimsy. It has the craftsmanship of the expert and partakes of Schuman's compositional penchant for writing polyphonically, but with the interwoven voices just short of full contrapuntalism. This produces a liveliness of rhythm not common to many of the linear-concerned composers. Schuman's symphony has long lines, magnificent color, and a meaningful excitement. Its argument outlines a work with six distinct sections, each defined by a tempo change. This logic is not difficult to follow, even if the lines are not those that thrive in the melodic realm of "tunes."

The playing of the Philadelphians is superb. All the subtle points are made clear for the ear, though this symphony needs patience from the listener to disclose its secrets. An excellent disk, with two major American symphonies, offers the buyer an impressive acquisition.

——Philadelphia Orchestra, Eugene Ormandy, cond. COLUMBIA ML-4992 (with Piston: Symphony No. 4).

UNDERTOW, CHOREOGRAPHIC EPISODES FOR ORCHESTRA

A suite taken from the ballet by Anthony Tudor, composed for the Ballet Theatre and first presented by them in 1945. The story is a shock-piece, concerned with an adolescent's obsession with sex, traceable to infantile frustration. This deprivation has set up problems which remain unsolved in his encounters with whores, drunks, and others. The climax is the murder of a lascivious woman. Only his capture makes possible the purging of the protagonist's soul. A score for such torturous events must necessarily be quite grim, with little lightness to bring relief. Expressionism is the style of Schuman's morbid musical tale. He is most certainly a successful exponent of this aesthetic.

It is not important to know which sections of the ballet have been used to construct the orchestral version. Heard as a symphonic piece in three major sections, the music has sufficient continuity and is self-explanatory. "Undertow" is constructed on a number of chordal motives and themes with an interlocked development; the orchestration is lean and this serves to underline the dramatic expressivity of the score. Levine's performance is convincing, with all the dance essences properly distilled.

——Ballet Theatre Orchestra, Joseph Levine, cond. CAPITOL P-8238 (with Copland: Billy the Kid).

String Orchestra

SYMPHONY FOR STRINGS

Actually the fifth in Schuman's set of symphonies, but the only one for strings. This is another of the successful works resulting from a commission from the Koussevitzky Foundation. Invigorating rhythmic life is predominant; still this is no musical vehicle in which contrapuntal drive is achieved quite often at the expense of musical justification. To a certain degree Schuman's string piece is a study in textures, with polyphony and muted sonorities marking the meditative inner movement, plus the pigmentation of plucked sounds as an important factor in the final part. The writing is a tour de force. Schuman utilizes old forms, holding them up, however, to the newest lighting scheme.

One cannot but compare the Steinberg performance with the old Concert Hall Society version (CHS-1078), still purchasable, though not from ordinary sources. The Capitol release is intense, dramatic, and tightly drawn, whereas the Concert Hall (the orchestra on that is a pick-up group, conducted by Edgar Schenkman) gives the feeling that the seams of the music will burst any moment. Little argument possible—the Steinberg-led recording is defined and definitive.

——Pittsburgh Symphony Orchestra, William Steinberg, cond. CAPITOL P-8212 (with Bloch: Concerto Grosso).

Band

CHESTER (OVERTURE FOR BAND)

Among the important serious American composers Schuman has been one of the few partial to this medium, this overture being the third work he has conceived for band. It has the correct characteristics for its special sonority plan. The Billings theme on which it is based also serves Schuman in the third part of his orchestral work, the "New England Triptych." Goldman's men play in an exhilarating fashion; the album contains some real ear-openers—downright originals for band by Mendelssohn, Bruckner, and Wagner!

——in "Band Masterpieces," Goldman Band, Richard Franko Goldman, cond. DECCA DL-8633.

GEORGE WASHINGTON BRIDGE

This "impression" is rather somber; it is not the usual rehash of hash, as are so many attempts at writing serious band music. It lacks only constructive efficiency; it takes much too long to make its point and still retain an auditor's interest. Doubtless not destined to be one's favorite Schuman piece. As for excellence of band performance, no one can surpass Fennell and his musicians.

——in "American Concert Band Masterpieces," Eastman Symphonic Wind Ensemble, Frederick Fennell, cond. MERCURY 50079.

INSTRUMENTAL

Piano

VOYAGE

This cycle of five pieces acquired its titles ("Anticipation," "Caprice," "Realization," "Decision," and "Retrospection") after the fact—they were added by the composer after he had seen his work set to a dance by Martha Graham. Unconscious though they may be with him, dark emotional contours surround Schuman's music. They make of "Voyage" a successful score for the modern dance, but they are of such proportions that one wishes the music had been recorded in its choreographic chamber orchestra version. Webster does all he can with the set of pieces, but it seems a halfway measure; the keyboard instrument sounds confined.

——Beveridge Webster. COLUMBIA ML-4987 (with Thomson: String Quartet No. 2).

22. Roger Sessions
(1896—   )

ROGER SESSIONS HAS BEEN CALLED A CEREBRALIST, A POLYTONALIST, as well as a man who expresses Germanic heaviness in terms of so-called "American" art music. He is none of these. He is a superb craftsman (one of the best in America, as well as one of the most admired by those who take time to think, know, and recognize) who composes music similar in its intensity to late Beethoven, but not to Beethoven's style (thus, *not* German). His music is complex, to be sure, but art has a way of expressing itself according to the demands made upon it. Sessions' music is not less worthy merely because it is of complex tissue. Though some may argue a certain involved pedantry, Sessions' art is of a type which makes him a composer's composer, and it should be recalled that no composer admires pedantry. His music is played rarely; sometimes, paradoxically, this is a mark of true value.

His harmony achieves diatonic stability by the contradictory use of chromatic placements which act as strengthening rods. Hypertrophy of key does not set in, as it does with the late nineteenth-century composers. Thus, Sessions composes a vital type of music, which is related to the most creative and intellectual past, but is new. At the risk of lecturing, it is suggested that the auditor endeavor to orientate himself to this factor of free tonal technique. Once it is accepted, Sessions' music becomes the impressive art it most definitely is.

A representative amount of his work has been recorded, affording a listener the opportunity to come to know this music, with its devotion to an ideal—music that refuses to play to the gallery, repudiates the habits of a romanticist, declines to be anything other than the product of an independent mind. Three of Sessions' major works are available on records, each the second work composed in its respective medium—symphony, sonata, and string quartet. (It is good to know that CRI will soon issue the first symphony, an early, but excellent work.)

ORCHESTRAL

SUITE FROM "THE BLACK MASKERS"

Early Sessions is represented, in this instance. The suite was drawn from incidental music composed for the Andreyev play, when it was produced at Smith College in 1923. It comprises four movements: a "Dance," then a "Scene," which includes the music Sessions composed for the third scene of the drama, followed by a "Dirge," and a finale in moderately slow tempo. The orchestral sounds are a mine of information, though no specific line-by-line musical explication of the text was attempted. Present, however, is a fevered, ultracolored spirit. One example of this is when the music delineates "malicious laughter, cries of agony and despair." The wondrous effect of the organ in the latter part of the work is a timbre stroke to be anticipated. It is not the Sessions of the Second String Quartet or Second Symphony one hears in this work; it is, rather, the young Sessions who wrote this heady and exciting music to complement the visual-verbal magic of dramatic art.

In terms of interpretation and sonic qualities this record deserves a triple-A rating.

——Eastman-Rochester Symphony Orchestra, Howard Hanson, cond. MERCURY 50106 (with Hovhaness: Prelude and Quadruple Fugue, and Lo Presti: The Masks).

SYMPHONY No. 2

Begun in 1944 and completed in 1946, Sessions' symphony is dedicated to the memory of Franklin Delano Roosevelt, who died during its composition. The music is of great expressiveness, with a tonality span that is as far-reaching as possible without intruding upon the domain of free tonality, or the reconstitution of harmonic materials into the regulated order of a twelve-tone composition. This symphony is on the scale of late Beethoven, with comparable introspective qualities. It is not an attempt to compose in imitation of Beethoven; Sessions expresses the most convincing aspects of a true, unified art work. In working with such serious, musically creative intent, his music seems to be free of sentiment; it sounds cold. But that is simply a matter of his refusing to direct his sounds toward the undiscriminating.

There are four movements, the tempi reflecting the classical compound of end divisions at fast speed, with a capricious second movement, followed by an expressive slow movement. The symphony was commissioned by the Ditson Fund, administered by Columbia University, and received two prizes: the Naumburg Award and the 1951 New York Music Critics' Circle Award. This is the type of music that shows Mitropoulos at his best, thus the performance is a most understanding one.

——New York Philharmonic Symphony Orchestra, Dimitri Mitropoulos, cond. COLUMBIA ML-4784 (with Milhaud: Symphony No. 1).

INSTRUMENTAL

Organ

CHORALE (No. 1)

A convincing work of virtuosity for the instrument; toccatalike in determination, though titled otherwise. Both renditions are characterized by excellence of registration and balance. The question of choice depends on whether the listener wishes an all-American-music disk or not.

——Marilyn Mason. COUNTERPOINT 522 (with Three Chorale Preludes, and Thomson: Variations on Sunday School Tunes).

——Mildred Andrews. UNIVERSITY RECORDINGS 2 (with Krenek: Sonata; Luebeck: Complete Organ Preludes and Fugues; and Piston: Chromatic Study on the Name of Bach).

THREE CHORALE PRELUDES

A modern slant on Bachian polyphony. Bach's chorale preludes had counterpoint woven around a basic melody; Sessions eliminates the fundamental and merely knits counterpoints. Stern stuff? A bit. But anyone who has heard academic counterpoint knows how much is gained when the rule book is thrown away. Mastery of idiom by the composer and mastery on the part of the performer, plus truly vivid reproduction.

——Marilyn Mason. COUNTERPOINT 522 (with Chorale No. 1, and Thomson: Variations on Sunday School Tunes).

Piano

FROM MY DIARY

No program accompanies these four pieces. Sessions states they were once called "Pages from a Diary," and nothing more. They are like etchings, with somber qualities alternating with lighter ones. None of the pieces could be considered opulent, but none are as dry as Ajemian considers them. Neither are they as vivid as Abramowitsch makes them, however. A major objective of performance is the discovery of the primary element in the music played; neither pianist has accomplished that in this case. Since a choice must be given, the headier approach by Abramowitsch is the less negative of the two performances.

——Bernhard Abramowitsch. MUSIC LIBRARY RECORDINGS MLR-7003 (with Second Sonata).

——Maro Ajemian. MGM E-3218 (with Krenek: Double Concerto for Violin, Piano and Small Orchestra, and Riegger: Sonatina for Violin and Piano).

SECOND SONATA

A symphony for piano, spelling forbidden territory for most pianists. The *"durchkomponiert"* means of this composition do not form the usual symmetries. It is divisible into fast, slow, and relentless (the composer marks the tempo at this place *"misurato e pesante,"* meaning "measured and heavy") sections, but one merges into the next. Sessions' music covers a wide tonal terrain. The road is dissonant but that is merely the modulatory direction in which the harmonies move. One might call this music "atonal," but what an error! Sessions writes in definite tonalities, strengthening and enlarging his music by dissonantly edged sounds; these do not embellish but establish the tonal polarity. The key pole is vibrated but not loosened by the chromatic sounds.

The playing of the sonata is a challenge to any pianist, merely in terms of placing the sounds properly. Abramowitsch accomplishes more than a mere mechanical reading. His musicianship and understanding bring the sonata into perspective; the textures are varied and arresting, the contrasts vivid, and the climaxes arrived at artistically. A high mark for this young German musician.

——Bernhard Abramowitsch. MUSIC LIBRARY RECORDINGS MLR-7003 (with From My Diary).

CHAMBER MUSIC
SECOND STRING QUARTET

Ecstatic, exotic, and extraneous music pours out in such quantity that one wishes fewer composers would devote themselves to such primal escapades. Sessions, whose art is of the most highly elaborated (but undoctrinaire) design, is one composer who does not so indulge himself. Logical unity must not be confused with metaphysical ruminations, else Scriabin becomes the equal of late Beethoven. But behind any technical tale there must be the creative experience of wonder for the listener.

In this quartet Sessions erects a tremendous inner scaffolding for his five-movements-in-one structure. (The work opens with a double fugue, which leads into a very exciting allegro, followed by a slow-paced section—cast in the form of a theme and five variations, then a scherzo, and the closing part in slow tempo, balancing the pace of the opening portion.) The blueprint reveals the composer's inquiring mind; it also attests to his lively imagination. Further, it demands the attention of the listener. And it will hold it. With a creativity that is rare, Sessions takes one through a significant exploration that cannot be described in other than intricate technical prose. But the constructive and artistic consistency of the quartet will be clear to the alert person even if he cannot read a score or fathom a technical dissertation.

The music of this quartet is of such quality that it nullifies the pertinence (or impertinence) of the charge of imitation that haunts so many musical compositions. Sessions' phenomenal newness is akin to the freshness—the lasting freshness—of the music of the great: Beethoven or Bartók; he never can be accused (as Cézanne implied in his criticism of a painting) of writing music that is "horribly like the real thing."

The New Music Quartet disbanded several years ago. Its performance of the Sessions opus is proof of what a loss this was to the chamber-music world. Theirs is truly a wondrous reading of an arch-difficult score.

One question: if a work is composed to be played without a

pause, why separate it by bands on a record? This makes matters easier for a lecturer, for he can find his sonic illustrations, but it does not follow the score or the composer's intentions. Such interruption breaks the continuity which is psychologically important to the total design.

——New Music Quartet. COLUMBIA ML-5105 (with McPhee: Concerto for Piano with Wind Octette Accompaniment).

VOICE WITH ORCHESTRA

IDYLL OF THEOCRITUS

A setting of the tragic love poem concerning Simaitha, in love with Delphis, who has left her. She relates the story of their love, Delphis' desertion and her vow to poison him. The scope of the poem is huge and the task of translating it into a huge dramatic solo piece for voice and orchestra might well have confounded many a composer, but not Roger Sessions. His music is magical— every part of its over-forty-minute length. No conservative splicing of words to musical description is attempted, save at a few points, and then the implication is subtle. The music spins out with sheer power, convincing by its tragic coloring, its checked and unchecked frenzy. There is no declamation, no song-speech; it is totally an aria of symphonic dimensions, framed by the richly-textured orchestral background. The all-encompassing viewpoint gives this old tale the form of a modern monodrama.

The entire text is furnished with the recording and, with the soloist's excellent diction, is a great aid in listening to the work. Miss Nossaman's voice is superb and only rarely does the orchestra overpower her. No Sessions piece is easy to perform; the Louisville group deserve plaudits for their excellence. No less credit belongs to those who made the decision to request this composition—still another in the long list of credits that mark the Louisville commissions.

——Louisville Orchestra; Audrey Nossaman, soprano; Robert Whitney, cond. LOUISVILLE COMMISSIONING SERIES LOU-57-4.

23. *Harold Shapero*
(1920—   )

HAROLD SHAPERO HOLDS A DISTINCT PLACE IN THE SCHOOL OF AMERI-
can composers due to his unstinting regard for the creative doctrines of the neoclassic school. It is not that he is an imitator.
What Shapero is bent on doing (and has done in an amazing
fashion) is giving musical classicism a thoroughgoing revival. The
sanctities of Beethoven are respected by way of (out of) Stravinsky. Combined with this is a tremendous rhythmic vitality, hewn
straight out of the clarity found in triadal associations.

His study with Slonimsky, Krenek, and Piston furnished a
strong background in essentials; the creative method of the last,
especially, can be found in the clean workmanship of Shapero's
music. Later study with Hindemith and Nadia Boulanger (Shapero's teachers constitute a blue-book of mentors) also left some
marks on his personality. The combined influences of these teachers might have resulted in a rather aimless musical sampling on the
part of a weak composer. Harold Shapero, however, is a powerful
personality. Whatever he does he does meticulously. He reminds
one of the phrase by Epictetus: ". . . consider what precedes and
what follows, and then undertake it." From intensive research
Shapero has constructed theories for his specific purpose that are
close to the classic ideal. His vocabulary is fortunately larger than
that used by the older neoclassic composers when they began their
work. His choice is not helter-skelter, or eclectic; he blends all his
materials together rather than using them as isolated techniques.
Thus the choice of pandiatonic materials for a dramatic climax
is not a stylistic impropriety. A remarkable newness (without a
completely new vocabulary) is to be recognized in the work of this
composer from Massachusetts.

Four works constitute Shapero's recorded catalogue. A fifth
work, the first piano sonata, has been deleted from the lists (New
Editions 1). Unlike one of his teachers, Hindemith, this creative
artist works at an extremely slow pace. The number of works recorded is in proper ratio to his output.

ORCHESTRAL

CREDO FOR ORCHESTRA

The spirit of this piece lies in its expressivity, cleanliness of musical thought, and preciseness of logic. This is music with a straightforward meaning, conveying a sense of positive creation, if not of startling discovery. The piece does not dig deeply; it has action but is of the type that exhilarates rather than excites—it is emotional. Such truthfulness must be accepted whether one is pro- or anti- the neoclassic school of composers. The performance is passably good and the engineering likewise.

——Louisville Orchestra, Robert Whitney, cond. LOUISVILLE COMMISSIONING SERIES LOU-56-5 (with Muczynski: Piano Concerto No. 1, and Orrego-Salas: Serenata Concertante).

SYMPHONY FOR CLASSICAL ORCHESTRA

Or: "Classical Symphony for Orchestra"—a slight tinge of Berlioz, but mainly the influence is Beethoven. No trickery is involved. Shapero's symphony is a remarkable manifestation of absolute music based on classical tenets. There is no story to be followed. Though predominantly harmonic, the textures are balanced; tonality is extensive, but based on a regular scale. The symphony's metrical order is equally extensive, but the phrases are determined with rigid attention to weight, length, and curve in their total relation to the placement of all accents (either directly stressed or of the agogic kind). The forms are dependent yet independent, being enrichments of classical models.

The initial thought when listening to this symphony will probably be Stravinsky. Incorrect. Shapero's expert music is related to Stravinsky as is early Haydn to the work of Beethoven's middle period. Warm rhythms, structural amplitude, limpid humor, combined with modern music substance make this symphony a wonder of emotional depth. The work is one of the very best produced by the composer.

The performance also is very good, despite its being by a pick-up band of musicians, and the sound is good. However, the liner notes (nearly four columns' worth) give nary a word about Shapero's symphony.

———Columbia Symphony Orchestra, Leonard Bernstein, cond. COLUMBIA ML-4889.

String Orchestra

SERENADE FOR STRING ORCHESTRA

The "Serenade" is an exploration of the byways of classical form and spirit, developed in a form of creative courtship. Shapero's music is diverting but not a divertimento. The composition is equivalent to a classical refresher course given in terms of modern pedagogy, its fresh spirit being further proof of an original production. (The rhythmic sweep of this music suggests that Shapero could well write exciting, classically clean ballet music.) The frictions are not on the surface, but integral, made by the placement of dynamics, the arrangement of chords, the spacing of sounds.

A difficult work to play: the composer's ideas result in subtly colored orchestration which is complex in its notation and minutiae, but Winograd achieves the best performance of the many he has made for MGM. An individual recording of top quality.

———Arthur Winograd String Orchestra, Arthur Winograd, cond. MGM E-3557.

INSTRUMENTAL

Piano Duet

SONATA FOR PIANO FOUR HANDS

Utilizing a rare medium in music today, Shapero's piano duet is a further example of his fine neoclassic craft.

Berlioz once described music as containing both sentiment and science. It is this principle that makes possible the enjoyment of complex art by both the technically wise musician and the non-technically-informed auditor. A misconception on the part of both, however, has sometimes been manifested in the approval of bad music by equally bad composers. The technician is deluded by false logic; the auditor is overimpressed by pretentious inflations which he mistakes for disciplined art. The ability to combine science with sentiment, but without sentimentality, is the sign of a good composer writing good music. Neither a fellow composer nor a listener will err in approving this duet. It consists of tight bands of counterpoint and rhythm. Shapero's music is crystal clear, its fricative warmth pointing up a twentieth-century pianistic tale.

The composer and Smit make a well-matched team. They play with smooth tone when required, or express themselves percussively when that dynamic needling is demanded. Columbia furnishes excellent sound for this excellent music.

——Harold Shapero and Leo Smit. COLUMBIA ML-4841 (with Cowell: Sonata No. 1 for Violin and Piano).

24. Virgil Thomson
(1896—   )

VIRGIL THOMSON IS AN EXTRAORDINARY MUSICAL INDIVIDUAL— successful in every possible endeavor. He is at home on the stage as a lecturer and conductor. His ability as a performer is no less outstanding. He has composed in virtually every medium, from sonatas to symphonies, from quartets to operas, from musical portraits, for which the person concerned sits while the composer sketches, to successful movie scores. But, to throw in a not unrelated aside, the facts of his career are more mundane than the homespun yet seminihilistic aesthetics of his music. Thomson may well be called an American prototype of Erik Satie, composing in the same neoclassic manner, but without the present-day pandiatonic obsession or polyharmonic greediness—a kind of creator of the concert-hall *Gemütlichkeit*.

His sensitivity and wide knowledge made him one of the most individual critics of all time, the kind of critic long absent from the American scene and, thus, thrice welcome. It is unfortunate that after years of the peppiest criticism known in the land Thomson has resigned his post as chief music critic of the New York *Herald Tribune*. Because of his many activities, one may regard Thomson as a one-man all-American musical team; yet he has nothing of the jack-of-all-master-of-none stigma. His imprint on contemporary musical life is deep and clear. Having avoided the plush comfort of any accepted style of the day, he stands by himself as one of the most individual of composers; yet he composes in a style that is immediately recognizable, understandable, and exportable, too.

His recording history has been marked by a number of ten-inch releases, now hard to come by. These include Ormandy's version of music from *Louisiana Story* and Thomson's own conducting of his "Five Portraits" (Columbia ML-2087). Another film suite— *The Plow That Broke the Plains*—was performed by the Little Orchestra Society on Decca DL-7527. Further, some cute "Synthetic Waltzes" were on Columbia 2147. In the twelve-inch class the most serious deletion has been of *Four Saints in Three Acts*, a major opus that should be revived without delay. It can be searched for among record rarities under Victor LCT-1139. Some other works also need recording: the piano etudes, the short orchestra pieces, and the Blake songs. What is available includes some good stuff, some run-of-the-mill items, and indicates that the scope can well be broadened. This is the eternal cry on behalf of the contemporary composer—in Thomson's case it is no less important.

ORCHESTRAL

ACADIAN SONGS AND DANCES FROM "LOUISIANA STORY"

Thomson's ability to underscore moods and plot sequence make him an excellent composer for the films. He is too individual for the commercial movie production, despite his easy-to-comprehend style, and is not eclectic in the manner of the Steiner coterie. Nonetheless, he conceived a refreshing and very original music for Paddy Chayevsky's *The Goddess*, a Columbia Picture. Thomson's talents have been mainly sought by documentary film producers, for whom his scores have been very telling. (Those for Pare Lorentz' *The Plow That Broke the Plains* and *The River*, with Robert Flaherty's *Louisiana Story*, are the most important.) The latter has the distinction of having won a Pulitzer Prize—the first ever given for film music. Orchestral suites have been drawn from these scores, the "Acadian Songs and Dances" being the second set of extracts from the full *Louisiana Story* score. It consists of seven movements. This folksy music is keyed to set designs and scored with a very fluid viewpoint, registering with an inconspicuous type of urbanity. Scherman's performance is acceptable, with no critical disagreement possible.

——Little Orchestra Society, Thomas Scherman, cond. DECCA DL-9616 (with Copland: Suite from "The Red Pony").

THE MOTHER OF US ALL—SUITE FOR ORCHESTRA

Opera without words. American as all get-out, with the Gertrude Stein libretto centering around the career of Susan B. Anthony, the pioneer woman suffragist. Thomson's synthesis covers overture material, a winter picture-scene with the swirl of leaves and whistling strings, hymn tunes, and general Americana. It is all a period piece, expressively descriptive, and makes nice music,

story or not. This is Thomson's forte: the genre painting for
musical instruments. Included in the score are themes which
sound like folk melodies, but which are Thomson's beautiful imitations of the real thing. This composer's reminiscences of old
dances, ballads, and hymns comprise a special class of national
music. Janssen's orchestra is good, in fact, it is very good. The
antonym describes the fact that it is no longer in existence.
——Janssen Symphony of Los Angeles, Werner Janssen, cond.
COLUMBIA ML-4468 (with Concerto for Cello and Orchestra).

Band

A SOLEMN MUSIC

Commissioned in 1949 to write a work to mark the birthday of
the famed Goldman Band, Thomson carried out his assignment
in a musical lament. The choice of theme was dictated by the
deaths of two very close friends; Gertrude Stein, the writer and
Christian Bérard, the painter.

This music is solemn indeed, and sometimes boring. This is not
because Thomson indulges in a type of purified twelve-tone technique. There are gentle clashes which can be termed neo-Grego-
rian. Whatever the description the music is unworthy of Thomson.
Fennell's group achieves homogeneity through stylistic attention
to the dissonant writing. The other works by H. Owen Reed,
Peter Mennin, Vincent Persichetti, and Howard Hanson are much
better. Band music wears long pants now—it is worth everyone's
attention.
——Eastman Symphonic Wind Ensemble, Frederick Fennell,
cond. MERCURY 50084 (with Hanson: Chorale and Alleluia; Mennin: Canzona; Persichetti: Psalm; and Reed: La Fiesta Mexicana).

SOLO INSTRUMENT WITH ORCHESTRA

Concertos

CONCERTO FOR CELLO AND ORCHESTRA

Thomson's concerto is a three-ply example of Americana. The
energetically alive first movement, titled "Rider on the Plains,"
is followed by "Variations on a Southern Hymn," and the work
is completed by a rondo-designed movement, "Children's Games."

This is homespun music, rather than having the basic formalism most usual in the concerto medium. The style seems to be an insolent intruder into the sanctity generally inhabited by a solo instrument with orchestra, but it must not be forgotten that Thomson's intention is to entertain and to hell with convention and praise be pleasurable convictions.

This concerto makes the cello ascend most often into the upper part of its range and the resultant tightness of sonority is not aided by unresonant sound. But take it or leave it, it is a gladsome work in the solo-with-orchestra sphere.

——Janssen Symphony of Los Angeles; Luigi Silva, cello; Werner Janssen, cond. COLUMBIA ML-4468 (with The Mother of Us All—Suite for Orchestra).

INSTRUMENTAL

Harpsichord

SONATA No. 4 (GUGGENHEIM JEUNE)

The Fourth Sonata is one of Thomson's musical portraits, written ("drawn," the composer says) from life; the sitter "posing" as he would for a painter. This is, without facetiousness, a clever means to an end, for the resemblance can only be projected in terms of the composer's inner subjectivity—it necessarily is heard quite differently by the auditor. One person's meat is, etc., etc. And how describe a fat person? By jocose music? Doesn't hair or lack of it affect a personality? The business of "drawing from life" is a crutch on which the composer leans with a snicker. Yet, the persons who have "sat" for Thomson have ranged from Picasso to Fiorello La Guardia, from Dorothy Thompson to Aaron Copland.

This three-movement work limns Peggy Guggenheim, who was (com)posed on May 1, 1940. From a hearing of the sonata she would seem to be a person of many facets, but it may be that knowing the subject influences one's thinking. In any event, a good sonata, with good ideas. Miss Guggenheim must have been very pleased with Thomson's study of her in black and white sonorities. From her performance Miss Marlowe must have been pleased with Miss Guggenheim also. And so are we pleased.

——Sylvia Marlowe. New Editions 3 (with Hovhaness: Quartet for Flute, Oboe, Cello and Harpsichord; Lessard: Toccata in Four Movements; and Rieti: Sonata All'Antica).

Organ

FANFARE

Approximately two minutes of Virgil Thomson concerning himself with the past and future simultaneously. Some *echt*-Bach, some *echt*-Thomson, mostly a progress through academic fields with some glances toward greener fields. Not an interesting essay, but most of the pieces in Ellsasser's recital are. (These include music by Vaughan Williams, Karg-Elert, and the organist himself.)

——in "A Richard Ellsasser Concert," Richard Ellsasser. MGM E-3005.

PASTORALE ON A CHRISTMAS PLAINSONG

Music in smooth-surfaced variation form. It is as picturesque as a floral arrangement. The pungency of dissonantal counterpoint marks some of the sections, but this is a Thomson device that adds fizz to the general flavor. The penultimate variant incorporates the carol "God Rest Ye, Merry Gentlemen," and again one is reminded of why Thomson has been called an American Satie, a make-funner of music. But he is serious even when he is witty. One enjoys listening to this type of musical conversationalist. The organ is given uncommonly excellent reproduction and Ellsasser is a musician who understands contemporary manners.

——in "Organ Music by Modern Composers—Volume 1," Richard Ellsasser. MGM E-3064.

VARIATIONS ON SUNDAY SCHOOL TUNES

The "king" of instruments is hardly ever the means of having some fun, but Thomson's set of "proof-fooling" variants is double-compounded wit. First, the heavy-heavy-hangs-over-your-head sound of the organ is especially prone to clumsiness if not treated properly and that means respectfully. Thomson mixes the serious with the profane here even to the extent of using tone clusters. Second, he minces the basic tunes into a sort of Gertrude Stein– E. E. Cummings amalgam. This might be called the Thomsonian power of Frenchified musical thinking in terms of high-class corn, but it is tasteful corn. It is nice to listen to music that does not dot all the i's and is purposely overpunctuated. Thomson's liking for hymns (they are used in at least two of his symphonies) is a true illustration of an American source fruitfully employed. But the Lord help the church-employed organist who dares to play these variations in his place of business!

Suggestion: listen to the first variation and then the third; these are the best of the four. Performance: inspired, and with faultless sound. Recommended for organists, music lovers, and all other semi-adventurous souls.

——Marilyn Mason. COUNTERPOINT 522 (with Sessions: Chorale No. 1; Three Chorale Preludes).

Piano

ECCENTRIC DANCE

This is a nervous type of music, acceptable (according to the publisher) for piano students in their third year of work. It illustrates fulfilling two objectives in two minutes of composition. It was composed in April of 1948, as another of Thomson's multitudinous portraits—this one of Kristians Tonny, an artist—and so it is not simply an exercise; to an extent an adult listener can also enjoy it. It is a good example of what one can do with little spurts of rhythms which run up and down and repeat themselves, chasing the tail of the precise and very neat harmonies which prop them. The collection covers ten composers and is worth acquiring.

——in "Piano Music for Children by Modern American Composers," Marga Richter. MGM E-3147.

CHAMBER MUSIC

STRING QUARTET NO. 2

The waltz that is almost inevitable in any Thomson chamber-music work is found in the second movement of this quartet. To dare to write a movement in strict waltz style attests to Thomson's honesty as a composer devoted to unostentatious music. As usual with this composer, the tonality frame is explicit. The key of D major moves to D minor, stirs itself to a chromatic section, then returns to D major. This folk movement is a pleasant contrast to the opening portion, which has Mozartian drive and grace in its neoclassic action. Movement three moves with gentle seriousness and also with a tango step in its central part. Though Thomson writes in a simple, fresh, and healthy manner, he does not hesitate to use refractional techniques. In the final part of the quartet (a rondo-formed section with its principal idea in dogmatic G major) the opening movement's theme is employed with changed tactics, and the slow movement's subject is elaborated by being propelled at almost twice its original speed and combined, as well, with the final movement's own initial theme. But such techniques of transmutation and transformation do not interfere with this quartet's exultant spirit. Still waters do run deep! The Juilliard gentlemen have done justice to this.

——Juilliard String Quartet. COLUMBIA ML-4987 (with Schuman: Voyage).

VOCAL

STABAT MATER FOR SOPRANO AND STRING QUARTET

An example of the sober charm, the salty elegance that distinguishes typically French music. And correctly so, one might argue, in music composed by an American to a French text (by Max Jacob). Though Debussy and Ravel walk through the pages of Thomson's vocal-string quintet, they are reflected in such features as paraphrased style accents, not directly imitated. There are no complex curvatures or stubby sounds in Thomson's music; it simply floats with dignified lightness. Both Tourel and the New Music group are sensitive to the finest degree. High-level Thomson music with comparable execution.

——Jennie Tourel, mezzo-soprano; New Music String Quartet. COLUMBIA ML-4491 (with Capital, Capitals, and Harrison: Suite for Cello and Harp; Suite No. 2 for String Quartet).

Vocal Ensemble

CAPITAL, CAPITALS

Formula: text by Gertrude Stein, music by Virgil Thomson. The text is word-bound sets of static articulations which give neither question nor answer, but produce verbal music through a cubistic jargon the equivalent of Stravinsky's "*Sacre*" rhythms; the music is bared of everything save simple chord support, close to a parody of Mozartian *recitativo secco.*

Gertrude Stein is both the hero and heroine of this "capital" work (a dialogue among four towns). Thomson is quite subsidiary, but that is to his credit, for in underplaying he steals the show in the long run. This underplaying takes a long time, but such is the strategy. No better proof can be offered of why Gertrude Stein should be read aloud. Off-beat in style, an open-and-shut illustration of musical hedonism. It will reward any listener.

——Joseph Crawford, tenor; Clyde S. Turner, tenor; Joseph James, baritone; William C. Smith, bass; Virgil Thomson, piano. COLUMBIA ML-4491 (with Stabat Mater, and Harrison: Suite for Cello and Harp; Suite No. 2 for String Quartet).

CHORAL

My Shepherd Will Supply My Need
Thomson has a gift for vocal writing, and setting a paraphrased psalm tune (by Isaac Watts) is his invitation to unpretentious composition. The merit of this work is its beauty of simplicity and the beauty is unmarred, save by the sound of the recording; one of vintage date by the standards of present-day LP. But, a worthy collection of choral music.

——Stanford Chorale, Harold Schmidt, cond. Music Library Recordings MLR-7022 (with Motets, Chansons, Madrigals, Folk Songs).

Psalm 123 and Psalm 136 (from "Three Antiphonal Psalms")
Listening to these unaccompanied two-part choruses it may well be realized how Virgil Thomson reflects his particular creative situation. This is music that is traditionally serious, yet the composer's actual conservatism is not as bland as one might think.

The first psalm is with few exceptions single-stranded. It spreads into two parts in one case, with ancient organum parallel running of the voices. But in no case is it antiphonal. In Psalm 136 naturalness gives way to the contrary treatment. The ostinato on five words is of unusual flavor. Intimate and sensitive music, right-wing *avant garde,* if one may use such a paradoxical term.

The collection in which these psalms are included is a cross-section that covers plainsong, the sixteenth century, Bach, early Americana, and Russian church music. A lively compilation, well done.

——Divinity School Choir, Yale University, James Borden, cond. OVERTONE LP-2.

BALLET

FILLING STATION

From the title it will be clear that this is an American opus. The characters and the plot are out of the Sunday supplements: the station attendant—a first-class mechanic and the typical American Boy—Pop and Mom (the latter the ruler of the roost), truck drivers, a nasty, precocious child, a state trooper, a gangster, *et al.* But the music, while simple in the extreme, is very appealing and not merely facile. Writing down is not Thomson's intent, though the American salon, *echt*-vernacular style that is employed comes dangerously close to concert vaudeville music. The score is a typical musical soufflé, including the clever use of "We Won't Be Home Until Morning," and is, with its variety-hall inclusion of a waltz, a tango, and the once-popular "Big Apple," music that one can drink cocktails to, work to, or merely listen to. The performance is adroit, the sound has some minor faults.

——New York City Ballet Orchestra, Leon Barzin, cond. Vox PL-9050 (with Kay: Western Symphony).

25. Edgar Varèse
(1885—   )

M<small>ULTITUDINOUS</small> "<small>ISMS</small>" <small>HAVE STALKED THROUGH THE ARTS, FROM</small> theoretical definitions and critical discussions of "classicism," "romanticism," etc., to manifestoes proclaiming "futurism," "dadaism," etc. Today we are in the midst of the age of "serialism" or what might be called "numberism." Consider then a man who really ran far ahead of the creative pack; who, as far back as the early '20's, conceived an entirely new means of composing music, one without any parallel until the present, when many of the young experimentalists are employing certain of the techniques he perfected.

To some Varèse is a god, to others he is a maker of noise; a few call him a primitive, and a fair number term him a fraud. Varèse is none of these, for he is simply a composer of honest music. He can be correctly called a pioneer—an innovator. Both terms are comfortable and fit. Pioneers do their pioneering deliberately. Varèse accomplished his by writing music that was spitting new because, strangely enough, he believed that no truthful creative person is ahead of his time, despite the fact that most people live with art of the dim past. This attitude toward the present happens to be very suspect in the arts, though it is the accepted view in the sciences, in the perfecting of language and communication, and in simple, day-to-day living.

The "ism" that Varèse espoused was pure "unacademicism." This commitment made him the first composer to employ totally pure atonalism. His innovations have resulted in his becoming a classic during his lifetime. The cry of catastrophe that marks any great newness in art—from Picasso to Joyce to Schoenberg—has always been proved wrong. Time heals all artistic wounds and brings understanding. Time has been kind to Varèse.

Varèse's teachers included Vincent d'Indy, Albert Roussel, and Charles Widor. Although his style is as far from that of these men as the earth is from Mars, the use of balance and contrast—preached in any academy—is mandatory in any art form. Only the means of application are different. As regards tonality, no har-

213

monic consonant-dissonant relationship is posited in Varèse's work. These antitheses are relative, after all, and the parallel concepts of passivity and activity, or the obverse, of tension and release, are given subtle formulation in his sound masses. No melodic subject (in the general meaning of the term) is utilized, since this would be foreign to his style and purpose. The chunks and hunks of tone —material Varèse sculpts—have been called "organized sound." This is his music, exactly.

This method of composition sets its own standards. The disciplines are violent color contrasts, timbre predicated not on average sounds but on utilization of instrumental ranges in which the extremes become the neutral territory, plus the most productive blending of opposites. Rhythm is paramount and is basically asymmetrical, both in apportionment and design. The ultimate concept of the rhythmic pulse evades outright definition, makes itself evident by being condensed into varied motival spurts, repeated like static and dynamic electrical shocks. In its way a Varèse composition is like the most modern of machines; streamlined, aluminum-bright, and as precision-built as any computer. This is not a music of sentiment; it is a music of power. To paraphrase a well-known saying: Varèse's music is frozen architecture.

Varèse's works are exceedingly few—just over a dozen. For a long time he refused to compose because he lacked the means to obtain the exact sonic effects he desired; absolute pitch, no oscillation of a tone by vibrato, and sound of inconceivable dynamic intensity or duration. His use of conventional instruments in an unconventional manner was a forced compromise. In 1953 the impasse was broken and he wrote *"Déserts,"* for winds and percussion with interpolated pre-recorded, taped material; in 1958 he composed the first work which embodied all his hoped-for effects, the *"Poème Électronique,"* for performance at the Brussels Exposition. This was first recorded and then performed by distribution over four hundred loudspeakers.

The four Varèse works available on records are, one can say, an adequate introduction to his music. "Arcana," a tremendous work for a huge orchestra and large percussion section, will make a fifth release, since it has been selected for recording by the American section of the International Music Fund.

ORCHESTRAL

Chamber Orchestra

INTÉGRALES

In this opus Varèse combines a percussion assemblage of eight metal, four membrane, and three wood instruments, plus a string drum (sometimes called a lion's roar) and a rute (a birch brush), with an extremely colorful assortment of melodic instruments. These include a pair of piccolos, high and normal-range clarinets, oboe, horn, two very high trumpets, and high, low, plus very low trombones. Thus a duple stream of sound is set into motion, forming its own special design—a design wherein tensility is of major importance, where ejaculatory portions of cutting timbres mix with bare, overpowering silences, and sonic weights are varied, forming manifold patterns within patterns.

A fantastic mastery of working materials and stylistic unity is displayed. Beauty is here as well—a beauty of cold instrumental logic that burns the ears with its magical diapason. Verily, strong music by a strong composer.

The performances of all the music that Waldman conducts on the EMS disk are truly amazing. Varèse's music is as difficult for performers as for those who hear it for the first time.

——in "Complete Works of Edgard Varèse—Volume 1," New York Wind Ensemble and Juilliard Percussion Orchestra, Frederic Waldman, cond. EMS 401. (*N.B. The use of "Edgard" is not correct, but was apparently sanctioned by the composer.*)

OCTANDRE

A rare musical title (a flower with eight stamens) and just as rare for the medium of the chamber orchestra. Although eight players equal an octet, "*Octandre*" demands a conductor and thus belongs in the category to which it has been assigned. Nor is the brutal explosiveness of its sound of chamber-music intimacy.

The timbres are allied in family name only: flute (also piccolo), oboe, clarinet (at times the small E-flat type), and bassoon (winds) are combined with a brass group of horn, trumpet, and trombone, plus the stringed bass. There are three movements but no suite design is implied. This is Varèse and the old formal categories do not apply; what we hear are streams of polyphony making eight sides of a musical edifice.

——in "Complete Works of Edgard Varèse—Volume 1," New York Wind Ensemble, Frederic Waldman, cond. EMS 401.

Percussion

IONISATION

Varèse was the first composer to use percussion instruments alone as a medium for artistic expression. "Ionisation" was completed on November 13, 1931, and represents both superfine creativity and prophetic sonoric discourse. It calls for 13 players who form a spanking-new type of orchestra, tri-divisional in structure. The constituents are metallic, membranous, and wooden. In addition there are rasping (guiro), swishing (maracas), and roaring qualities. (The last is made by an instrument consisting of a wooden barrel with a parchment head through which a rosined string is drawn. The player rubs the string with a piece of cloth or leather.) Tonal instruments complete the catalogue: tubular chimes, high- and low-pitched sirens, the delicate celeste, and the piano, treated frictionally—clusterwise. This is truly a percussive plutocracy.

Varèse's achievement is unique, particularly because he traces and presents the elements of musical architecture with percussion, not relying exclusively on his pitched instruments for the melodic representation or the unpitched instruments for rhythm. The tutti, as a unit and as separate members, perform in defined elucidations: harmonic, contrapuntal, melodic, within the formal design. They function in a way akin to that of the violent adjectives, verbs, and phrases found on a Picasso canvas.

For percussion players this work holds a place comparable to that of the Beethoven concerto for violinists; the word "famous" is most fitting. And it is not surprising, therefore, that three recordings (plus a sampling) are available of this work. One should have no difficulty in choosing among them. Paul Price's Urania group is masterful; so is Waldman's. But the EMS disk was made ten years ago (1950) and its engineering, good as it was, cannot come even close to Urania's. The real soul of the work becomes apparent with the stabilities, colors in clear perspective, and true sound of the "Sound Barrier" record. Price also is at the controls in the Illinois rendition. It is an excellent presentation, but the engineering of the Urania disk is cleaner.

A word of warning regarding the listing of this piece in the bible of record catalogues, the Schwann. "Ionisation" is listed in Folkways' zestful grab-bag of eighteen out-of-this-world examples titled "Sounds of New Music," and is so designated in the catalogue. But what Schwann does not indicate, nor does Folkways (either on album cover, record label, or booklet of notes), is that it is a mere snippet, some fifty seconds' worth taken from the full composition of almost six minutes' duration. The Folkways album is a real musical adventure of a titillating order, but in the case of Varèse it is unreliable. Further, Schwann lists for this album the same conductor and ensemble as are featured on the EMS disk. Again, there is no corroboration of this on the album's cover listing, label, or descriptive notes. This may be an oversight but the entire matter is misleading and quite irregular. (For those who wish the Folkways record, its number is FX-6160.)

——in "Breaking the Sound Barrier—Vol. 1—Percussion," American Percussion Society, Paul Price, cond. URANIA UX-106.

——in "Complete Works of Edgard Varèse—Volume 1," Juilliard Percussion Orchestra, Frederic Waldman, cond. EMS 401.

——University of Illinois Percussion Ensemble, Paul Price, cond. UNIVERSITY OF ILLINOIS CUSTOM RECORDING SERIES CRS-3 (with Colgrass: Three Brothers; Harrison: Canticle No. 3; and McKenzie: Introduction and Allegro).

INSTRUMENTAL

Flute

DENSITY 21.5

A work that bears the champion of all music titles. It is explained by the fact that Varèse wrote this piece for the famous Georges Barrère, who was planning to introduce a new platinum flute. The density of platinum is the quantity given in the title. Composed in 1936, Varèse revised the work ten years later. It demands a flutist who can obey the minute, ultra-refined markings that detail the homophonic line, in this manner projecting the unstated harmony and also the undulating colors in the various zones of the instrument's three-octave range. The shifts of dynamic are kaleidoscopic and occur at a dizzy pace: for example, sounds totalling one beat louden and immediately return to a very soft pitch, only to rise once again quickly to a still louder point.

Unfortunately, the only performance on records is far from what Varèse has written. Most of the time only three levels of dynamic strength can be distinguished; the music calls for more than a dozen different qualities. In part, this deficiency is due to old recording techniques. Thus, in certain measures the flutist is to articulate sharply, play softly, and hit the keys of his instrument to produce a quasi-percussive effect with the pitched sound. The striking of the keys is not heard at all; certainly the soloist is not at fault here. In concert performance Varèse's novel invention scores with immediate effect.

——in "Complete Works of Edgard Varèse—Volume 1," René Le Roy. EMS 401.

26. Heitor Villa-Lobos
(1887—1959)

THOUGH THE TRANQUIL WORKS OF SECOND-RATE COMPOSERS REQUIRE
little explanation, the quality of a creatively important person's
work cannot be understood merely through study, analysis, and
technical examination. If we are to comprehend the music of a
composer as individual as Villa-Lobos, if we are to get clues to his
thinking, we must take cognizance of his personality.

Villa-Lobos had a very vivid imagination (a boon to those who
listen to his music, but hard going for his biographers and essay-
ists); he was not a Machiavellian, but rather a romantic Paul
Bunyan. He retitled his compositions several times; adapted portions of one section of an old opus to fit in with a new one; believed to such degree in the mythical and apocryphal meanings of
his works that this aspect of them reached a startling level of make-
believe, no matter how he explained it. It is this side of his personality that shines through in the bravado, "derring-do," and verve
of his music; discipline and truth are conveyed by their direct
opposites. His embellishments were the products of an ego that
wrote important music but deceived itself at times, for if Villa-
Lobos and his music had been better controlled, he would not
have said that there were only two great composers—"Bach and
I." Yet exaggeration was the man's virtue; it was Villa-Lobos' big
paint brush swabbing the musical canvas.

It would take a small volume to attempt to explain and codify
his vast corpus of works, which total over two thousand. Such un-
phlegmatic *copia verborum* is more than mere prolific output; it
shows the man's abandon, his absolute unself-consciousness. Thus,
he would write the "fourth" work of a set in one medium, but
never trouble to compose the third! Villa-Lobos was neither personally nor in his music a Lilliputian.

But it must not be thought that his achievements are small. He
is, without a doubt, one of the big lights in twentieth-century
music (though on a lower level than, for example, Stravinsky,
Hindemith, Schoenberg, or Bartók). He is the greatest, and thus,
the most important composer of Latin America. Since he borrowed

heavily from himself, his work does not divide into specific creative periods; his compositions exist as a unit. There are so many different manifestations and irregularities that one can find maturity in an early work, and undiscipline in a late opus. The self-taught composer has proved his ability to play a valid role on the creative stage. Whether study would have diminished Villa-Lobos' fantastic and exotic, classical-romantic-experimental and folkloristic voice rolled into one, is anyone's guess.

Multilingual himself, Villa-Lobos speaks similarly in his music. The range is from the simple to the extreme; from uninvolved harmony to pseudo-atonality. The varnish of sonority is a favorite coloring—his colors are very graphic; the rhythmic forceps grip with the utmost strength (generally—there are exceptions—these rhythms are Brazilian to the core). These are immense values. But this musical Prodigal Son's music lacks trimming down, could do with a little discipline. However, if it had been contracted, if some of the coarseness and the musical errata had been removed, it would have ceased to be Villa-Lobos. It is just this profusion that makes Villa-Lobos come close to his audience, give them an accurate picture of the man through his music.

Bachianas Brasileiras

Ever the revolutionary (in use of instruments, in designing new effects, even to the matter of using the fingers to teach solfeggio), Villa-Lobos has made two formal devices his own. First, the *Chôros* (*discussed below*) and second, what is less a musical form than a type of creative principle—the nine suites (one existing in two versions) titled "*Bachianas Brasileiras*." A free translation of this is the only one possible—"Bachian Brazil Spirit."

These compositions are not imitations of Bach. They are rather exemplifications of the great universal spirit of Bach, so much admired by Villa-Lobos, transmuted into a Brazilian idiom. Thus, the genius of the great Bach sparks and is a guide to the expression of a folkloristic Brazilian spirit. Bachian polyphony is not a major element; there is only a simulation of counterpoint, though the general aspects hint at such style. Although at times the link with Bach is the result of reworking a piece that originally had no such connotation, the classic matter after the national fact is justified, since Villa-Lobos' objective is for the greater part simply homage to Bach. Who can prove that Bach's style (or its contemplation) was not at the source of the earlier conception?

The most complete fusion is obtained by utilizing Bachian titles. To make certain of the hybrid, a parenthetical Brazilian title follows each of these. Thus: in the first of the series an "Introduction" is accompanied by an *"Embolada,"* a *"Prelúdio"* with a *"Modinha,"* and a "Fugue" is partnered with a *"Conversa."* As varied as those of the *Chôros* are the forms, styles, and instrumentations of the nine *"Bachianas Brasileiras."* The fifth is for voice and eight cellos; the ninth is for string orchestra, or an orchestra of voices, etc.

This original and powerful conception contains some of the most creatively abundant music of Villa-Lobos. It is indeed fortunate that all nine suites have been recorded.

Chôros

Originally, the *chôro* was a type of Brazilian street dance, but its free improvisatory feeling, set in melodic lines with incisive rhythms, is merely the primitive mold that Villa-Lobos took and shaped into a new formal creation. The form of the *chôro* is entirely independent of categorization. It is more a generic title for this Brazilian composer's very individual and audacious setting of anything calling for from two instruments to a gargantuan disposition of musical forces (the fourteenth of the set, for example, calls for a large orchestra, plus a band and chorus!). Villa-Lobos has called the *chôros* "Brasilofonia," i.e., the sound of Brazil. It is an extemporaneous outpouring that varies with each work—in grab-bag tempi, in assorted designs, freed of any rigidity, and similarly unordered in its instrumentations.

Since the *chôros* are devoid of formula, each being of individual substance, some express a philosophical idea, or have a general programmatic basis and nothing more. The tenth, for example, concerns "the reaction of civilized man to stark nature"; the eleventh, according to Nicolas Slonimsky, pictures "the unity in diversity of the Brazilian landscape."

By the time Villa-Lobos had completed his eleventh *chôros* he already had produced the proverbial baker's dozen, for in addition to the numbered set he had written an "Introduction to the *Chôros*," and a second to the second! Additional pieces bring the final *chôros* total to sixteen—fourteen numbered ones plus the two special ones. Villa-Lobos had no equal either in complicating matters (as in the numbering plan for these pieces) or in expressing his ego. The "Introduction" was in anticipation of any future plan to present a festival of *chôros*; the "*Chôros* No. 2 *bis*" was to be ready in case of an encore!

From the *chôros* set the following are available on records: No. 1, for solo guitar; No. 4, for three horns and trombone; No. 5, for solo piano; and No. 7 subtitled Septet.

It is a listener's good fortune that no half measures have been applied to the recording of Villa-Lobos' music. Naturally there are important omissions, but in a catalogue of such amplitude this is understandable. There are immense riches in the choices offered in addition to the nine "*Bachianas Brasileiras*" and the several *chôros*. A hearty selection from the piano music is available, and a considerable amount of chamber music, guitar solos, and orchestral compositions. In the case of Heitor Villa-Lobos the record companies have indeed been friendly and sympathetically disposed.

ORCHESTRAL

BACHIANAS BRASILEIRAS No. 2

Most famous for its final movement, which has moved into the high-class division of the pops-concert repertoire, and is already represented in four miscellaneous collections of such material (*see immediately below*). The other parts of the work have an extreme richness of invention. Why the complete "*Bachianas Brasileiras* No. 2*" is given only rare performances is an enigma.

As usual, the parallel between classic titles and native subtitles gives the musical working plan. A "*Prelúdio*" fruitfully conveys the "Song of a *Capadócio*" (a boaster of low character); this is followed by an "*Aria*" ("Song of Our Land") and a "*Dança*" ("Remembrance of the Wild Country"), and finally the "Toccata" ("Little Train of a Rustic"). The intimate fusion of Bach style with the secular-popular music of Brazil is illuminating; new formal conditions thereby construct new musical notions.

It is worth realizing that despite this constructive partnership, all four movements are actually transcriptions; the third was originally a piano piece, the first, second, and fourth were cello and piano compositions. This is no startling fact; it is Villa-Lobos' way of convincing himself (and others) that a new work *is* a new work, but happens to have been an old work. The fact that it will fit into the general plan (here of Bach-Brazil) is coincidental, or it may be schematic—changing the data so it will fit the testimony regardless. One can afford to be liberal when the musical result is as exhilarating as this suite.

There is no choice of recordings, so Villa-Lobos' own will have to suffice. A much greater distinctness of voices and contrasts can be obtained, however. Villa-Lobos was a workaday conductor; his reading is good in terms of tempi, but it lacks expansive capacity. Nonetheless the sound is technically excellent and there is sufficient excitement about the music of this and three other *"Bachianas"* to give enjoyment. A tempting disk.

——Orchestre National de la Radiodiffusion Française, Heitor Villa-Lobos, cond. ANGEL 35547 (with Bachianas Brasileiras Nos. 2, 6, and 9).

BACHIANAS BRASILEIRAS No. 2 ("THE LITTLE TRAIN OF THE CAIPIRA")

It will be observed that the translation of this title does not match that mentioned above in the discussion of the complete work. This is due to the difficulty of literal, as compared with literate, translation. Some have avoided the problem by using a mixture of English with the original (*"caipira"*). Actually, a *"caipira"* is a rude, indolent, and shrewd person of the Brazilian interior. The best translation for this is "rustic," thus: "Little Train of a Rustic."

In any event, Villa-Lobos' train makes musical history. It is the second instance of such locomotion orchestrally pantomimed. The first huffed and puffed, was awesome, monstrous, a tremendous iron machine: Honegger's "Pacific 231." Villa-Lobos' is a special marvel, a wonderful ride of fun, of much better orchestral picture-painting, down to the puffing, the chugging, the screeching, speeding and stopping, and letting the-steam-out-of-the-funnel— plus a tune to travel by. This is far less than a miniature "231," being more of a third-class choo-choo almost ready for the scrap-heap.

Though Kostelanetz comes close, he cannot achieve, nor does the Gould recording achieve, the clarity and sharp outline of Lane's reading. Under this young conductor everything is in perfect balance and all in place. He produces a gem of orchestral camera work. (All the other items on the Lane disk are exceptional; the Epic people must be very happy with this issue.) Kostelanetz has marvelous sound, but his compilation cannot match Lane's assortment, nor can Gould's. Goossens' entry is first-class and with trenchant sound. However, only the desire to own the two major-length Ginastera works would warrant purchasing the Everest disk. For this Villa-Lobos sketch the number one listing is the miscellany bearing the Epic label.

——in "Pop Concert Latin America," Cleveland Pops Orchestra, Louis Lane, cond. EPIC LC-3626.

——London Symphony Orchestra, Eugene Goossens, cond. EVEREST LPBR-6041 (SDBR-3041) (with Ginastera: Estancia; Panambi).

——in "Clair de Lune and Popular Favorites," Andre Kostelanetz and His Orchestra, Andre Kostelanetz, cond. COLUMBIA CL-798.

——in "Grand Tour," Andre Kostelanetz and His Orchestra, Andre Kostelanetz, cond. COLUMBIA CL-981.

——in "Jungle Drums," Morton Gould and His Orchestra, Morton Gould, cond. RCA VICTOR LM-1994.

BACHIANAS BRASILEIRAS NO. 4

Of the nine *"Bachianas Brasileiras,"* this is the only one that exists in two settings. (Menahem Pressler's sterling performance of the original version is discussed in the piano section—*see below, under* Instrumental.) Villa-Lobos made his symphonic transcription in 1941. Result: neither loss nor gain. The peculiarly uncompromising quality of the solo-piano conception highlights the music's dynamic character; it is somewhat softened in the orchestral panorama. Nonetheless, the totally dramatic identity of the Bach–Villa-Lobos compound is revealed either way. It would be worthwhile owning both versions. This would make it possible to have a presentable (if not the best) reading of the first *"Bachianas"* and a handsome recorded interpretation of the seventh.

——Orchestre National de la Radiodiffusion Française, Heitor Villa-Lobos, cond. ANGEL 35674 (with Bachianas Brasileiras No. 7).

BACHIANAS BRASILEIRAS NO. 7

Neither form nor date of composition affected Villa-Lobos' style. He was always true to himself, no matter the difficulty this presented in terms of projecting his technique as a whole. Spontaneity is always present; the sense of improvised music-making suggests a script from which an excellent actor departs.

A first-rate example is available in the rather romantic dress of this classic-national *"Bachianas."* The end movements are patterned on the usual prelude and fugue, save that the latter is of imposing size, a neobaroque transmutation. The middle portions form the rhythmic sandwich which is a feature of the Villa-Lobos menu. Beautifully recorded, certainly definitively conducted.

——Orchestre National de la Radiodiffusion Française, Heitor Villa-Lobos, cond. ANGEL 35674 (with Bachianas Brasileiras No. 4).

BACHIANAS BRASILEIRAS NO. 8

Villa-Lobos' eighth work in the *Bachianas* series is warmed by intense nationalistic expressions. It is (though a certain amount of French impressionism filters into the style) full of both strange, wonderful sonic notions and exotic Brazilian fantasy. It superimposes upon the primitive the sophisticated, plus some compositional manners found in the composer's adored Bach. All of it is logical. Hearing this work, one can understand the creativeness of Villa-Lobos, true to his surroundings, speaking a natural musical language not dictated by hyperacademic tenets.

The highlight is the heart-rending "Aria," subtitled, as is always the case in this set of works, with the native equivalent: *"Modinha."* Villa-Lobos' melody is unforgettable. Bachian dialect will be found in translation in the final fugue, but more especially in the *"Catira Batida,"* which resembles a gigue, adorned newly (and natively) with the percussive sounds of hollowed coconuts of differing pitch. The performance is rather pedestrian but does not dim the beauty of the work.

——Orchestre National de la Radiodiffusion Française, Heitor Villa-Lobos, cond. ANGEL 35179 (with Momoprecoce).

CAIXINHA DE BÔAS FESTAS (*or* VITRINE ENCANTADA)

A children's ballet score. Villa-Lobos must have had real fun in writing this to order for a youth concert by the Philharmonic Orchestra of Rio de Janeiro. (I recall the conductor Burle Marx, now resident in Philadelphia, telling me that Villa-Lobos did not complete this work until just a little before the première. Some fancy-dan copying and emergency rehearsals were necessary.)

The music is grist for this Brazilian composer's mill—merely a succession of tunes strung together, conceived in the spirit of a choreographic potpourri. The cast of characters is engagingly described by the highly colored orchestration, though the story is not necessary for the enjoyment of the music.

Victor calls this work "The Surprise Box," but actually it should be translated as "The Small Holiday Box" (Slonimsky translates it as "Little Box of Holy Night"). Neither does Victor list the second title, which means "Magic Window." But Victor's release is an instance of bright, well-executed orchestral performance, with plenty of brilliant sound.

——Rome Symphony Orchestra, Juan José Castro, cond. RCA VICTOR LM-2143 (with Falla: Homenajes).

DAWN IN A TROPICAL FOREST

Villa-Lobos states that a Brazilian tropical forest is "an *overture* of colors accompanied by the magic singing and chirping of the tropical birds," together with the multitudinous sounds of the native Indians. So be it. No one has bettered him in what might be described as tropical symphonic sound. This humidity of timbre combination, of musically translated febricity, is the principal quality of this piece.

Villa-Lobos' singular orchestrational imagination in music of this kind has been an important guide for the Hollywood boys in their scoring of films dealing with jungle themes. But theirs is an imitation of Villa-Lobos' imitation.

The performance is very good and the clear sound has proper

resonance. Once more an auspicious example of what value has resulted from the Louisville Orchestra's commissioning project. ——Louisville Orchestra, Robert Whitney, cond. LOUISVILLE COMMISSIONING SERIES LOU-545-1 (with Creston: Invocation and Dance, and Stevens: Triskelion).

EROSION—THE ORIGIN OF THE AMAZON RIVER
    A Villa-Lobos musical newsreel. There is no husbanding of materials in this case. Despite a preface which presumably tells the story the music is to document, this is mainly a mural of lush orchestral colors and a sonorous overabundance. In a way, this is Villa-Lobos codifying Villa-Lobos—a kind of sampler of his composition. "Erosion" is an indigenously mirrored manifestation which could only have been conceived by this composer. If the form is uncertain and rhapsodic, the blend is distinctly personal: primitive and cosmopolitan; banal and imaginative. Music worth hearing just occasionally; it will not bear frequent re-hearing. Thus, a commission fulfilled to the letter of the contract and no more. ——Louisville Orchestra, Robert Whitney, cond. COLUMBIA ML-4615 (with Dello Joio: The Triumph of St. Joan Symphony).

UIRAPURÚ, SYMPHONIC POEM
    Early Villa-Lobos, composed in 1917 but revised 31 years later. Nonetheless it has all the characteristics of a mature work, since Villa-Lobos' output cannot be portioned out in the period-of-work pattern which marks that of most other composers. His creative picture is kaleidoscopic; the youthful work and the very latest composition cannot rightfully be compared, for each is singular —paradoxically, time did not play any role in his career or determine his style.
    Taking into account what he had observed during a trip into the Brazilian interior, Villa-Lobos composed this orchestral poem about a legendary enchanted bird. The story is replete with jungle and animal sounds, plus tonal simulation of insects, owls, enchanted toads, bats, glowworms, and so forth. The persuasiveness of the music stems from its folk authenticity. In its way *"Uirapurú"* is Villa-Lobos' *"Sacre."*
    Stokowski is the ideal conductor for this colorful score. It is a welcome addition to the recorded catalogue, filling the gap left by

the deleted Columbia version, which was made under Efrem Kurtz's baton.

——New York Stadium Symphony Orchestra, Leopold Stokowski, cond. EVEREST LPBR-6016 (SDBR-3016) (with "Modinha" from Bachianas Brasileiras No. 1, and Prokofiev: Cinderella-Ballet Music).

String Orchestra

BACHIANAS BRASILEIRAS No. 9

Music of almost formal classic proportions, cast in the form of a prelude and fugue. Bach has had his day in the court of many composers. In this Brazilian's domain he rules regally. The prelude glitters with lyrical splendor; all else is from Bach's polyphonic jewel case.

Why do fugues so often cause a dull performance? Though Villa-Lobos' orchestral direction is not spiritless, the fugue is not as clear as the score shows it should be. Surinach's conducting is prosaic and the playing sounds like professionals sight-reading: the notes are all performed, but sometimes with shaky rhythmic conjunction. MGM offers two possibilities. The all-Villa-Lobos album has four piano works also available on MGM E-3158, while the fifth composition, "*Chôros* No. 7" receives its best rendition on a Capitol disk. If Surinach's performance is chosen, therefore, it is suggested that one buy the E-3444 album which illustrates the work of an outstanding Chilean composer.

——Orchestre National de la Radiodiffusion Française, Heitor Villa-Lobos, cond. ANGEL 35547 (with Bachianas Brasileiras Nos. 2, 5, and 6).

——MGM String Orchestra, Carlos Surinach, cond. MGM E-3444 (with Santa-Cruz: Sinfonia No. 2).

——in "Music by Heitor Villa-Lobos," MGM String Orchestra, Carlos Surinach, cond. MGM E-3516.

Cello Orchestra

BACHIANAS BRASILEIRAS No. 1

Villa-Lobos gives as good as he gets, in this unusual work for a rare grouping of instruments. In reciprocation of the Bach spirit he offers Brazilian ethos, and sets this blend for an orchestra unlike any other—one of eight cellos. This combination makes a rich instrumental mintage. The forms of the end movements dip into Bach waters by way of a prelude movement and a "*Conversa*," meaning "conversation"—a true synonym for a fugue. Likewise the middle movement; the deep sentiment which imbues this part's long line, together with the music's scope, are Bachian exemplifications.

Ringing changes on the old and creating something new is not a sign of compromise. Villa-Lobos is often an unrestrained composer, but he is in this "*Bachianas*" a controlled, powerful, contributory creator.

Of the versions listed below the palm goes to Janssen because he plays the fugue as a piece of musical colloquy and not as a heavy academic lecture. Otherwise, both the Janssen and Slatkin releases are ideal. Bloomfield takes a pedestrian pace in the slow movement and is perfunctory in his contrapuntal survey. There is this to note: all three disks are completely given over to the Brazilian composer's music; Janssen's is the most important in this respect.

——Chamber Group, Werner Janssen, cond. CAPITOL P-8147 (with Chôros No. 4; Chôros No. 7).

——Concert Arts Cello Ensemble, Felix Slatkin, cond. CAPITOL P-8484 (SP-8484) (with Bachianas Brasileiras No. 5, and Bach-Villa-Lobos: Prelude and Fugue No. 8 for orchestra of celli).

——Cello Ensemble, Theodore Bloomfield, cond. MGM E-3105 (with Bachianas Brasileiras No. 4).

BACHIANAS BRASILEIRAS NO. 1 ("MODINHA")
Used as filler material, but elegantly accomplished; in this regard, a bonus for the purchaser.

——New York Stadium Symphony Orchestra, Leopold Stokowski, cond. EVEREST LPBR-6016 (SDBR-3016) (with Uirapurú, and Prokofiev: Cinderella—Ballet Music).

FANTASIA CONCERTANTE
Instrumentalists tend to be sectarian in their associations. There have long been separate groups of pianists, singing teachers, organists, string players, and the like. The New York Flute Club is a highly respected and important organization. While no oboe society exists, or group of trombonists, the time may yet come

when such lodges will be formed. The latest of these fraternities to be formed is the Violoncello Society, founded in May, 1956. Villa-Lobos' piece was especially written for this group, premièred on December 10, 1958, and then recorded under the composer's direction.

It is not a work written merely to keep a promise—a commission delivered. The "Fantasia" represents music of authenticity, of nationalistic classicism as observed and practiced by the composer—personal in sound, with Villa-Lobos (read: Brazil) for its source. Especially compelling is the melting beauty of the haunting slow movement; the others are of more idiomatic Bachian order.

Villa-Lobos' fondness for the cello derives from the fact that early in his career he played the instrument in the theaters and moving-picture houses of Rio de Janeiro. His consideration of the special color of a cello orchestra (no trickery; it does give an individual blend, not one disposed to imitate other instruments) has resulted in a pair of *"Bachianas Brasileiras"* (Nos. 1 and 5); this work could really be listed with them, as a third.

Despite a collection of 32 distinguished cellists (Bernard Greenhouse of the Beaux-Arts Trio, Claus Adam of the Juilliard String Quartet, and the soloists Janos Scholz and Luigi Silva among them), some sloppy intonation in unisons, especially in the high tessitura, occurs; it is inconceivable it was unheard by the composer or the editor. This is the only flaw. Otherwise don't hesitate: this is a distinguished work and performance to match. Powerful sound.

——Violoncello Society, Heitor Villa-Lobos, cond. EVEREST LPBR-6024 (SDBR-3024) (with Bach–Villa-Lobos: Preludes and Fugues from *The Well-Tempered Clavier*, transcribed for orchestra of violoncellos).

SOLO INSTRUMENT WITH ORCHESTRA

BACHIANAS BRASILEIRAS NO. 3, FOR PIANO AND ORCHESTRA

Quite often, when a composer thinks he has fashioned a brand-new structural pattern he (more often, we) will discover that no matter what disposition he makes of his material a fundamental relationship exists between it and the forms followed through the centuries. Villa-Lobos' third *"Bachianas"* is a compound of free design plus established tenets. Because it is related to the old (by way of a *"Prelúdio,"* "Fantasia," "Aria," and "Toccata"), the new (these movements translated into *"Ponteio,"* and the Brazilian equivalents of a "Revery," a "Love Song," and a "Woodpecker") is not shining bright. Neither is it hackneyed. Much of the time the music is mere tune-plus-accompaniment, thus much Brazilian and little Bach. No pedantic strictness, mostly picturesque structures.

The performance report is not too favorable. The pianist, a resident in South America, is knowledgeable, and technically able; the orchestra and the conductor are the opposite. Balances are twisted; the playing is somewhat of a struggle, and scarred by intonation lapses. Rough going all the way—the piano is nasal and the sound is thinned in the high gamuts.

——Filarmonica Triestina; Felicja Blumental, piano; Luigi Toffolo, cond. Vox PL-10070 (with Albéniz: Spanish Rhapsody, and Saint-Saëns: Wedding Cake).

MOMOPRECOCE, FOR PIANO AND ORCHESTRA

Some sour with this sweet. *"Momoprecoce"* is based on a cycle of ten piano pieces titled *"Francette e Pia,"* which combine French and Brazilian melodies. Using one's own work and recasting it is perfectly justified, but it may sometimes result in weakening what was a strength. The short pieces have conviction; strung into a large-scale composition they wamble, sound belabored, and are totally diffuse—unordered in this day of orderliness. Villa-Lobos refuses to let go and overargues. What can a soloist do with this kind of music? But do consider the companion work.

——Orchestre National de la Radiodiffusion Française; Magda Tagliaferro, piano; Heitor Villa-Lobos, cond. ANGEL 35179 (with Bachianas Brasileiras No. 8).

INSTRUMENTAL

Guitar

CHÔRO NO. 1

Villa-Lobos once told the famous critic Olin Downes, "I compose in the folk style. . . . He [the composer] must select and transmit the material given him by his people." The maxim is perfectly illustrated, but overemphasized by the undue length of this piece, in which the plaintive principal theme returns again and again. Much of a muchness, and what is, to quote the liner note, "irresistible," becomes quite resistible.

There is little difference between the pair of performers. De la Torre is no Segovia (comparisons may be odious but we are rarely indifferent to them), yet he is a discriminating musician. Almeida diffuses as much color, is slightly less concerned with sharp detail. However, there is some difference in the disks that include this initial *chôro*. Almeida's survey is for the lover of guitar music Villa-Lobos-made, while de la Torre offers some good, some fair, and some questionable music by other hands. Vignettes by Llobet and Tárrega, with the *"Fandanguillo"* of Turina, are in the first class; a Giuliani composition is somewhat pedantic, totally unoriginal; questionable are transcriptions from Falla's *"El Amor Brujo."* Why? Why?

Villa-Lobos' fondness for creating ordered confusion by the re-use of themes, and the transfer and retitling of entire movements from earlier pieces without acknowledging such practice, will require a Brazilian Köchel to iron out. But it is not cricket to muddle this farrago further. Where Capitol (or Almeida) found the title *"Chôro Typico"* one knows not; it is not listed in Villa-Lobos' catalogue. This *chôro* is "typical," to be sure, but it becomes *"Chôro No. 1"* the moment one puts needle into groove and hears the music. Accordingly, it is discussed here under its proper title.

——in "Virtuoso Guitar," Rey de la Torre. EPIC LC-3479.
——in "Villa-Lobos: Music for the Spanish Guitar," Laurindo Almeida. CAPITOL P-8497 (SP-8497).

CHÔRO TYPICO
    See "Chôro No. 1" for guitar.

ETUDES NOS. 1 AND 8
    Villa-Lobos chose the guitar for the first of his many *chôros.* He also wrote two suites, a pair of waltzes, and some eight individual numbers for the instrument, in addition to a dozen etudes and a set of preludes. It is not always cast in this solo role; the

guitar has an important place in a number of this composer's chamber-music works.

The twelve etudes (composed in 1929) are not all of exemplary merit, but none of them is arid. An etude for pedagogic use is one thing; a concert etude, designed for the public's ears and not solely for the practice room, is another. Both of those under consideration (for another, *see below*) have expressive content. If Chopin, Liszt, and Debussy are in the first rank of composers of concert etudes for the piano, Villa-Lobos is without doubt the kingpin composer of concert etudes for the guitar.

The initial etude is called "studies of arpeggios," and those acquainted with the first unaccompanied cello suite of Bach will note a resemblance. Such warm eclecticism, delighting the ear, is never unwelcome. No. 8 is more melodic than it is concerned with design—Villa-Lobos often refused to be guided by formal documentation.

Segovia is the monarch of guitarists, yet the younger men such as Almeida, Bream, de la Torre, and others have learned so much from him that (as is the case here) the choice is almost in favor of one of the disciples. In the first etude Segovia illuminates matters generally. Almeida seeks the harmonic meaning and thus projects the music with straightforwardness. Both guitarists demonstrate the *innigkeit* of the eighth etude, a song-rhapsody. Nonetheless, *ne quid nimis*, Almeida's performance is with a full complement of other Villa-Lobos guitar music, while Segovia's is contained in a mixed bag. Both are intended for lovers of the guitar, but without snobbishness I might say that an entire disk of one composer's music for this special instrument may be a little too much of the real thing. This is not to deny that the music *is* the real thing. Two other points: Capitol's sound is better than Columbia's; Segovia's Villa-Lobos contribution is hidden in the assortment under the bland title of "Two Studies." Why such tissue-papered disguise? ——Andrés Segovia. Columbia ML-4732 (with Castelnuovo-Tedesco: Concerto for Guitar and Orchestra; Ponce: Rondo on a Theme by F. Sor; Sonatina Meridional; Torroba: Arada and Danza; and Turina: Fandanguillo).
——in "Villa-Lobos: Music for the Spanish Guitar," Laurindo Almeida. Capitol P-8497 (SP-8497).

ETUDE NO. 7

A mixture of some lyricism with much more scalic rhapsodizing make this etude of semi-improvisational type. Almeida's playing is clean, clear, fundamentally suitable. He plays this etude much better than many of the other pieces, most of which have a constrained dynamic range. The other etudes on the disk (Nos. 1 and 8 of the total dozen—*see above*) hold much more interest.

——in "Villa-Lobos: Music for the Spanish Guitar," Laurindo Almeida. CAPITOL P-8497 (SP-8497).

FIVE PRELUDES

Villa-Lobos composed a set of six guitar preludes in 1940, but the manuscript of one somehow disappeared. Considering his jumbo output, one can understand such loss. (It may well be that Villa-Lobos, who had a perfervid imagination, *thought* he had written a sixth prelude. Quite often he planned a work but never executed it, or pretended he had.)

In a way these preludes are as close to the essence of Villa-Lobos as Villa-Lobos ever came. Much music is a set of platitudes, some is designed for the snob-elect, and a certain percentage is what we might term "player's" music—music for the instrumentalist, without didacticism. The last is the first here, very little of the first makes that category come last, if at all, and there is none of the second classification. Above all, the guitar is an instrumental medium for rich-blooded Latin music and so Villa-Lobos poured into these preludes much of his true self. His language is proportioned, defined, shows less reticence in the command of instrumental technique, and thematic material that is personally indigenous.

The first of the group is a keen, haunting music, with a smidgen of nostalgia that is like a Brazilian blues, minus any jazz relationship. Fantasy and fancy mark the second and fourth preludes. In the third, one recognizes the composer's great admiration for Bach, whose music Villa-Lobos felt was a resource available to any composer, regardless of era or country of origin. Bachian hat-tipping can be noticed in this gentle piece, in a repetitive sequential passage that has direct (or was it merely subconscious?) reference to a Bach piano concerto. The last prelude is one of the special love songs of the composer's country—the *"modinha."* However, it is rather cool and detached for such emotional material.

Bream's execution gives a resplendent effect. There is contrast, almost implied dialogue, in his greater stressing of dynamic planes, whereas Almeida (who only plays the odd-numbered items in his all-Villa-Lobos album: *see below*), though technically excellent, performs in the manner of a reticent tête-à-tête. Both players are superlative in the first prelude, one of the most typical of the works Villa-Lobos wrote for the guitar. In the fifth of the group Bream's dynamic controls are magnificent, while in the third his use of changing strings on repeated sounds is an example of timbre differentiation that makes him eligible to share the Segovian throne. Those who are interested only in the preludes need not hesitate in preferring Bream's recording, except for the fact that he plays them *in toto*. There are other factors that must be considered in judging Almeida's version—these are discussed below.

One concluding criticism. Both disks were recorded extremely close. Accordingly annoying finger swishes, hand shifts in making position changes, and glide noises mar both releases. Is this aural jarring necessary to guitar microphoning?

——in "Guitar Music of Villa-Lobos and Torroba," Julian Bream. WESTMINSTER XWN-18137.

FIVE PRELUDES (Nos. 1, 3, AND 5)

These are three of the eight works on Almeida's Villa-Lobos record. Though a worthy project, one wonders whether it is not a risky one, in view of the specialized color of the guitar plus the fact that some of the music is of only average quality. Three etudes together with three preludes, plus a pair of *chôros*, offer little formal modulatory variety. Regardless of one's admiration and respect, Villa-Lobos is no Bach. There are a number of good things on this disk, but the comprehensive spark will not ignite unless segments are played. Listening to the eight works in succession one realizes how a single attitude rules the music throughout. Monotony may breed the usual contempt.

Almeida's playing of the preludes is good, but Bream's interpretation is better; further, he performs the complete set of five. (For a discussion of the music and a detailed comparison of the two performances, *see above.*)

——in "Villa-Lobos: Music for the Spanish Guitar," Laurindo Almeida. Capitol P-8497 (SP-8497).

Gavotta-Chôro

Since the *chôro* is already a synthesis of Brazilian Indian and popular music, it is apparent that the joining of an old French dance form with it makes the compound a triple one. But two's company and three make a crowd. Q.E.D.: Formal preoccupation, an uninspired demonstration. (For data concerning the suite of which this is a part, *see* "Schottish-*Chôro*" *below*). The music by the younger Brazilian, Gnattali, included in these recorded "Impressions," is a far different matter.

——in "Impressoes do Brasil," Laurindo Almeida. Capitol P-8381.

Schottish-Chôro

When source material is available the supplying of inadequate liner notes is annoying. It is exasperating to read that a "schottish-*chôro*" is a "stylized recreation of the *Schottische*, a nineteenth-century round dance reminiscent of a slow polka." The rest of the data is as uninformative. One does not ask for hyperattenuated technical analysis, but proper information is important to place a work within a composer's output.

This lengthy piece (too long for its simple idea) is one of five Villa-Lobos wrote between 1908 and 1912, and thus represents his early style. The "*Suite Popular Brasileira*" is considered as his eighteenth work and the "Schottish" is the second part of that. All the portions of the suite contain *chôro* hybridizations: in the first it is crossed with a mazurka, in the third with a waltz, in the fourth of the set with a gavotte (*see* "*Gavotta-Chôro*" *above*), and finally there is a small "*Chorinho.*"

As an historical point of reference, this piece is interesting; as compared with Villa-Lobos' preludes and etudes for the guitar it is very stilted and mere filler material for the disk.

——in "Villa-Lobos: Music for the Spanish Guitar," Laurindo Almeida. Capitol P-8497 (SP-8497).

Piano

BACHIANAS BRASILEIRAS NO. 4

A partita by Villa-Lobos, with much Bach and no semblance of folkloristic accompaniment until midway in the third movement. At that point there is no mistaking the direction or purpose of the music. Thus, there is not too much insistence on either aspect of the duality that the *Bachianas* compositions express, but rather, artful fusion. Villa-Lobos shows he is a master of piano composition in most of his works for the instrument—this one is no exception. Pressler does a dedicated job with the music, especially in the third movement, with its exciting pedal point, and in the toccata commentary of the final *"Danza."*

(For a different version of this work *see under* Orchestral.)

——Menahem Pressler. MGM E-3105 (with Bachianas Brasileiras No. 1).

CHÔROS NO. 5—"ALMA BRASILEIRA" ("SOUL OF BRAZIL")

A mellowed impression that conveys true Brazilian nationalism. No native quotations, but as close to the precious treasure of folk music as any composer might come. Villa-Lobos, the creative sponge, absorbed all the pertinent traits of his country's folklore and made them his own.

By all means choose the MGM release rather than the mélange offered by Westminster. Echániz plays poetically but Engdahl plays a healthy amount of Villa-Lobos, and that's the speciality in which the listener is presumably interested. Which MGM, then? While both offer the same four piano works, that listed first below has another *chôro* with the ninth of the *"Bachianas Brasileiras"* series; the second disk is completed with some good Milhaud.

——in "Music by Heitor Villa-Lobos," Leonore Engdahl. MGM E-3516.

——Leonore Engdahl. MGM E-3158 (with Poema Singelo; Saudades das Selvas Brasileiras; Suite Floral; and Milhaud: Saudades do Brasil).

——in "Latin American Rhythms," José Echániz. WESTMINSTER XWN-18430.

CIRANDAS

Aside from creating melodies that have the essence of folk material, Villa-Lobos utilized unchanged original native sources, or cut them to fit, as in this cycle of 16 pieces. (*"Cirandas"* should not be confused with the set of 12 pieces bearing an almost similar title: *"Cirandinhas."* Both works were composed in 1925, and although each is concerned with specific native idioms *"Cirandinhas"* is much simpler in concept and falls in the category of children's teaching pieces.) Each part of *"Cirandas"* is based on a Brazilian folk song and is permitted full sway in the enlarged, yet concentrated development employed. *"Cirandas"* illustrates the most personal side of Villa-Lobos' music.

——Joseph Battista. MGM E-3020.

POEMA SINGELO

Though the melodic tracery resembles a Tchaikovsky salon favorite and the eclectic touch is heavy (Liszt, modal harmony at times, and even Chopin!) there are enough characteristic Brazilian elements to warrant listening time. If one is pro-Villa-Lobos the *"Poema"* will be pleasantly interesting.

——Leonore Engdahl. MGM E-3158 (with Chôros No. 5; Saudades das Selvas Brasileiras; Suite Floral; and Milhaud: Saudades do Brasil).

——in "Music by Heitor Villa-Lobos," Leonore Engdahl. MGM E-3516.

PRÔLE DO BÊBÊ ("THE BABY'S FAMILY")—SERIES 1 AND 2

This double collection of enchanting pieces contains some of Villa-Lobos' most delightful and attractive music for the piano. From the titles it might be assumed the music was conceived for educational purposes, but, on the contrary, these are full-fledged concert works.

The first set of eight was composed in 1918 and did not have a subtitle. When they were republished in America they bore the definitive and apt description of "The Baby's Dolls." (Abram's recording on EMS-10 terms the set "The Children's Doll Suite.") A second group of nine pieces appeared three years later, identified as "The Little Animals." Although both these suites have been recorded neither publication nor recording has been accorded the third set of nine "Games," written in 1926.

Expert invention is illustrated in the manner in which Villa-Lobos limns the various toys and dolls, without resorting to cartooning via the keyboard. Some of the pieces display facets of the Impressionist style. Others are indigenous, as in the samba rhythm that marks "The Clay Doll" or the toccata power that triggers "The Little Glass Wolf." This is quite an interesting gallery—from "The Rubber Doll" to "The Little Rubber Dog," etc. A highly original set of 17 small musical artworks, each bearing Villa-Lobos' clear signature.

It is not only completeness that argues for taking the Echániz version in preference to that by Abram (*see below*). What is offered is an exceptional performance, a conception that makes each piece come alive, that delineates the musical idea with sharp-tooled playing of line and rhythm. Westminster's sound has marvelous presence.

——José Echániz. WESTMINSTER XWN-18065.

PRÔLE DO BÊBÊ ("THE BABY'S FAMILY")—SERIES 1

This is contained on an EMS disk which includes two other works not otherwise represented on records. Because of these ("*Rude Pôema*" and "The Three Maries") the release is worth acquiring. For Villa-Lobos' exceptional piano description of eight dolls the buyer is directed to Echániz' superlative version (*see above*). Abram plays the program pieces efficiently, but is not inquisitive as to their content. The result is a lack of color and even potency. EMS sound is excellent; Westminster's is excellent plus.

The Regules version is high-class razz-ma-tazz. The Siena pianoforte is an attempt to obtain string-plucking sonority with variety of timbre in the different sections of the total keyboard. One thinks immediately of electric attachments to pianos, chord organs, and they-laughed-when-I-sat-down-to-play ads (I fooled the hell out of them—I didn't play; the pushbuttons did). This is supposed to be *ye compleat piano*, but it will never replace the Steinway, Baldwin, or even the economical spinet type. Miss Regules performs a Spanish program of Albéniz, Mompou, and

Turina to support the Villa-Lobos. She plays cleanly, nicely, even attractively. But, those piano sounds—zounds!
——Jacques Abram. EMS-10 (with Rude Pôema; The Three Maries).
——in "Siena Pianoforte," Marisa Regules. ESOTERIC ESP-3002.

PRÔLE DO BÊBÊ ("THE BABY'S FAMILY")—SERIES I (MORENINHA ["THE PAPER DOLL"])
The second of the set of eight. As an example from the set it is as good as any. A fine sense of maturity and imagery is exhibited by the once-prodigy in her playing.
——in "Encore," Ruth Slenczynska. DECCA DL-9991.

PRÔLE DO BÊBÊ ("THE BABY'S FAMILY")—SERIES I (O POLICHINELLO ["PUNCH"])
This is the penultimate piece in the group and often serves as encore fare. Its popularity is deserved. Brailowsky tosses it off with proper puppet presumption.
——in "Brailowsky Encores," Alexander Brailowsky. RCA VICTOR LM-2276.

RUDE PÔEMA
Details: five years in the making; first performed by Artur Rubinstein, for whom it was written. It was later orchestrated. Description: this is music of volcanic vehemence, of vibrating violence, a music unfriendly save to the vested interests of virtuosi. Results: few perform Villa-Lobos' dynamistic piece, which is harmonically and rhythmically involved.

The abilities of Jacques Abram are tested—he comes through with superb virtuosity, and without a note out of place. What takes place? Everything—cadenzas, nostalgic impressionism, percussive primitivism, an improvised plan of bravura, and the transmittal of musical shock without recourse to serialism, pointillism, or any "ism" save pyrotechnicalism. Hearing is believing.
——Jacques Abram. EMS-10 (with The Children's Doll Suite; The Three Maries).

SAUDADES DAS SELVAS BRASILEIRAS ("RECOLLECTIONS OF THE BRAZILIAN FORESTS")
This miniature suite of two movements (both in animated

tempo) conveys a well-balanced vitality. Although it lacks dominant individuality its tastefulness is immediately recognizable.
There are sufficient Brazilian rhythms to identify its national
habitat.

——Leonore Engdahl. MGM E-3158 (with Chôros No.
5; Poema Singelo; Suite Floral; and Milhaud: Saudades do Brasil).

——in "Music by Heitor Villa-Lobos," Leonore Engdahl. MGM
E-3516.

Suite Floral

Some Brazilian music with profuse French dressing. The ratio
is 1:2. "Floral" does not signify flowery music; it is simply the composer's way of applauding Brazil's annual Festival of the Garden-
ers. Villa-Lobos is rather conservative in the lyrical, quasi-Debussy
sounds of the opening movement, a "Summer Idyll." The melodic
flow and light rhythms of the second part ("A Singing Country
Girl") are in direct contrast to the brilliant dance picture illustrated by the final movement, "Joy in the Garden."

——Leonore Engdahl. MGM E-3158 (with Chôros No. 5; Poema
Singelo; Saudades das Selvas Brasileiras; and Milhaud: Saudades
do Brasil).

——in "Music by Heitor Villa-Lobos," Leonore Engdahl. MGM
E-3516.

The Three Maries

No matter what Villa-Lobos wrote the music had personality.
Thus, piano music based on a fairy tale, "The Three Maries of
Earth," almost fits the three names (Alnitah, Alnilam, and Min-
tika) with musical onomatopoeia. In this instance Villa-Lobos is
as clear as is Debussy in his "Children's Corner." The two works
have in common the quality of objective simplicity. Expertly performed.

——Jacques Abram. EMS-10 (with Rude Pôema; The Children's
Doll Suite).

Violin

Song of the Black Swan

A quite unfamiliar piece, given no explanatory data on the
liner note. In fact, the descriptive notes are anything but informa-

tive. This lack covers all the dozen works on the record. And who conceived the ridiculous heading? Of course the gentleman "plays Gershwin." He also plays 11 other composers. He plays well— exceedingly well.

This piece is the *"O Canto do Cisne Negro"* that Villa-Lobos wrote first for cello and piano, having extracted it from an early, unpublished symphonic poem, composed in 1916, titled *"Naufrágio de Kleônicos."* In 1917, Villa-Lobos transcribed his own transcription, for violin and piano. It is short, simple and almost sweet.
——in "Bezrodny Plays Gershwin," Igor Bezrodny, violin; Abram Makarov, piano. Monitor MC-2028.

CHAMBER MUSIC

Bachianas Brasileiras No. 6, for Flute and Bassoon

The high and low colors of the two wind instruments afford a propitious contrast for duet composition. Both instruments are equally treated, to a degree, for, though the part writing is proportioned, the flute is given the lion's share of soloistic assertion. A great deal of the opening "Aria" (*"Chôro"*) is constructed sequentially. This gives balance and correlation to the music, but not much development. The "Fantasia" has a very segmented design, with very little freedom of musical flow. The performers are capable; their instruments have the special French woodwind tone.
——Fernand Dufrène, flute; René Plessier, bassoon. Angel 35547 (with Bachianas Brasileiras Nos. 2, 5, and 9).

Duo for Violin and Viola

While some string duets go beyond the two-voice possibilities and form trio and even quartet combinations, Villa-Lobos' predilection for thickness is here restrained; only occasionally is the writing for more than two parts. The first movement has a novel sound because it travels on quartal, intervallic paths. Though smoothness is presumably a concomitant of intervallic spans of thirds and sixths, this is an excellent example of how limited the musical vocabulary can sometimes be, for the entire effect is one of relaxed flowing sound, yet all stemming from the distance of fourths. The slow movement has haunting lyricism. In the final movement the theme sounds as though it will break any moment into a fugue. Perhaps this is the trick up Villa-Lobos' sleeve, for it never does. It moves with attention to counterpoint, never, however, taking it vigorously by the hand.

Since chamber music is basically *hausmusik*, there is nothing nicer than a family performance. The Persingers live up to their famous name. Stradivari's miscellany is very interesting; it includes Hindemith's piece for solo viola with strings, Turina's "*Scène*" for the odd combination of violin, piano, and string quartet, plus the once very familiar, now rarely performed Halvorsen duo version of a movement from Handel's G Minor harpsichord suite. The sound is of lifelike quality.

——Louis Persinger, violin; Rolf Persinger, violin. Strad 608 (with Handel-Halvorsen: Passacaglia; Hindemith: Trauermusik; and Turina: Scène Andalouse).

Première Sonata-Fantaisie, for Violin and Piano

Throughout, a work of rich musical tapestry. Despite the textural thickness and constant instrumental motion, the structures remain clearly apparent through the timbre fog.

Not an easy recording to locate. However, the healthy virtuosity of the composer and the performers, plus the heady romanticism of the music, make the search a worthy project.

——in "Album of 20th Century Music," Ruth Posselt, violin; Allan Sly, piano. Academy Records ALP-304.

Trio for Oboe, Clarinet and Bassoon

Design is of secondary importance in many of Villa-Lobos' compositions. It is color that governs the tactics of this wind trio, illustrative of a mailed timbre fist in the musical glove. Thus, syncopations, full-scale deployment of dynamics, plus wholesale instrumental distribution lend a rashness to the music that is otherwise of simple nature. Magnificent performance with choice sound.

——Members of the New Art Wind Quintet. Westminster XWN-18651 (with Quartet for Flute, Oboe, Clarinet and Bassoon; Quintet—en forme de Chôros).

Chôros No. 4

Leave it to Villa-Lobos to think of unusual instruments and combinations. A composer who utilizes a violinophone (a violin with an electrical attachment) and metronomes as instruments in his music would not hesitate to write a brass quartet for the rare partnership of three horns and a trombone. The music is typical; the tune that appears in the middle is no folk item, but a true "pops" melody in terms of origin. Nonetheless, nationalism is just as genuinely proclaimed. Well-played, not so well-sounding. The companion *chôros* has resonance, this one does not.

——Chamber Group, Werner Janssen, cond. CAPITOL P-8147 (with Bachianas Brasileiras No. 1; Chôros No. 7).

String Quartet No. 6

Although all national dances have their precise rhythmic plots set in definite pulses, the composer who seeks to idealize one of them in an art work is liable to replace set formulas by different arrangements. The various Brazilian flavors present in this quartet are not the exact equivalents of such rhythmic entertainments. The persistence of syncopation and defined metrical patterns in the Sixth Quartet are taken from the dance—Villa-Lobos' absorption of folk culture is being stated again. Even more expressive are the turns of the slow movement. The minor keys that regulate this part of the work once again exhibit the abiding sentiment of which Villa-Lobos is a master illustrator. It can be said that the instances of this emotional character (the "Aria" in the fifth *"Bachiana"*; the *"Modinha"* in the eighth of the set, etc.) are the masterpieces within the sprawling output of this composer. This is melody of a significant turn. And it is the kind of music that enjoys long life.

The Hollywood foursome play Villa-Lobos' quartet with beautiful tone, impeccable ensemble, and penetrating style. America can boast, rightfully, that it has the best quartet teams on the scene today.

A question: why in heaven's name try to separate a string quartet by stereo technique? Integration is the acme of the medium, anything else is subversion and stupid.

——Hollywood String Quartet. CAPITOL P-8472 (SP-8472) (with Kodály: Quartet No. 2).

QUARTET FOR FLUTE, OBOE, CLARINET AND BASSOON

Casualness of form defines each of the three movements. Villa-Lobos has other affections that come first. Rhythmic excitation, color melodrama—these stir the ear. One cannot but react to this composer's vehemence, even when refusing to praise his free discourse. Mozartian finesse cannot be expected in Villa-Lobos' woodwind music. This composer's best arguments are propounded by avoiding such logic. Sonorescence and fantasy come first with this Brazilian; harmony, counterpoint, and form are second in consideration. Sit back and enjoy organized wind *sound.*

——Members of the New Art Wind Quintet. WESTMINSTER XWN-18651 (with Quintet—en forme de Chôros; Trio for Oboe, Clarinet and Bassoon).

QUINTET—EN FORME DE CHÔROS

Villa-Lobos makes a slight change in the old order here. The combination of a flute, oboe, clarinet, bassoon, and the brass French horn is incorrectly described as a woodwind quintet, but such is the way of tradition. In this work the true designation of "woodwind quintet" can be applied, since the French horn is exchanged for an English horn. This combine gives a lusher, thicker color, far more appropriate to the ad libitum, jam session format that is essential to the *chôros* form. The sum total is exciting music, modifying formal practices in a creative fashion that is distinctly unusual. Perfectly recorded—in fact one of the best wind recordings, stereo notwithstanding. The New Wind performers are star musicians.

——New Art Wind Quintet. WESTMINSTER XWN-18651 (with Quartet for Flute, Oboe, Clarinet and Bassoon; Trio for Oboe, Clarinet and Bassoon).

CHÔROS No. 7—"SETTIMINO" ("SEPTET")

It is not very well known that Villa-Lobos played and had great fondness for the saxophone (it appears in many of his works). To find it in his seventh *chôros* is an example of the freedom of his chamber-music instrumentation—as free as the *chôros* form that Villa-Lobos designed. This piece is a compendium; as mixed and unspecific as the composer himself, assorted as the instrumentation itself is, and yet held together by the sheer force of invention and fantasy. Popular song, unreserved national dances, and the improvisational take turns in appearing. Slow-paced, exotically colored sections merge into dance patterns (there is even an outright waltz in one place). Thus, the primitive jungle accent is related to an almost savage keenness of tone color. Oddest of all is the extraordinary chamber-music use of a tam-tam. This writer knows of no similar employment of the instrument. It plays nine sounds and then drops out. Other writers seem to have overlooked this more-than-ordinary point. For this "septet" (for five wind and two string instruments) is, therefore, an "octet"!

The significant virtue of a conductor having rare insight into the ways of a composer is illustrated by Janssen. His conception is so far superior to that of Solomon there is no hesitation in placing his recording first. Janssen's performers (one understands the need of a conductor for this difficult music) play in tune; Solomon's play him false. But why approve a tape for mastering if it lacks at least consolidated intonation? Both of the MGM combinations are of more than ordinary interest. The assortment is a better choice, especially for the inclusion of Chávez and Revueltas.

——Chamber Group, Werner Janssen, cond. CAPITOL P-8147 (with Bachianas Brasileiras No. 1; Chôros No. 4).

——in "Spanish and Latin-American Music for Unusual Instrumental Combinations," MGM Chamber Orchestra, Izler Solomon, cond. MGM E-3155.

——in "Music by Heitor Villa-Lobos," MGM Chamber Orchestra, Izler Solomon, cond. MGM E-3516.

VOCAL

CARANGUEYO ("THE CRAB SONG")
MODINHA (SERESTA NO. 5)
NESTA RUA ("ON OUR STREET")
NHAPOPÉ
PAI-DO-MATO ("FATHER OF THE WOODS")
REDONDILHA (SERESTA NO. 11)
XANGÔ

Only a paltry number of Villa-Lobos' songs have been recorded, despite the huge wealth of vocal music he composed. In his gigantic output there are close to seventy individual songs with piano accompaniment, and more than a dozen large song cycles, which account for about one hundred additional vocal pieces. Villa-Lobos also wrote a good number of works for voice and organ and still others for voice with orchestral, or small instrumental ensemble accompaniment. A rarity in the vocal category is his suite of three movements for soprano and violin, composed in 1923.

The seven songs released by Washington Records are an appetizer that whets one's appetite. It is regrettable that the group does not include the haunting "Song of the Oxcart Driver," made famous by the late Elsie Houston, whose magnificent performance on a 78 r.p.m. disk became an overnight hit.

"*Carangueyo*" is a well-known Brazilian folk song. Cute and properly styled by the vocalist.

From the opening rhythmic figure of the "*Modinha*" it will be realized that this music is drawn from the wellsprings of native material. Villa-Lobos composed a set of twelve "*Serestas*" in 1925 (the eleventh of the series—"*Redondilha*"—is discussed below). These "serenades" are of varied character and can be considered among the very best of his vocal compositions. Once again Villa-Lobos inaugurates a formal device; like the "*Chôros*," the "*Serestas*" are an amalgam of folk tunes plus original material plus imitations of folk tunes. In Villa-Lobos' oven these are baked into a fully individual product. The sentimental love song ("*Modinha*") is a very representative example.

"*Nesta Rua*" is also a love song, folkloric and quite popular; Villa-Lobos' individual harmonization make it his song-property.

There is a dark quality, with a strange, Russian cast, in "*Nhapopé*," a song about a Brazilian bird. (This piece is the sixth of a set of seven "*Modinhas e Canções*," which Villa-Lobos composed between 1933 and 1942.)

In 1930 Villa-Lobos wrote a song cycle titled "*Canções Indígenas*," consisting of three pieces. The first of these is "*Pai-do-Mato*"—an ordinary song, not typical of Villa-Lobos' vocal-composition expertness. The lyrics are by Mario de Andrade, a contemporary Brazilian poet.

The title of "*Redondilha*" applies to a specific verse form (a quatrain with each verse consisting of five or seven syllables). The music is concerned with life's deception. Mournful, but beautiful Villa-Lobos music, refined and intimate. Beautifully sung.

The hybrid Afro-Brazilian qualities of *"Xangô"* are derived from the Macumba rites. *"Xangô"* is from the set of 13 *"Chansons Typiques Brésiliennes,"* composed between 1919 and 1935. These are quasi-original, exemplifying musical reciprocity—Villa-Lobos' harmonizations of folk tunes and popular airs. The common interest is served and the end result is very effective musical interaction.

Miss Gloria has a fair voice, is not too concerned with anything but straightforwardness. She displays flexibility but some of the songs lack conviction. In *"Xangô,"* for example, her singing does not have the drive and savagery required by the piece. Her accompanist is satisfactory. (N.B. The liner for this record and the four-page insert giving the English translations of the texts are amateurish productions. The buyer should not expect much information.)

——in "Songs of Brazil," Sarita Gloria, soprano; Anthony Chanaka, piano. WASHINGTON RECORDS WR-408.

Voice with Cello Ensemble

BACHIANAS BRASILEIRAS No. 5

There are very few people who are unmoved by the exquisite melody that spans the opening of this two-movement work, scored for a soprano voice and eight cellos. A contemporary melody that has come to be honored with the term "celebrated" is unique. In this chant Villa-Lobos has captured the full essence of his formal amalgamation of Bach (classic purity) and nationalism (striking color and rhythm) and drawn the maximum of expressivity from minimal instrumental means. This, too, is a singular achievement. The second movement is another combination idea; a love-dance song. It is showy, without the incontrovertible individuality of the opening movement.

All performances must be measured against the "Aria" recorded by Bidú Sayão on a ten-inch disk some 15 years ago (*see below*). It is rare to hear such astonishing stylistic profundity in the delivery of a song. None of the singers listed is more than adequate, but if one wants the complete work then one will have to accept less than Sayão's recreative powers. De los Angeles sings correctly, but strict behavior is rather deadly in this case. Nixon is cool; she thins and curtails the sensual passion that lies in the song. Curtin's voice is directed with poor taste—it sounds as though she were singing a heavy Strauss role. One would rather settle for Sayão, despite the poor, pinched recorded sound and only one-half of the work. She is memorable.

(For the sake of giving the complete picture mention should be made of a setting for low voice and guitar, included in an album "Duets with the Spanish Guitar," issued by Capitol on PAO-8406. The performers are Laurindo Almeida, guitar, and Salli Terri, contralto. The arrangement is not the composer's. This writer not having heard the recording, no other data can be given.)

——Orchestre National de la Radiodiffusion Française; Victoria de los Angeles, soprano; Heitor Villa-Lobos, cond. ANGEL 35547 (with Bachianas Brasileiras Nos. 2, 6, and 9).

——Concert Arts Cello Ensemble; Marni Nixon, soprano; Felix Slatkin, cond. CAPITOL P-8484 (SP-8484) (with Bachianas Brasileiras No. 1, and Bach–Villa-Lobos: Prelude and Fugue No. 8 for orchestra of celli).

——New Orchestral Society of Boston; Phyllis Curtin, soprano; Willis Page, cond. COOK 1062 (with Bach: Brandenburg Concerto No. 3; Bach–Bachrich: Suite for Strings; and Stravinsky: Concerto in D for String Orchestra). (The same Villa-Lobos performance, but paired with music by Héctor Campos-Parsi, is available stereophonically on: RONDO ST-540.)

BACHIANAS BRASILEIRAS NO. 5 (ARIA—CANTILENA)

A magnificent display of performance art by Sayão, despite the dated sound. The recording was transferred from an old 78 r.p.m. and it will be so recognized. But old-play or long-play, warmth, style, passionate conviction, and throat-catching vocalism are here in abundance. Even if one owns the complete work it is still strongly recommended that Sayão's recording be acquired. (The other items on the record are dull.)

——Instrumental Ensemble; Bidú Sayão, soprano; Heitor Villa-Lobos, cond. COLUMBIA ML-5231 (with Braga: Folk Songs of Brazil, and Puccini: Five Arias).

CHORAL

AVE MARIA, No. 20

The number after the title is not an error. This is simply another example of the composer's prolificacy. In 1909, Villa-Lobos wrote his first *"Ave Maria"* and his catalogue shows this prayer of the Catholic faith as the subject of innumerable compositions thereafter. The one recorded example is simple in style, a forthright and straightforward choral item.

——San José State College A Cappella Choir, William J. Erlendson, cond. MUSIC LIBRARY RECORDINGS MLR-7007 (with Copland: In the Beginning; Corsi: Adoramus Te, Christe; Handl (Gallus): Ascendit Deus; and Tallis: O Nata Lux De Lumine).

Choral with Orchestra

FOREST OF THE AMAZON

Actually, this is the music that Villa-Lobos composed for the motion picture *Green Mansions*. As has often been the case with incidental music or background scores, the music was far superior to the film. True to his usual practice, Villa-Lobos' music has practically nothing to do with the Hudson story. Hudson's tale was a point of reference, an extraneous item for the Brazilian's flexible, coloristic imagery. And as is to be expected, Villa-Lobos departs very freely from his own indications. The sections comprise an accumulation of thoughts, indifferent to formal considerations, but quite alive to developing bold ideas from the minimal material. The main concern is to render the freedom of fantasy to the exclusion of all else. In this the music is quite successful. The orchestration is of the hothouse type, of Rousseau luxuriance, with some portions exclusively for the orchestra, others for either chorus or soprano with orchestra.

Despite Sayão's long career her voice retains a personality and a gentle luminescence. The orchestra plays with brilliance and the sound is a five-star affair. Since this was one of the last works Villa-Lobos composed it is worth owning if only for historical reasons.

——Symphony of the Air; Bidú Sayão, soprano; chorus; Heitor Villa-Lobos, cond. UNITED ARTISTS UAL-7007 (UAS-8007).

27. Ben Weber
(1916—   )

DISCUSS TWELVE-TONE MUSIC THESE DAYS AND YOU WILL FIND THE battle lines as severely drawn within the dodecaphonic area as they once were between the tonalists and the twelve-tonalists. Some regard Schoenberg as the master, others deride this once-radical. The first group retains and practices the dogma: pure and total chromatic equality without a trace of diatonic relationship; the others take the system and make of it an incidental partner of disintegration, bombing the tones into total fragmentation. Their lust for serial atomization is the equivalent of dodecaphonic rape.

Now, no one has ever accused the dodecaphonic composers of turning out musical milk and honey. Neither is the finger pointed at the newer experimenters. None of us can (or should) avoid the worst of the truths that are doubtless in the process of being developed by the post-Boulez, pro-Stockhausen school. But we cannot deny the need for strong links in the creative chain. One such composer is Ben Weber.

This man is an independent, but not independent of twelve-tone technical resources. Weber embraced the dogma and then found sufficient strength to free himself and achieve a sensitive, serious, romantic integration within the science of dodecaphonic arrangement. In this respect he parallels Alban Berg, but is more aloof (not being from Vienna?). His music has a passionate vehemence; its sounds are not mere technical platitudes. He has been called an atonalist—a misnomer, for atonality shies away from re-identification with pertinent reference points, be they major-minor or twelve-tone. Weber writes in twelve-tone style, but is not of the cold twelve-tone system. This proves the validity of serial music, which can be as flexible in its give-and-take as any other. It proves also that no matter the type of creative discovery, eventually it can be shaped in different ways if it has any evolutionary force. Weber is an elucidator of twelve-tone technique, by way of his own manner of creative invention.

For one of the newer lights on the American musical horizon, Weber has fared well with the recording industry. The latest re-

251

lease in the Fromm Music Foundation Twentieth-Century Composers Series consisted of three of his compositions. Seven major works are therefore available for the listener who would enjoy effective contemporary music.

ORCHESTRAL

PRELUDE AND PASSACAGLIA, OP. 42

The mistake of thinking formal definition the equivalent of artistic reality has haunted more than one composer. Thus variation or the related passacaglia form can turn out to be a mere ornamentally extensive exercise, instead of yielding the rich fullnesses resultant from clear thematic comprehension. Weber's absorbing nineteen variations contain colorful tensions, deal with the main argument, and reach their goal beautifully. The music's climax is prepared and is not the result of mere technical rule of thumb. In contrast, the somberness of the preamble is an example of artistic orchestration.

This is an impressive-sounding performance. The Louisville Orchestra certainly commands respect for its ability to play music as stylistically disparate as Sowerby and Weber. Good engineering balance on this disk.

——Louisville Orchestra, Robert Whitney, cond. LOUISVILLE COMMISSIONING SERIES LOU-56-6 (with Badings: Louisville Symphony [No. 7], and Sowerby: All on a Summer's Day).

SOLO INSTRUMENT WITH ORCHESTRA

RAPSODIE CONCERTANTE FOR VIOLA AND SMALL ORCHESTRA, OP. 47

A long aria-like composition in which the bronze-brown timbre of the viola enhances the music's intense cast of thought. Weber handles his own rhapsodic defense by the use of a row, but does not orate. This is quiet, almost cool music; by its understatement it develops a strength, most apparent after several hearings. Like all art, its secrets will be disclosed if given time.

Trampler's viola playing is most informative, appealing, of full tonal beauty. Formerly the violist of the New Music Quartet, this musician enjoys the highest reputation; his guest appearances with the Budapest Quartet in quintet performances prove the esteem in which he is held. His playing of all three works on this recording deserves triple-star rating.

——MGM Chamber Orchestra; Walter Trampler, viola; Arthur Winograd, cond. MGM E-3559 (with Glanville-Hicks: Concerto Romantico, and Richter: Aria and Toccata).

INSTRUMENTAL

Piano

EPISODES, OP. 26a

Stage works have more than once served as a source of adaption for absolute music. Weber's set of pieces originally constituted a ballet, "The Pool of Darkness," scored for flute, violin, trumpet, bassoon, cello, and piano.

The "Episodes" are romantic, almost ecstatic pieces. However, the music is far from perfumed in sound, fussy effect, or reasoning. Weber has emotional reserves and employs a free twelve-tone method for projecting them. Though in separate parts, the music gives the sense of a totality, an impression of sonority scaled for the most part in mysterious recesses—music of no pomp but much circumstance.

Masselos is to the contemporary school as Schnabel was to Beethoven. Enough said.

——William Masselos. MGM E-3556 (with Griffes: Sonata for Piano, and Rudhyar: Granites).

FANTASIA (VARIATIONS), OP. 25

Weber writes with the conviction of a composer who knows his way. He conceives his "Fantasia" in one solid chunk, but splits it to form the actuality of a triple-movement work played without pause. The plan: a theme with variations, passacaglia variants, and a final "Fantasia." Although texturally heavy, the clear lines supercharge the composition, intensifying the dodecaphonic language. There is a unity of conception that shows a truly creative mind at work in this opus of integrity and conviction. The superfine performance is by the very gifted protagonist of present-day piano music, for whom Weber wrote his work (in 1946).

——William Masselos. EPIC LC-3567 (with Concertino for Flute, Oboe, Clarinet and String Quartet; Serenade for Strings).

CHAMBER MUSIC

SERENADE FOR STRINGS, OP. 46

Weber's string composition has enjoyed singular success. Commissioned by the Fromm Foundation, it was first performed at a concert sponsored by that organization, held at Tanglewood in the summer of 1956. The following year it gained the distinction of two New York City performances in one day—given by the group that recorded the work.

This is music not to slumber by; its sinewy and hard-knit contrapuntal travels can well cause travail unless performed by virtuoso musicians, and these must be well rehearsed. Weber is the new type of composer—astute, knowledgeable, resolute in his desire to be understood, but unequivocal in his demands on his listeners. This is not to deprecate his music, it is rather to emphasize an attitude of listening that must share the optimum knowledge of the composer. The difficulty of the idiom commands respect, if not total acceptance. It is akin to seeing through the glass darkly. There is no gainsaying that Ben Weber is one of our important composers. His handling of counterpoint, freedom of line for tension, and use of the instrumental palette are excellent.

The "Serenade" has a coherence brought about by the employment of definite designs: like Schoenberg, Weber uses the march form to balance the end parts of his work; an aria marks the second movement, and this is followed by a minuet formation (Weber describes it as "off-kilter"). The fourth part is mainly polyphonic. These establish the quintet's symmetry, but no tedious, uninteresting music results from employing traditional structural balances. By his very orthodoxy Weber proves the unorthodoxy that marks twelve-tone music (or its derivatives) as the distinct relative of tonal music. Weber refuses to wear compositional false colors; he wishes to have his music heard by those trained to enjoy classical style sounds, but whose ears can be attuned to his contemporary accent.

The Galimir group with the assistance of a fine double bass player give a refined performance—every phrase within the whole is defined and thorough. Rare indeed is the projection of such warmth and spirit in a work of difficulty. The sound is realistic.

——Galimir String Quartet; David Walters, contrabass. EPIC LC-3567 (with Fantasia [Variations]; Concertino for Flute, Oboe, Clarinet and String Quartet).

CONCERTINO FOR FLUTE, OBOE, CLARINET AND STRING QUARTET, OP. 45

This work fuses modern style with baroque form—thus, merging sophistication with Handelian clarity (plus chromatics). The title gives a clue to the composition, but may lead one to expect the split-off characteristics of the concerto grosso. Weber's "Concertino" rarely uses prime solo characteristics; the wind instruments' rhythms partake of athletic spirit, giving a decided Bachian swing to the work as a whole.

Weber's forms are precise. Each movement has a distinct personality, yet contributes to the total. Within each of the designs there is a relaxation generally inherent in music of unchecked fantasy. Weber balances all the factors necessary for a rewarding aural experience.

The performance of this septet is exceedingly accomplished. Epic is to be congratulated not only on its artistic idealism but on its choice of magnificent artists as performers.

——Julius Baker, flute; Harry Shulman, oboe; Alexander Williams, clarinet; Galimir String Quartet. EPIC LC-3567 (with Fantasia [Variations]; Serenade for Strings).

VOCAL

Voice with Orchestra

SYMPHONY ON POEMS OF WILLIAM BLAKE, OP. 33

A musical synthesis, whereby the sung poetry is put to use and ordered for symphonic purposes. "To Autumn" is of moderate tempo; the second part, featuring the voice, is like a slow movement. Movement three is a dogmatic scherzo in conduct, though not in scherzo tempo. A lighter element concludes Weber's vocal-instrumental symphony.

The composer's intent is described as a "cyclic expression of mystery, despair, madness and love reborn." In a sense these moods run over their boundary lines and intermingle, save for the very individual third part. Weber's writing is exceedingly free and the contrasts are somewhat blurred. Excellently performed with a first-rate singer as a bonus.

——Leopold Stokowski and His Orchestra; Warren Galjour, baritone; Leopold Stokowski, cond. COMPOSERS RECORDINGS CRI-120 (with Goeb: Symphony No. 3).